Learn Android Studio 3

Efficient Android App Development

Ted Hagos

Apress®

Learn Android Studio 3: Efficient Android App Development

Ted Hagos
Manila, National Capital Region, Philippines

ISBN-13 (pbk): 978-1-4842-3155-5
https://doi.org/10.1007/978-1-4842-3156-2

ISBN-13 (electronic): 978-1-4842-3156-2

Library of Congress Control Number: 2018933042

Managing Director, Apress Media LLC: Welmoed Spahr
Acquisitions Editor: Steve Anglin
Development Editor: Matthew Moodie
Coordinating Editor: Mark Powers

Distributed to the book trade worldwide by Springer Science+Business Media New York, 233 Spring Street, 6th Floor, New York, NY 10013. Phone 1-800-SPRINGER, fax (201) 348-4505, e-mail orders-ny@springer-sbm.com, or visit www.springeronline.com. Apress Media, LLC is a California LLC and the sole member (owner) is Springer Science + Business Media Finance Inc (SSBM Finance Inc). SSBM Finance Inc is a **Delaware** corporation.

For information on translations, please e-mail rights@apress.com, or visit http://www.apress.com/rights-permissions.

Apress titles may be purchased in bulk for academic, corporate, or promotional use. eBook versions and licenses are also available for most titles. For more information, reference our Print and eBook Bulk Sales web page at http://www.apress.com/bulk-sales.

Any source code or other supplementary material referenced by the author in this book is available to readers on GitHub via the book's product page, located at www.apress.com/9781484231555. For more detailed information, please visit http://www.apress.com/source-code.

Printed on acid-free paper

For Adrianne and Stephanie.

Table of Contents

About the Author

Ted Hagos is the CTO of RenditionDigital International, a software development company based out of Dublin. Before he joined RDI, he had various software development roles and also spent time as trainer at IBM Advanced Career Education, Ateneo ITI, and Asia Pacific College. He spent many years in software development dating back to Turbo C, Clipper, dBase IV, and Visual Basic. Eventually, he found Java and spent many years there. Nowadays, he's busy with full-stack Javascript and Android.

About the Technical Reviewer

Wallace Jackson has been writing for leading multimedia publications about his work in new media content development since the advent of Multimedia Producer Magazine nearly two decades ago. He has authored a half-dozen Android book titles for Apress, including four titles in the popular Pro Android series. Wallace received his undergraduate degree in business economics from the University of California at Los Angeles and a graduate degree in MIS design and implementation from the University of Southern California. He is currently the CEO of Mind Taffy Design, a new media content production and digital campaign design and development agency.

Acknowledgments

I don't think a lot of people read the acknowledgement section of any book, probably not even the people I'm going to thank. But just in case they do read this book (and this section), I'd like to extend my thanks to them.

Thanks to Mark Powers and Matthew Moodie for guiding me through the manuscript development process. I used to have a romantic notion of the writing life; now I know better. Thanks also to Wallace Jackson, who did the technical review, and to Massimo Nardone, who helped out in the author review of the last four chapters. Special thanks to Steve Anglin, who got me into Apress.

Thanks to Steph and Adrianne for understanding why I skipped some of my house chores while writing this book.

Covering a topic as vast as Android and a tool as rich as Android Studio requires the effort of many individuals whom I haven't really met and know personally, but they do deserve gratitude. This is a tough section to make because I know I am bound to miss some names, so if I miss some, it's not because of ingratitude, it's because of ignorance.

Introduction

Welcome to *Learn Android Studio 3*. This book will help you get started in your programming journey with the little green robot. You already bought the book, so you don't need to be convinced that programming for the mobile platform offers a lot of opportunity for software developers.

While the book is aimed at beginning Android programmers, it isn't for people who are completely new to programming. The book assumes that you have prior coding experience with any of the CFOL (C family of languages, e.g., C, C++, Java, C#, JavaScript). Ideally, you are already a Java programmer trying to get your feet wet in Android; in case you're not, don't worry. Basic Java programming is covered in the Appendix, and you can refer to that as you try to feel your way into the language.

The book covers two fronts: the fundamentals of Android programming and the use of Android Studio 3. Android programming concepts and the use of the IDE are explained using a combination of graphics and code walkthroughs: there's plenty of those in the book.

Chapter Overviews

Chapter 1 - Introduces Android. It deals with a bit of Android's history and the technical makeup of its OS.

Chapter 2 - Walks you through to the setup of Android Studio and its requisite software. Whether you use macOS, Linux, or Windows, this chapter has you covered.

Chapter 3 - We start dipping our toes into Android programming. We'll start with creating a basic project and then run it on an emulator. This activity is something that you will do many times in the course of your Android programming career. Well finish up with a discussion of what makes up an Android application and how it is different from a desktop application.

Chapter 4 - This chapter deals with building user interfaces, one of the most basic and probably widely used components in Android.

Chapter 5 - Continuing from Chapter 4, after you've built some UIs, you might want it to actually do something. This chapter deals with how to respond to user-generated events.

Chapter 6 - This chapter deals with Intents. We've used Intents in the previous chapter, but this chapter digs in deeper. Intents are uniquely an Android thing; it truly embraces loose coupling. The chapter shows plenty of examples on how to use Intents for component activation on a multiactivity application and how to pass data between activities.

Chapter 7 - This chapter is shorter than the rest but it will help you put a bit of polish into your app. It deals with UI design, themes, styles, the AppBar, and Fragments.

Chapter 8 - Android is very protective of the user experience; it doesn't allow apps to freeze the UI leaving the user clueless as to what to do next. If you've seen ANR (Application Not Responding) errors before, this chapter shows you how to avoid these things.

Chapter 9 - Shows some of the things you can do to debug your apps in Android Studio 3. It goes through a list of the kinds of errors you might encounter while coding and what you can do in Android Studio to respond them.

Chapter 10 - At some point in time, you need to be able to save all the data you've created in the application. This chapter shows you the basics of saving data using a file, shared preferences, and the internal storage.

Chapter 11 - When you're ready to distribute your app, you'll need to sign it and list it in a marketplace like Google Play. This chapter walks you through the steps on how to do it.

Appendix - This chapter breezes through the Java language. It deals with some of the basic language concepts you will need to get started in Android programming.

Chapter 1

Introduction

Most people would think of Android as a phone or tablet; or at least, that is what end users would think. A developer would probably think of Android as an operating system (OS), and for the most part, it is. Android was designed originally to work as a mobile OS, but as it progressed, it found its way to some other places like TVs, car systems, watches, e-readers, netbooks, game consoles, and so forth.

Android includes quite a bit of stuff. It is a comprehensive platform. Apart from the OS and prebuilt applications, it includes a very capable software development kit, libraries, application frameworks, and reference design. We will explore some of them in considerable detail in the coming chapters. In the meantime, we'll look at Android's history, some statistics, and the Android platform architecture.

History

Android has an interesting and very colorful history. It first came to life in 2003 when a company called Android Inc. was founded by Andy Rubin. Android Inc. was backed by Google, but they did not own it yet. In 2005, Google bought Android Inc. to the tune of 50M+ dollars. Sometime in 2007, the Open Handset Alliance was born, and the Android OS has been officially open sourced. At this point, Android had not even reached version 1.0 and it was far from mainstream; it reached V1.0 sometime in 2008, but they had not thought about dessert names just yet.

The year 2009 up to 2010 saw a torrent of rapid releases. Android was picking up steam. Cupcake, Donut, Froyo, éclair, and Gingerbread were released during this two-year period. 2011 is a major milestone because up until this point, the Android OS remained confined to mobile phones. Honeycomb, the successor to Gingerbread, was the first Android version to be installed on tablets. There was a bit of controversy with Honeycomb because Google did not release its code to open source immediately. The following is a quick summary of Android's history.

2003	Android Inc., founded by Andy Rubin and backed by Google, was born
2005	Google bought Android Inc.
2007	Android was officially open sourced. Google turned over its ownership to the Open Handset Alliance (OHA)
2008	version 1.0 was released
2009	versions 1.1, 1.5 (Cupcake), 1.6 (Donut), and 2.0 (Eclair) were released
2010	versions 2.2 (Froyo) and 2.3 (Gingerbread) were released
2011	3.0 (Honeycomb) and 4.0 (Ice Cream Sandwich) were released
2012	version 4.1 (Jellybean)
2013	version 4.4 (KitKat)
2014	versions 5.0–5.1 (Lollipop); Android became 64-bit
2015	version 6.0 (Marshmallow)
2016	version 7.0-7.1.2 (Nougat)
2017	version 8 (Oreo)

One other thing that makes Android's history colorful is the lawsuits. Sometime in the past, Oracle sued Google, alleging that the latter infringed some copyrights of Java. But the Java implementation of Android isn't based on Oracle's Java language implementation; it is instead based on OpenJDK. Before Android Studio 2.2, installation of a separate Java SDK was a prerequisite for Android Studio; that is no longer the case because OpenJDK is now part of the installation. Then, there were the lawsuits between Apple and Samsung; the main part of all that was about Android. There were some bumps in the past but the little robot marched on.

Statistics

7.2 billion

Number of Android devices. It already has exceeded the total number of people in the planet

3

Number of decades it took for mobile devices to go from zero to 7.2 billion

1.5 million

Number of Android devices being activated daily

2,617

Number of times users touch their mobile devices in a day

2 billion

Number of active Android users monthly

87

Percentage of share of Android in the mobile OS market

I know you are already into Android development; you are reading this book after all. If you weren't aware of these statistics before, I hope this gives you extra motivation to continue your journey toward mobile development. Mobile computing usage is growing at a rapid pace, and Android has the lion's share of it.

Operating System

The most visible part of Android, at least for developers, is its OS. An OS is a complex thing, but for the most part, it is what stands between a user and the hardware. That is an oversimplification, but it will suffice for our purposes. By "user," I don't literally mean an end user or a person. What I mean by it is an application, a piece of code that a programmer creates, like a word processor or an e-mail client.

Take the e-mail app, for example; as you type each character on the keys, the app needs to communicate to the hardware for the message to make its way to your screen and hard drive and eventually send it to the cloud via your network. It is a more involved process than I describe it here, but that is the basic idea. At its simplest, an OS does three things:

- manages hardware on behalf of applications

- provides services to applications like networking, security and memory management, and so forth

- manages execution of applications; this is the part that allows us to run multiple applications (seemingly) almost at the same time

Figure 1-1 shows a logical diagram of Android's system architecture; it is far from complete, since it doesn't show all the apps, components, and libraries in the Android platform, but it should give you an idea on how things are organized.

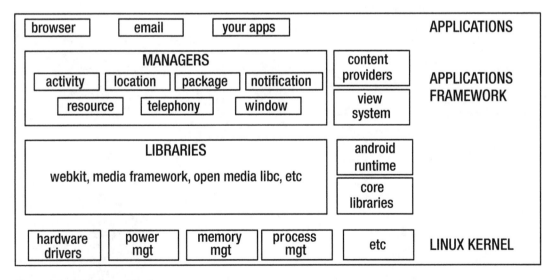

Figure 1-1. Platform architecture

The lowest level in the diagram is the one responsible for interfacing with the hardware, various services like memory management, and executions of processes. It should sound familiar because these were the three things I said that OSes do. This part of the Android OS is Linux. Linux is a very stable OS and is quite ubiquitous itself. You can find it in many places like server hardware on data centers, appliances, medical devices, and so forth. Android has an embedded Linux inside it which handles hardware interfacing and some other kernel functions.

On top of the Linux kernel are low-level libraries like SQLite, OpenGL, and so on. These are not part of the Linux kernel but are still low level and as such, are written mostly in C/C++. On the same level, you will find the Android runtime (Android class libraries + Dalvik virtual machine), which is where Android applications are run. Unlike other Java programs, Android executables are not *.class* files; they are *.dex* files. Dex files are not run on a typical Java virtual machine (JVM) like the one installed on your desktop. The dex files are meant to run on a VM that is optimized for low-powered handheld devices. The compilation cycle could be summed to the following: .java files (source code) ➤ Java compiler (.class) ➤ dex compiler (.dex) ➤ packaging (.apk)

> **Note**   The Dalvik VM was written by Dan Borstein; the VM was named after a fishing village in Iceland.

Next up is the application framework layer. It sits on top of both the low-level libraries and the Android runtime because it needs both. This is the layer that we will interact with as an application developer because it contains all the libraries we need to write apps.

Finally, on top is the application layer. This is where all our apps reside, both the ones we write and the ones that comes prebuilt with the OS. It should be pointed out that prebuilt applications which come with the device do not have any special privileges over the ones we will write. If you don't like the e-mail app of the phone, you can write your own and replace it. Android is democratic like that.

Chapter 2

Android Studio

Developing applications for Android was not always as convenient as today. When Android 1.0 was released sometime in 2008, what developers got by way of a development kit was no more than a bunch of command-line tools and ant build scripts. Building apps with vim, ant, and some command-line tools, that wasn't so bad if you were used to that kind of thing, but many developers were not. The lack of integrated development environment (IDE) capabilities like code hinting, project setups, and integrated debugging was somewhat a barrier to entry.

Thankfully, the Android development tools (ADT) for the Eclipse IDE was released, also in 2008. Eclipse was, and still is, a favorite and dominant choice of IDE for many Java developers. It felt very natural that it would also be the go-to IDE for Android developers.

From 2009 up until 2012, Eclipse remained to be choice of IDE for development. The Android SDK has also undergone both major and incremental changes in structure and in scope. In 2009, the SDK manager was released; we use this to download tools, individual SDK versions, and Android images that we can use for the emulator. In 2010, additional images were released for the ARM processor and X86 CPUs. 2012 was a big year because Eclipse and ADT were finally bundled; this was a big deal because until that time, developers had to install Eclipse and the ADT separately, and the installation process wasn't always smooth. So, the bundling of the two together made it a whole lot easier to get started with Android development. 2012 was also a big year because it marked the last year of Eclipse being the dominant IDE for Android.

In 2013, Android Studio was released. To be sure, it was still on beta, but the writing on the wall was clear. It will be the official IDE for Android development. Android Studio is based on Jetbrain's IntelliJ. IntelliJ is a commercial Java IDE that also has a community (nonpaid) version. This is the version that would serve as the base for Android Studio. In this chapter, we will cover the following.

- Setup

- Configuration

© Ted Hagos 2018
T. Hagos, *Learn Android Studio 3*, https://doi.org/10.1007/978-1-4842-3156-2_2

- Hardware acceleration

- Some basic parts of Android Studio 3

> **Note**   Before you can install Android Studio, you need the Java 8 JDK. JDK installation instructions are in the appendix.

Android Studio Setup

The AS3 installer is available for macOS, Windows, and Linux. The download page detects the OS you are using, so you should be able to spot the download button fairly quickly. You will be asked to agree to some terms and conditions before you can proceed with the download. Read it, understand it, and agree to it so you can carry on. After that, the AS3 installed will be downloaded in a zipped file.

If you have an existing installation of Android Studio, you can keep using that version and still install the preview edition. AS3 can coexist with your existing version of Android Studio; its settings will be kept in a different directory.

macOS

You must have seen the installation instruction after the terms and conditions screen; if you haven't or you skipped through it, I suggest that you give it a once-over, because there is an installation warning in case you have an existing version of Android Studio. It says that if you downloaded Android Studio version 2.3 or earlier, the application name on macOS installer does not include the version number. So, you may want to rename your existing Android Studio prior to installing the preview version. You can rename your existing Android Studio installation by opening a finder window; then, select "Applications" from the sidebar, find Android Studio, activate the context menu (press Ctrl + mouse click), and choose rename. The installation notes for AS3 are at `https://developer.android.com/studio/preview/install-preview.html`

1. Unpack the zipped file

2. Drag the application file into the **Applications** folder

3. Launch AS3

4. AS3 will prompt you to import some settings; if you have a previous installation, you can import that (it is the default option)

Windows

1. Unzip the installer file

2. Move it to a folder location of your choice (e.g., `C:\AndroidStudio`). Drill down to this folder

3. Inside, you will find a `bin` folder; inside it, you will find `studio64.exe`. This file is what you need to launch. If you are on a 32-bit Windows, the launcher file is named `studio.exe`

Tip   If you right-click `studio64.exe` and choose **Pin to Start Menu**, you can make AS3 available from the Windows Start menu; alternatively, you can pin it to the Taskbar.

Linux

The Linux installation requires a bit more work than simply double-clicking and following the installer prompts. In future releases of Ubuntu and its derivatives, this might change and become as simple and frictionless as its Windows and macOS counterparts, but for now, we need to do some tweaking. The extra activities on Linux are mostly because AS3 needs some 32-bit libraries and hardware acceleration.

Note   The installation instructions in this section are meant for Ubuntu 64-bit and other Ubuntu derivatives: Linux Mint, Lubuntu, Xubuntu, Ubuntu MATE, and so forth. I chose this distribution because I assumed that it is a very common Linux flavor, hence, readers of this book will be using that distribution.

If you are running a 64-bit version of Ubuntu, you will need to pull some 32-bit libraries in order for AS to function well.

To start pulling the 32 bit libraries for Linux, run the following commands on a terminal window.

```
sudo apt-get update && sudo apt-get upgrade -y
sudo dpkg --add-architecture i386
sudo apt-get install libncurses5:i386 libstdc++6:i386 zlib1g:i386
```

When all the prep work is done, the AS3 installation can be managed using the following steps.

1. Unpack the downloaded installer file. You can unpack the file using command-line tools or using the GUI tools; you can, for example, right-click the file and select the "Unpack here" option, if your file manager has that option

2. After unzipping the file, rename the folder to AndroidStudio

3. Move the folder to a location where you have read, write, and execute privileges. Alternatively, you can also move it to /usr/local/ AndroidStudio

4. Open a terminal window and go to the AndroidStudio/bin and execute ./studio.sh

5. At first launch, AS3 will ask you if you want to import some settings; if you have installed a previous version of Android Studio, you may want to import those settings into AS3

Configuring Android Studio

Before we can dive into programming, we need to do a couple of things to complete the development setup. We need to

▪ Get some more software so we start creating programs that target a specific version of Android

▪ Make sure we have all the SDK tools we need, and optionally

▪ Change the way we get updates for AS3

Launch AS3 if you haven't done so yet. From the opening dialog, click "Configure" and choose "SDK Manager" from the drop-down list. This should take you to a window where you can select the SDK platforms to download (Figure 2-1).

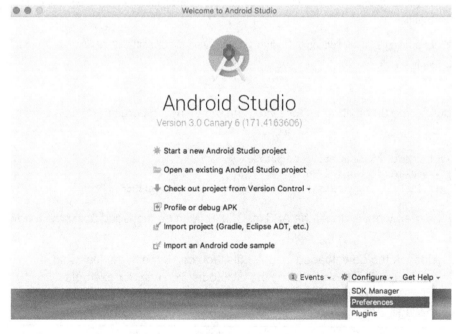

Figure 2-1. Preferences window

When you get to the SDK window, enable the "Show Package Details" option so you can see a more detailed view of each API level. We don't need to download everything in the SDK window. We will get only the items we need.

SDK levels or platform numbers are specific versions of Android. Android 8 or Android "O" is API level 26, and Nougat is API level 24 and 25. You don't need to memorize the platform numbers anymore, because AS3 shows the platform number with the corresponding Android nickname.

If you have a pretty fast Internet connection, you may choose to download everything. That way, you can create projects that target multiple versions of Android all the way down to Eclair. For our purposes, we will only download Nougat (platforms 24 and 25) and Oreo (platform 26). Make sure that together with the platforms, you will also download "Google APIs Intel x86 Atom_64 System Image". We will need those when we get to the part where we test run our applications.

> **Note**   Another way to build applications for earlier Android versions without having to download all the API levels is to use the Android Support Libraries; these libraries afford us backward compatibility.

Once you have completed the selection, click the "OK" button to start the download process (Figure 2-2).

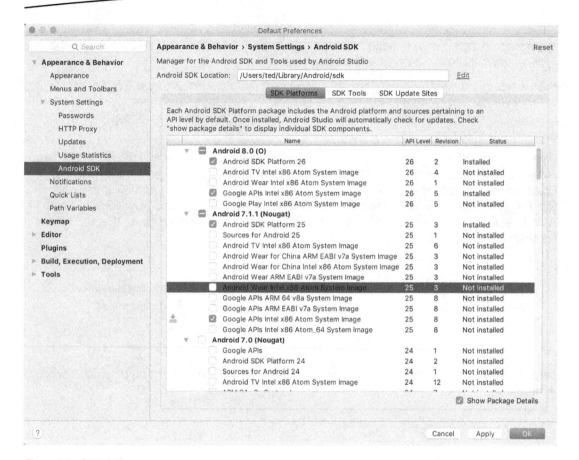

Figure 2-2. *SDK platforms*

Next, we head to the "SDK Tools" tab. This is in the same section on the Preferences window; just click the tab in the middle to view the details of the tools (Figure 2-3).

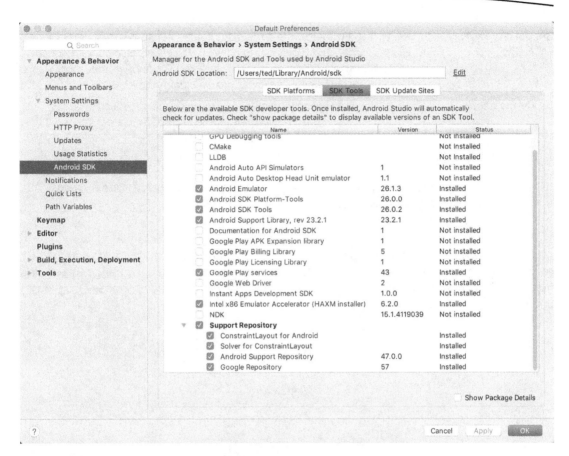

Figure 2-3. SDK tools

You don't generally have to change anything on this window, but it wouldn't hurt to check that you have the following packages.

Android SDK Platform Tools	This contains important tools like adb, which will help us do diagnostics and debugging, and sqlite3, which we can use when we create applications that use databases, plus a couple of other tools.
Android SDK Tools	This includes essential Android tools like ProGuard. You don't need to deep dive into the details of these tools (for now). Just make sure this box is ticked and you're good to go.
Android Emulator	You will definitely use this. This is a device emulation tool. We will use this to test our applications in a virtual device.

Support Repository	If you want to write code that targets Android Wear, Android TV, or Google Cast, you want to download this. This also contains local Maven repository for support libraries. The support repository also allows you to use new features on older Android versions.
HAXM Installer	If you are using a macOS, or a PC with Intel processor, you can use this. It is an accelerator for the Android Emulator.

> **Note**   If you are on the Linux platform, you cannot use HAXM even if you have an Intel processor. KVM will be used in Linux instead of HAXM.

After you've downloaded some target platforms and checked the SDK Tools, we can move on to the last configuration item, which is the "Update Channel". You can change this setting from the "Preferences" dialog window. From the opening dialog window, choose "Configure" and then "Preferences" (Figure 2-4).

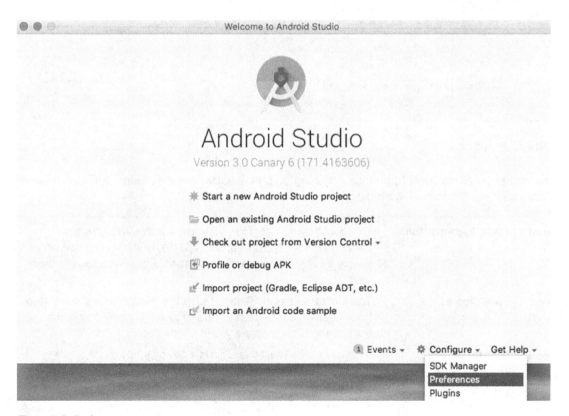

Figure 2-4. Preferences

On the left side of "Default Preferences", choose "Updates" (Figure 2-5).

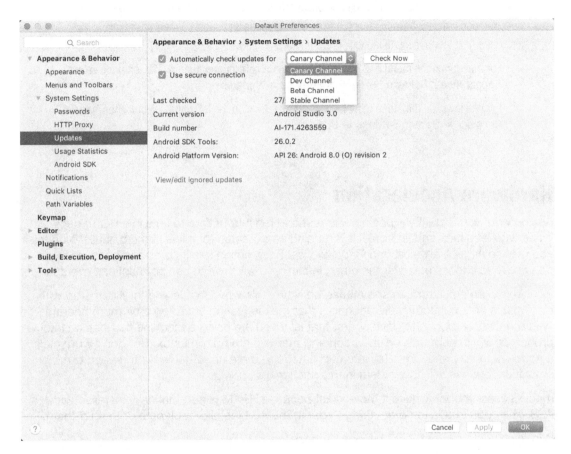

Figure 2-5. Update Channel

AS3, just like any Android Studio installation is configured by default to get updates from the channel where you originally downloaded the installer. At the time of this writing, AS3 was downloaded from the "Canary" Channel (also known as the Preview Channel), hence, it gets the update from the Canary Channel by default. You can change the channel to any one of these four:

- Canary Channel: This has bleeding-edge releases; it could be updated every week. You don't want to use this for production codes

- Dev Channel: Just like the Canary Channel but a bit more stable. You still don't want to use this for production

- Beta Channel: This contains release candidates. The devs are basically waiting for feedback before they get fed to the Stable Channel

- Stable Channel: This is the official stable release and is suited for production work

> **Note**   The "Preferences" window can be accessed within AS3 when a project is opened in full view. You don't always have to launch it from the AS3 opening window. When you're inside AS3, follow the next instructions to launch "Preferences":
>
> - For macOS: on the menu bar, **Android Studio ➤ Preferences**, then on the left pane select **Appearance & Behavior ➤ System Settings ➤ Updates**
>
> - For Windows: on the menu bar, **File ➤ Settings**, then on the left pane select **Appearance & Behavior ➤ System Settings ➤ Updates**

Hardware Acceleration

As you write your app, it will be useful to test and run it from time to time in order to get immediate feedback and find out if it is running as expected, or if it is running at all. To do this, you will use either a physical or a virtual device. Each option has its pros and cons, and you don't have to choose one over the other; in fact, you will have to use both options eventually.

Running on an emulator can sometimes be slow;, this why Google and Intel came up with HAXM. It is an emulator acceleration tool that makes testing your app a bit more bearable. This is definitely a boon to developers, that is, if you are using a machine that has an Intel processor which supports virtualization and that you are not on Linux. But don't worry if you're not lucky enough to fall into that category; there are other ways to speed up emulation, and we will cover them in this section.

macOS users probably have it the easiest because HAXM is automatically installed with AS3. They don't have to do anything to get it; the AS3 installer took care of that for them.

Windows users can get HAXM in one of these ways:

- Downloading it from https://software.intel.com/en-us/android. Install it like you would any other Windows software, double-click, and follow the prompts.

- Alternatively, you can get HAXM via AS3's SDK manager; this is the recommended method.

For Linux users, the recommended software is KVM instead. KVM (Kernel-based Virtual Machine), is a virtualization solution for Linux. It contains virtualization extensions (Intel VT or AMD-V).

To get KVM, we need to pull some software from the repos. But before doing anything else, you need to do two things.

1. Make sure that virtualization is enabled on your BIOS or UEFI settings. Consult your hardware manual on how to get to these settings. It usually involves shutting down the PC, restarting it, and pressing an interrupt key like F2 or Del as soon as you hear the chime of your system speaker, but like I said, consult your hardware manual

2. Once you made your changes, and rebooted to Linux, find out if your system can run virtualization. This can be accomplished by running the following command from a terminal egrep -c '(vmx|svm)' /proc/cpuinfo. If the result is a number higher than zero, that means you can go ahead with the installation

```
sudo apt-get install qemu-kvm libvirt-bin ubuntu-vm-builder bridge-utils
sudo adduser your_user_name kvm
sudo adduser your_user_name libvirtd
```

You may have to reboot the system to complete the installation.

> **Note**   There are other ways to check if virtualization is available on your Linux machine. You can run the following command on a terminal. You will need to run this command as root
>
> ```
> grep --color vmx /proc/cpuinfo
> ```
>
> Another way is to is to use "cpu-checker", which you will need to get it from the repos. See the following command
>
> ```
> sudo apt-get update
> sudo apt-get install cpu-checker
> ```
>
> Now you can check if the CPU has acceleration capabilities
>
> ```
> kvm-ok
> ```
>
> If the acceleration is available, you should see something like
>
> ```
> INFO: /dev/kvm exists
> KVM acceleration can be used
> ```

The Android Studio IDE

The following section points out some common features of AS3. We will create our first project in the next chapter, so you may want to refer back to this section once we've started creating some projects. For now, let's just familiarize ourselves with AS3.

AS3 is based on Jetbrain's IntelliJ IDE, so if you have occasion to use that, AS3 will be very familiar. Even if you are coming from another IDE such as Eclipse or Netbeans, a lot of AS3 features should be very familiar. Figure 2-6 shows some of the basic parts of AS3.

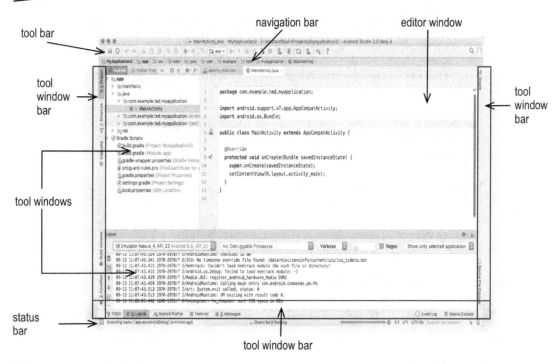

Figure 2-6. Android Studio IDE

Editor window	This is the most prominent window and it has the most screen real estate. The editor window is where you can create and modify project files. It changes in appearance depending on what you are editing. If you are working on a program source file, this window will show just the source files. If you are editing layout files, you may see either the raw XML file or a visual rendering of the layout, just like you what you have seen in the last chapter
Navigation bar	This allows you to navigate the project files. It is just a more compact view of the "Project files" window. It's a horizontally arranged collection of arrow boxes which resembles some sort of breadcrumb navigation that you can find on some web sites. You can open your project files through the navigation bar or through the project tool window
Toolbar	The toolbar lets you do a wide range of actions: save files, run the app, open the AVD (Android virtual device) manager, open the SDK manager, undo/redo actions, and so on.
Tool windows	The tool windows gives you access to very specific tasks: look at the project files, view all the TODO annotations, view the logcat window, access the profiler, and so on. Each of the tool windows is expandable and collapsible. You can pop them open when you need them then tuck them away when you're done
Tool window bar	The tool window bar runs along the perimeter of the IDE window. It contains the individual buttons you need to activate specific tool windows
Status bar	This part of the IDE shows what's going on with your project and with AS3 itself. It displays context-sensitive messages such as error messages, running processes, repository messages, and so on.

AS3 offers many ways to navigate the IDE, as you have seen in Figure 2-6, but the primary way of navigating AS3 is through the main menu bar. This bar sits at the top of the IDE, and it is the most complete and comprehensive way to navigate it (Figures 2-7 and 2-8).

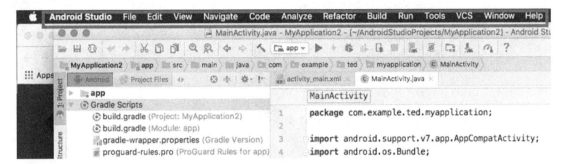

Figure 2-7. Main menu bar in macOS

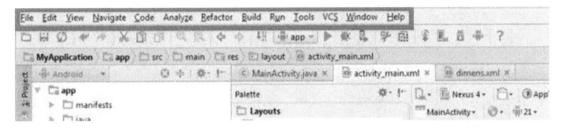

Figure 2-8. Main menu bar in Windows

Chapter 3

Application Fundamentals

We will create a simple project. It will not do anything but simply display a text field. The point of the exercise is to familiarize ourselves with the Android Studio development environment.

Creating a Project

Launch the Android Studio IDE if it isn't open yet. You will be greeted by the opening screen (Figure 3-1).

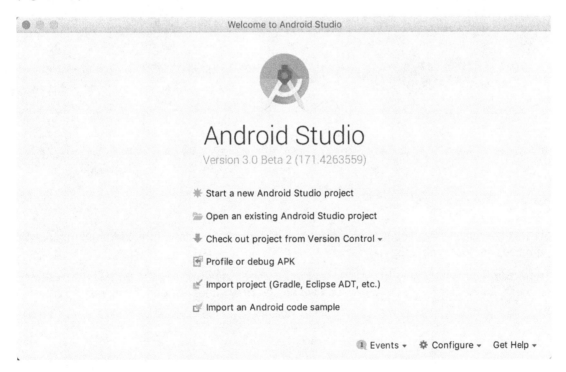

Figure 3-1. Welcome to Android Studio

© Ted Hagos 2018
T. Hagos, *Learn Android Studio 3*, https://doi.org/10.1007/978-1-4842-3156-2_3

There are a couple of things you can do from this opening dialog window, but the only thing we will do is to start a new Android project. We will explore the other options as we go further along. Click the "Start a new Android Studio Project" to launch the new project wizard. Before you go further, make sure that you are connected to the Internet. Android Studio uses a build tool called gradle. It pulls several files from Internet repositories whenever you create a new project (Figure 3-2).

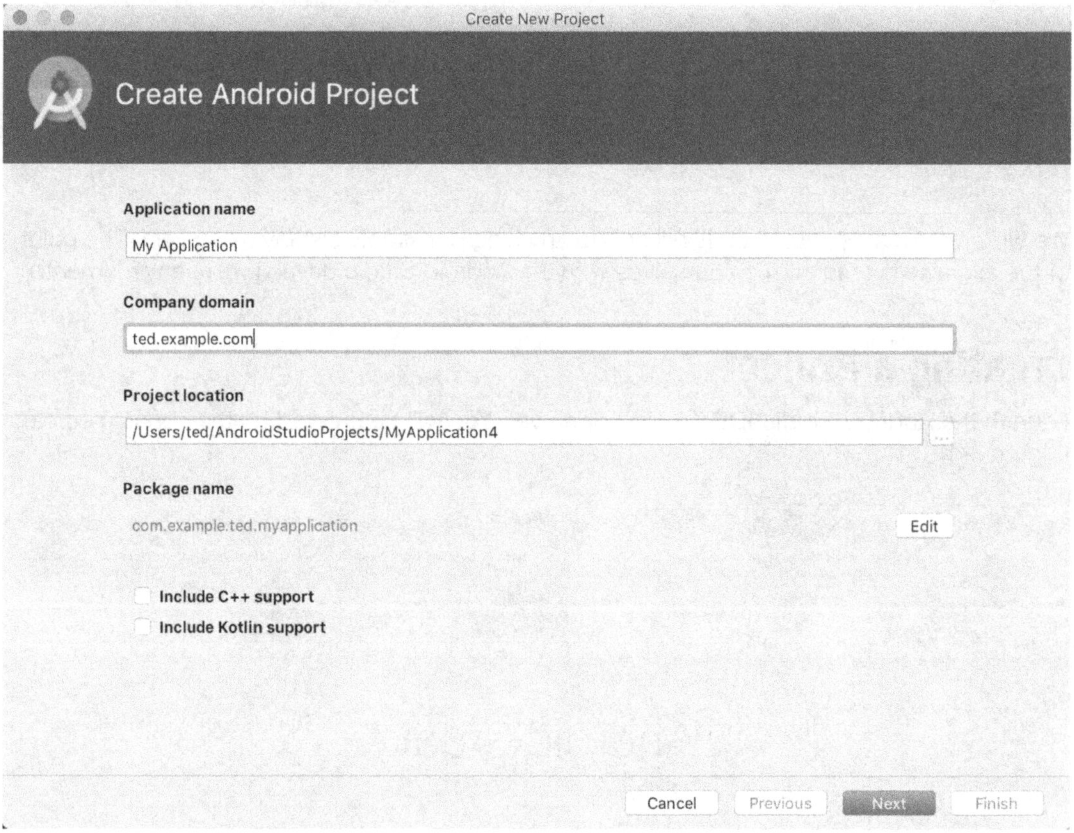

Figure 3-2. *Create new project*

You will need to provide a couple of things for the wizard. You need to type in the application name and the company domain.

The wizard shown in Figure 3-2 will accept input about the details of the project you want to create; it will be filled with default values which you may accept or edit if you wish.

application name	What you want to call the application. This is known also as the project name. The application name not only becomes not only the name of the top-level folder which contains all the project files in your disk, but also becomes a part of your application's identity should you release it in Google Play
company domain	This is your organization or company's domain name in reverse DNS notation. If you don't have a company name, just type anything that resembles a web domain name (e.g., myname.com). Since we are just trying to get started for now and we won't release this application to Google Play, it doesn't matter if the company domain is real or not
package name	This is the company domain plus the application name. This will uniquely identify your application should you choose to release it in Google Play. You will not input this field; this is automatically constructed from the application name and company domain. The wizard will fill this up automatically for you but you can edit it if you wish. Generally, it is best just to leave this alone
project location	This is a place in your disk drive where the project files will be kept. It is almost similar to the workspace idea of Eclipse, if you have used that. Unlike Eclipse though, the project location is simply that, a location for your project files. It does not contain settings information like in Eclipse

We need to specify which version of Android we would like to target (Figure 3-3). We'll just choose Marshmallow for now (API level 23). This doesn't mean that our application will run only on Marshmallow; instead, it means our app will run on devices that have Marshmallow or higher versions. The *minimum sdk* entry in this screen will dictate the lowest version of Android that our app will support. There is no hard-and-fast rule on how to select the minimum sdk, but it's enough to remember that the lower the sdk version, the more devices your app can support. Best keep in mind also that lower Android versions may offer fewer application features. On the other hand however, the support libraries allow us to use new features on older Android versions. Selecting a min sdk could be more of a business decision rather than a technical one because you need to consider how wide your audience of target users will be.

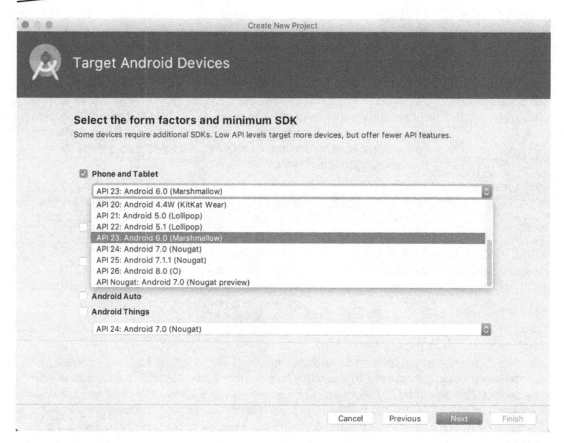

Figure 3-3. Select target version

Leave the other check boxes untouched. We are only interested in the phone/tablet application for the moment.

Next thing to do is choose a type of activity. An activity is an Android component that facilitates user interaction. It is the visible part of your application. There are many kinds of activities, as you can see on the wizard options in Figure 3-4, but for our purpose, we will select the "empty activity" option.

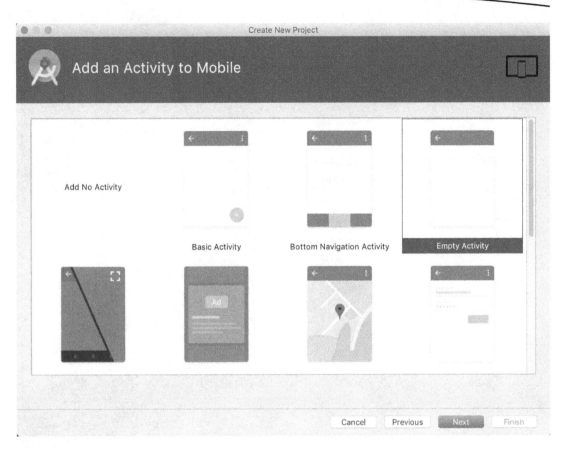

Figure 3-4. *Choose type of activity*

Choosing the "empty activity" option does not mean we won't get any activity class. The wizard will generate an activity class for us, but it will be empty. It won't have any widget or controls except for a single text field that says "Hello World". The empty activity is the basic building block of other activities. It is a good idea to be acquainted with this most basic version of the Activity class.

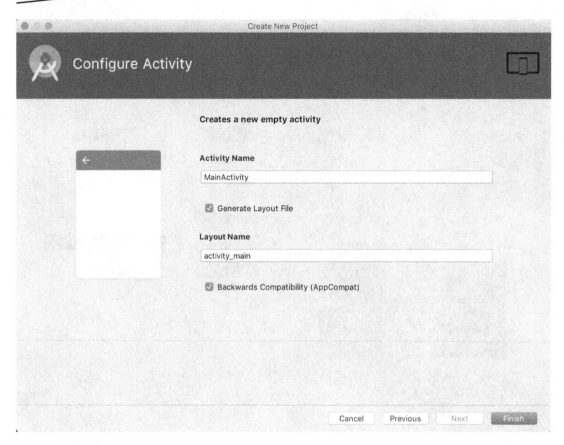

Figure 3-5. *Configure activity*

Once we've chosen the type of activity, there are two other inputs that remain: the *activity name* and *layout name (Figure 3-5)*. The activity name will be used to generate a Java file which will contain all the program logic for this activity. The layout name will be used to generate an XML file that will contain the user interface definition.

When you click the "Finish" button, AS3 will kick into high gear to generate the project. You need to be connected to the Internet when this is happening because AS3 will pull quite a few resources from the Web.

During the very first run of AS3, you may see some error messages; that's just a result of the building process. AS3 will usually give you directions on how to correct those errors. It may be as simple as clicking a link at the top right of the IDE in yellow, which shows the error message itself.

Using Android Studio

When things have finally settled, you will see a screen similar to Figure 3-6.

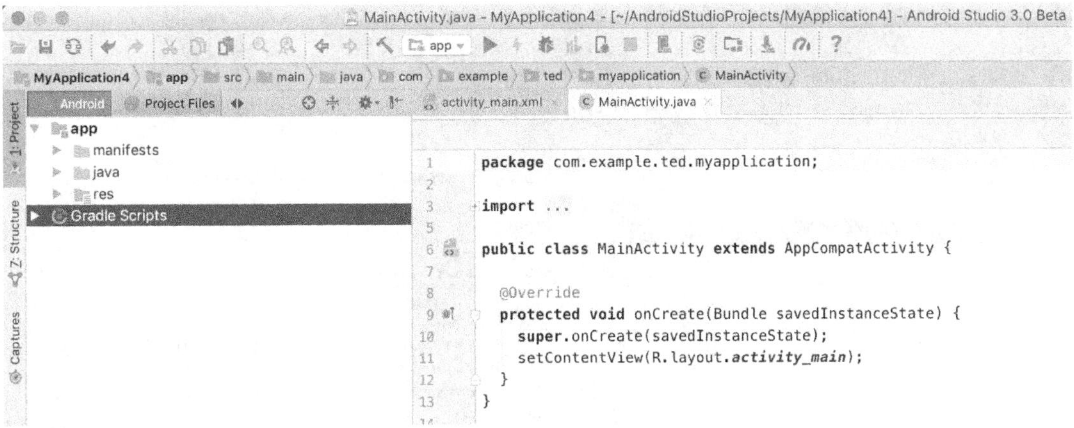

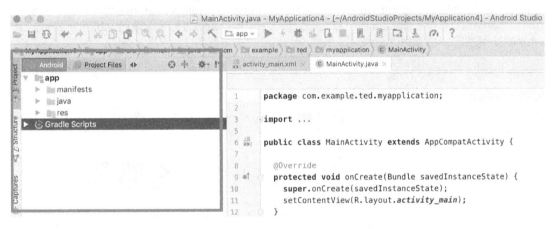

Figure 3-6. *Main AS3 window*

On the far left of AS3 main window, you will see a section with a tree-like layout where the files and folders of our app are displayed (see Figure 3-7). You can use this to navigate the project and open a file by double-clicking it.

Figure 3-7. *Project window*

The main editing area uses tabs. When you open a file for editing, it becomes a tab in here. You can use the tabs to switch from one file to another. There are two tabs currently open: choose the `activity_main.xml` tab so we can view how our app looks (Figure 3-8).

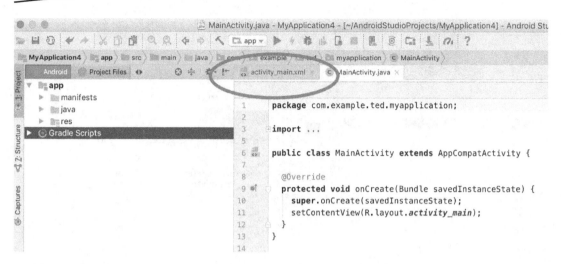

Figure 3-8. Tabbed editing area

You will notice that when you switched to view activity_main, the context of AS3 changed as well. Once the UI layout became available for editing, the "Palette" became visible as well. What we are seeing in Figure 3-9 is a rendering of our app's user interface. This UI is defined on an XML file (activity_main.xml) . As you can see, there isn't much on it yet but a simple "Hello World" that the wizard built for us.

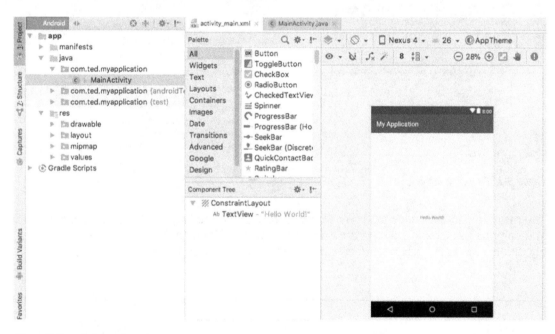

Figure 3-9. activity_main.xml

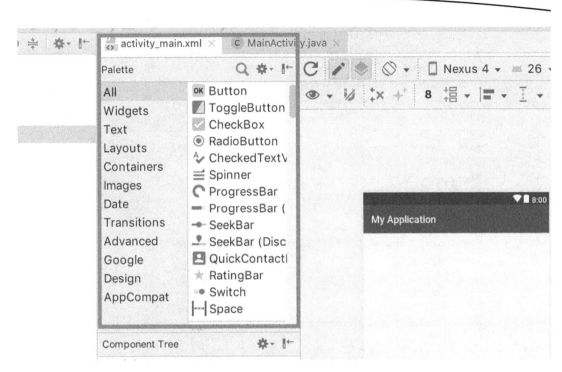

Figure 3-10. Palette

The "Palette" area contains all the views or widgets that we can use for our app. The basic idea is to simply drag and drop views from this palette and onto the design canvas.

While you are still viewing `activity_main`, you will notice that there are two tabs the lower left part of AS3. These tabs correspond to two modes of viewing the layout screen. The "Design" mode shows a visual rendering of the UI, and the "Text" mode shows us the XML code. The layout file can be manipulated either way. Switching between design and textual mode is a great way to learn and familiarize yourself with the XML markup.

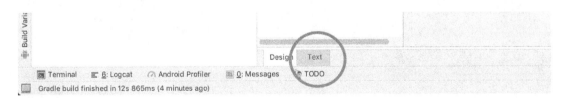

Figure 3-11. viewing modes of activity_main.xml

Figure 3-12 shows the XML markup content of the layout file (`activity_main.xml`).

```
1     <?xml version="1.0" encoding="utf-8"?>
2     <android.support.constraint.ConstraintLayout
3         xmlns:android="http://schemas.android.com/apk/res/android"
4         xmlns:app="http://schemas.android.com/apk/res-auto"
5         xmlns:tools="http://schemas.android.com/tools"
6         android:layout_width="match_parent"
7         android:layout_height="match_parent"
8         tools:context="com.example.ted.myapplication.MainActivity">
9
10        <TextView
11            android:layout_width="wrap_content"
12            android:layout_height="wrap_content"
13            android:text="Hello World!"
14            app:layout_constraintBottom_toBottomOf="parent"
15            app:layout_constraintLeft_toLeftOf="parent"
16            app:layout_constraintRight_toRightOf="parent"
17            app:layout_constraintTop_toTopOf="parent"/>
18
19    </android.support.constraint.ConstraintLayout>
```

Figure 3-12. Textual view of activity_main.xml

We don't need to add or do anything else to this app. The purpose of this first exercise is to simply get acquainted with the most common features of AS3. The steps we did so far are quite boilerplate. Most of the applications you will create will go through the same steps.

The next thing to do is run the application. We will execute the app inside an AVD (Android virtual device). The AVD is an emulator; it runs an actual image of an Android OS rather than just simulating its behavior. To run the app, click the "Run" button on the toolbar.

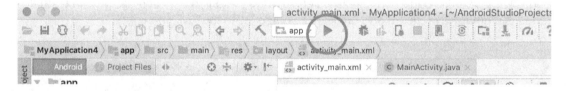

Figure 3-13. Run button

AS3 will look for either a connected physical device or an already running emulator. Since we have neither one, none are listed in "Connected Devices". There are a couple of entries already in "Available Virtual Devices" because I have created them already. Your setup will be quite empty since you have not created an AVD before.

Create a new emulator by clicking "Create New Virtual Device" as shown in Figure 3-14.

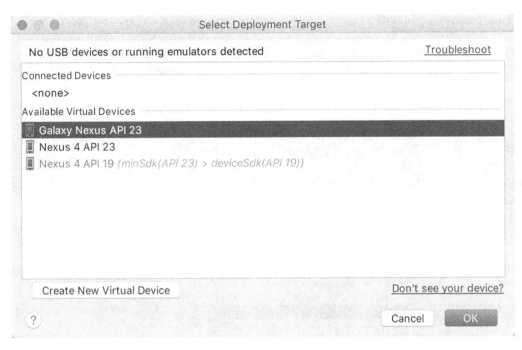

Figure 3-14. Deployment target

Choose a device definition. In this example, I chose the 4.7" Nexus 4. Click "Next".

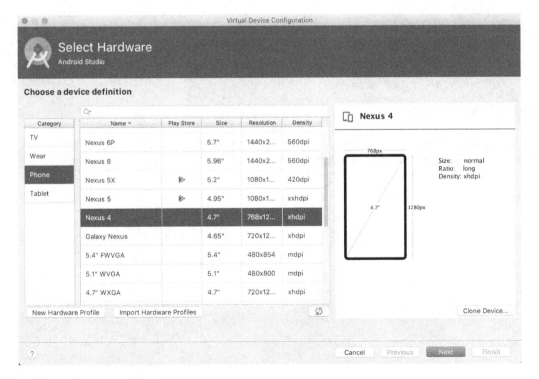

Figure 3-15. AVD configuration

We should choose an OS image for our new emulator. This project was created with a min sdk of 23 (Marshmallow), so we will choose API 23 as the system image as well. In your workstation, the Marshmallow entry might appear with a clickable "Download" link; if that is the case, just click "Download" so that the OS image will be downloaded. When that is done, click "Next" to configure the new emulator.

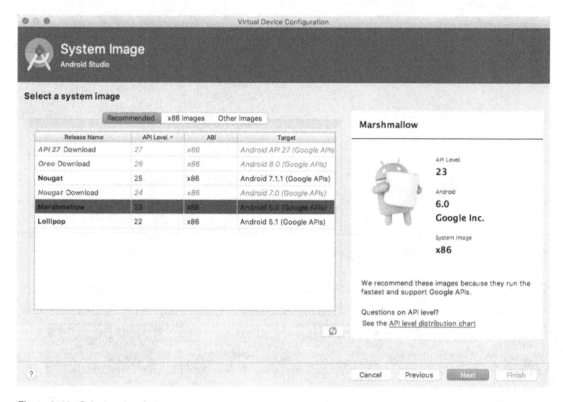

Figure 3-16. Select system image

You can change the name of the newly created emulator, or you could just accept the default name. Click the "Show Advanced Settings" if you want to see some more options for configuration.

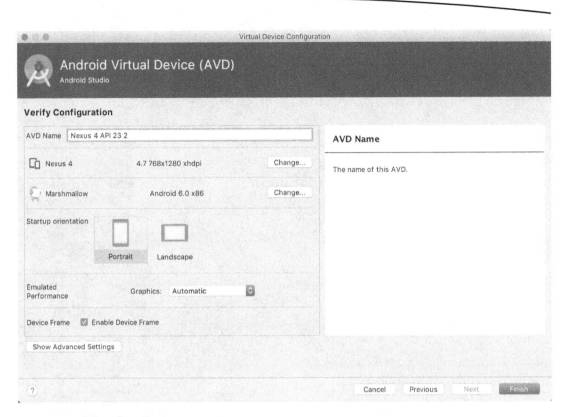

Figure 3-17. AVD configuration

You can change a couple more options when advanced settings are visible. You can tweak these values later depending on the needs of your app. You can give your emulator more memory or internal storage space if you need to test that in your app. For now, we will simply accept the default values. Once the AVD is created, you should be back the "Select Deployment Target" screen.

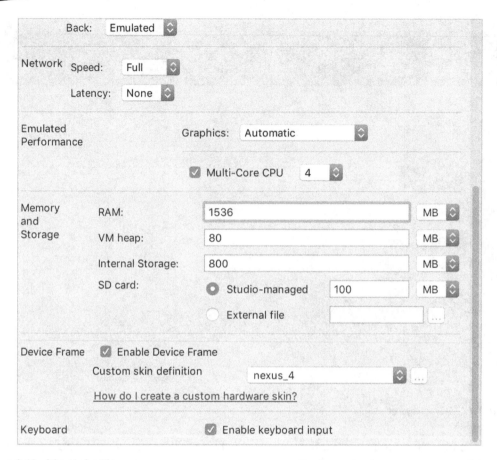

Figure 3-18. Advanced settings

Select the newly created emulator, and then click "OK". It could take a while for the emulator to start, but when it finishes, you should see (Figure 3-20) a virtual machine representation of the Nexus 4 running on a separate window.

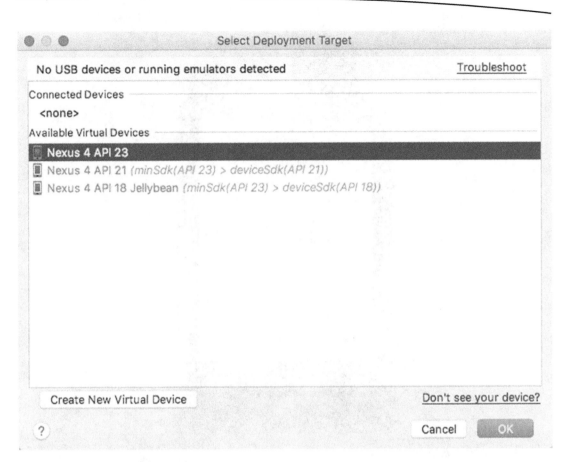

Figure 3-19. Select deployment target

Go back to AS3 and click the "Run" button so we can run the app on the emulator with our "Hello World" application running.

Figure 3-20. *Hello World running in the emulator*

Compilation and Runtime

Android components are written using either the Java or Kotlin language; this is why AS3 ships with its own embedded JDK. The compilation process however, is not the same as what you might have been used to with either Java SE or Java EE.

Android executables are dex files and not class files. Program compilation is a two-step process in Android. The java source files are first compiled into class files, just what you did in Java SE/EE. After that, the resulting class files are converted into to dex files by the dx tool. Dex files are the ones that are run inside the Android runtime (ART).

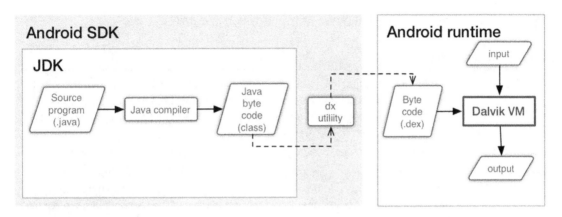

Figure 3-21. Compilation and runtime

Android Components

Applications in Android are not quite the same as apps written for the desktop. They might have some striking similarities as far as appearances go, but structurally they differ quite a lot. Desktop apps are pretty much self-contained. The exe files contain all needed routines and subroutines within them. From time to time, it may rely on some dynamically loaded library, but pretty much the exe is self-sufficient. That is not the case with Android apps.

An Android app is not a monolithic package like an EXE file in Windows. It is a bundle of loosely related or loosely coupled components and other resources, and they are held together inside an APK file (Android package file).

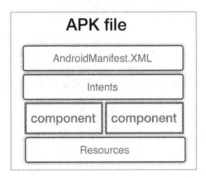

Figure 3-22. Logical view of an Android app

Table 3-1 describes an Android app and its composition in detail.

Table 3-1. An Android App

APK file	The Android package file has extension of *.apk*. It basically a form of archive that was based on the jar (Java archive), which in turn was based on a zipped file. It holds everything together in an Android app. This file is what is downloaded on a user's device when they install an app
Resources	You may include other resources like audio, video, or pictures in your app
Manifest	The *Android manifest* is an XML file. It defines quite a few things: for example, what the application can do, what kinds of requests or "Intents" can it respond to, what makes it up, whether it can go to the Internet, and so on. Here are some other things you will find on the manifest file: • The name of the application • Which screen will show up first when a user clicks the application • What kinds of components does the app have? Does it have Activities? What are their names? Does it have BroadcastReceivers Services, Content Providers? • What kinds of things can it do with the mobile device? Can it access the network? The Internet? The camera? Will it record GPS locations? Can other applications interact with this application? If so, what kinds of permissions should these other applications have? • Does the application use external libraries (usually jar files that another programmer wrote)? • What versions of Android will this application run on?
Components	Components are application building blocks. They are quite unique to Android's architecture because the other mobile computing platforms do not build their applications the same way. A component can be created to do one thing: show a screen, run a background process, provide data, and so on. This component can make the functionality or behavior available to other components (even to other applications outside its APK). This kind of loose coupling makes it possible to achieve reuse at an application level
Intents	If components make loose coupling possible in Android, Intents are what connects these components. We will use intents in lots of ways: for example, to call another screen, to respond to some other application or another component, or to pass data from one component to another (or to another application)

Components

Components are key building blocks for any Android application. They are high-level abstractions of useful things like showing a screen to the user, running a background task, broadcasting an event, and so on. They are precoded Java classes with very specific behavior. We need to extend them, of course, so we can add functionality that is unique to our application.

Think of building an Android application like it is building a house. Some people build houses the traditional way: they assemble beams, struts, floor panels, and so forth. They build the doors and other fittings from raw materials, by hand like an artisan. If we built Android applications this way, it would take us a long time and it could be quite difficult. The skill necessary to build applications from the scratch could be out of reach for many programmers. In Android, applications are built using components. Think of it as prefabricated pieces of a house. The parts manufactured in advance and all it requires is assembly. We don't build the house from raw materials. Instead we use prebuilt components and assemble them together. If you could remember the parts of the Android operating system from Chapter 1, the OS includes quite a lot of things, not only hardware drivers and applications, it also includes prebuilt components. We can build our own applications on top of these components, thus saving us valuable amounts of time. Figure 3-23 shows a logical representation of the Android architecture.

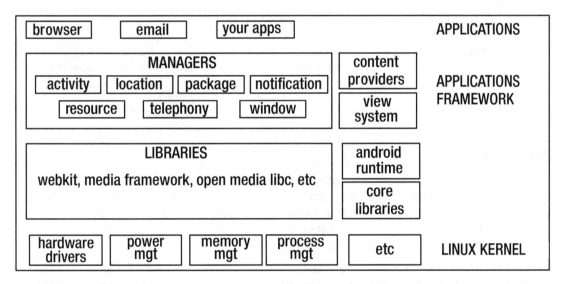

Figure 3-23. Android architecture

Table 3-2. Android Components

Component	What It Does	Example
Activity base class: android.app.Activity	Holds, displays the user interface elements (View and ViewGroups). It's a focused thing a user can do with your application	View a single e-mail message, take notes
Service base class: android.app.Service	Run a process in the background	Download a large file from the Internet, play background music
BroadcastReceiver base class: android.content.BroadcastReceiver	Receive messages either from the Android system or from applications	Display a warning message when the device battery dips to below 10%
ContentProvider base class: android.content.ContentProvider	Store and retrieve data, like a database	Contacts or address book on your phone. Any application can look up and add data to the phonebook

Activities

An activity is a single focused thing that a user can do (this definition is from the Android developer web site, developer.android.com). It's a very succinct definition of the Activity component because it is exactly that, a focused thing that interacts with a user. The equivalent of an Activity in your PC desktop would be a window that is blown up in full screen. It grabs your attention and gets you focused.

The activity component is part of the applications framework, as shown in Figure 3-1. The basic idea to use this component is to extend (inherit) from the class *android.app.Activity* and then compose the user interface by aggregating UI elements (text fields, buttons, etc.) inside the activity class. All of these user interface elements are capable of reacting to events such as click and swipe.

Some applications have only one Activity, and some other applications will have more than one screen. For applications that have more than one screen, you will need a way to launch activities. There are also times when you will need to pass data from one activity to another. We will address those needs by using *Intents*.

Services

Sometimes you will need to write code that is invisible to the user, one that doesn't have a user interface. Surely you will need to launch it somehow from an Activity, but once launched, the application just keeps on running, even if the UI that launched it has already disappeared from view. A music player is such an example of this kind of app. A GPS-enabled application which updates your location every now and then is another example.

If you need to build these kinds of apps, you will use Services. These are long running operations that are executed in the background. A Service is independent of the Activity that launched. Even if the UI screen that was used to launch the service has already died, the Service code just keeps on going.

Content Providers

Each application runs on its own process: its own virtual machine. This behavior of Android protects each application. If one badly written application goes wonky, it cannot bring the other running applications down. It is good for application stability. But this makes it nearly impossible for one application to access data from another.

Content Providers solves the problem of data sharing between applications. It is possible for you to write an application and share whatever data it has with other applications. The Contacts and Calendar apps in Android are good examples of apps that use Content Providers.

Don't confuse Content Provider with your own database. If you create an application that uses a SQLite database, of course your application can access that. If, for example, you want to allow other applications to gain access to your app's data, you can build a Content Provider. Your application will make the data available to other apps using standard URIs.

Broadcast Receivers

Broadcast receivers are used if you want to execute some program logic in your app as a response to events generated by either the Android system or other applications. You can, for example, initiate a database write when the phone receives an SMS message. You probably want to examine the SMS message and if it fits certain criteria, you will record it to the database. This is one example of how to use Broadcast receivers.

You can make your application listen to certain events. To do this, you need to register your application to listen to a specific event. It is the same concept when you subscribe to a mailing list. When there is a new mail, you get notified.

Apart from listening to broadcasted events, you can also make your application broadcast specific events. To do that, you will extend a specific Android class called the BroadcastReceiver.

BroadcastReceivers typically don't have user interfaces. But you can create notifications that will show up on the status bar.

Chapter 4

Activities and Layouts

Most apps will need one or more screens that they will use to communicate with the user. It is possible to write applications that don't need a UI (e.g., apps that run in the background), but for the most part, when you create an application it will need a user interface, and for this reason, we need to understand activities. Building user interfaces is one of the fundamental skills that an Android programmer must have. In this chapter, we will take a look at how to build an app with a single and simple user interface. You have already created such an app back in Chapter 3, but we did not take a closer look at the activity component.

Our goals for this chapter are the following:

- Understand the basic things that make up an application with a user interface: these are activities, View objects, and layout (view groups)

- Understand the basic relationship between an activity and a layout file

- Understand the basics of ConstraintLayout

Building the Hello Screen

Back in Chapter 3, we built a project with an empty activity. This new project will be very similar to that one. If you want to work on this code sample, you can use the project information in Table 4-1; that way, it will be easier to follow.

© Ted Hagos 2018

T. Hagos, *Learn Android Studio 3*, https://doi.org/10.1007/978-1-4842-3156-2_4

Table 4-1. Project Information

Application name	Hello
Company domain	Use your web site, or invent something; remember that this is in reverse DNS notation
Project location	This usually best left alone; use the default value, but make sure to take note of this location in case the need to access it arises. Ignore the C++ and Kotlin support
Form factor	Phone and tablet only
Minimum SDK	API 23 Marshmallow
Type of activity	Empty
Activity name	If you leave the default alone it alone, this will be *MainActivity*, which is fine
Layout name	If you leave the default alone it alone, this will be *activity_main*, which is fine

Once the creation wizard finishes, you will have quite a few files in the project folder, but only two of them are important for us right now: we are particularly interested in `MainActivity.java` and `activity_main.xml` (Table 4-2, for details).

Table 4-2. Important files for this project

File	Location	Purpose
Layout file	app/src/main/res/layout/ activity_main.xml	This is the layout file of our application. All user interface elements are written in here. Whenever you drag and drop any element from the palette, this file gets updated to reflect what you changed in design view
Program file	app/src/main/java/ MainActivity.java	This Java file is the main program; all the program logic goes in here. If you want to do something as a reaction to some user-generated event, this will be the place to write that code

The Layout File

Open `activity_main` if it isn't already open yet; in case it isn't or if you closed the tab previously, you can launch it from the project tool window.

The project tool window shows us a tree-like structure of our project files. When you double-click any file, it will be launched and opened as a tab in the main editor.

The project tool window allows you to change perspectives or views. Most developers just leave the view to "Android" as shown in Figure 4-1, but you can switch the view to *Project*, *Packages*, *Scratches*, *Project Files*, and so on. Try to open the different views by clicking the spinner button right beside "Android" so you can explore each view for yourself.

When the layout file is opened in main editor, you may view it in design mode (wysiwyg) or text mode. In design mode, you may see both the design and blueprint of the layout file.

Figure 4-1. Project tool window

You can switch between design and text mode while editing the layout file by clicking either "text" or "design" tab; you can find these tabs somewhere in the lower left portion of the main editor. These tabs appear only when you are editing the layout file (i.e., they are context sensitive). Figure 4-2 shows the layout file in "design" mode.

Note   The AS3 UI elements in your installation may not be consistent with what's shown in Figure 4-1. AS3 is progressing at a rapid pace, and your version of AS3 may not be the same as what's been used in this book.

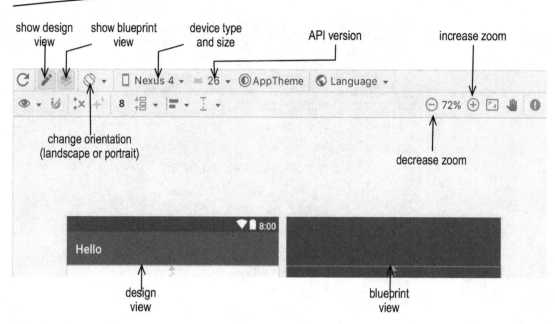

Figure 4-2. Design editor

Table 4-3 describes the elements of the Design editor

Table 4-3. Elements of the Design Editor

show design view	Toggles between showing and hiding the design view (see Figure 4-2)
show blueprint view	Toggles between showing and hiding the blueprint view
change orientation	Changes the orientation of the layout. This will be useful if you are trying to simulate what the layout would look like if the user switches between portrait and landscape orientation
device type and size	Selects the device type, whether it's a phone, tablet, TV, or Android wear. You can also change the screen configuration (size and density)
api version	Selects the version of Android you would like to preview the app
design view	Shows a color preview of the layout
blueprint view	Shows an outline preview of the layout
increase zoom	Increases the magnification of the layout on the design editor
decrease zoom	Decreases the magnification of the layout on the design editor

There may be two windows represented in the design editor: as you can see in Figure 4-2, both of these two windows are actually representations of the same layout file (our activity_ main). The design view shows a color preview of the layout file, while the blueprint view shows only the outline. You can choose to switch off either of these views or you can view them both.

Listing 4-1 shows the layout file in "text mode". In this mode, you could see XML code that AS3 generates as you make changes to the layout in design mode. This process of wysiwyg to code generation is bidirectional: if you edit the xml directly, the changes will be reflected almost instantaneously back to the design view, although I don't imagine that you would like to build the UI by editing the XML directly.

Listing 4-1. app/src/main/res/layout/activity_main.xml

```
<?xml version="1.0" encoding="utf-8"?>

<android.support.constraint.ConstraintLayout  ❶
  xmlns:android="http://schemas.android.com/apk/res/android"
  xmlns:app="http://schemas.android.com/apk/res-auto"
  xmlns:tools="http://schemas.android.com/tools"
  android:layout_width="match_parent"
  android:layout_height="match_parent"
  tools:context="com.example.ted.hello.MainActivity">

  <TextView  ❷
    android:layout_width="wrap_content"
    android:layout_height="wrap_content"
    android:text="Hello World!"
    app:layout_constraintBottom_toBottomOf="parent"
    app:layout_constraintLeft_toLeftOf="parent"
    app:layout_constraintRight_toRightOf="parent"
    app:layout_constraintTop_toTopOf="parent"/>

</android.support.constraint.ConstraintLayout>
```

❶ The root node of the XML file, this line defines the layout for this activity to be a `ConstraintLayout`

❷ Defines `TextView` widget as the first child of the root node. A TextView is a noneditable text widget, which are commonly used as labels

In most situations, you won't need to mess around with the xml code of the layout file because the design editor is sufficient for designing and building the user interface.

Main Java Program

The other file of interest is the main program. If it isn't opened in the main editor yet, launch `MainActivity.java` from the project tool window.

Figure 4-3 shows the main program in the editor window. You will see a bunch of visual guides in here, including code folding outline, line numbers in the gutter, and icons of related files (when applicable).

Figure 4-3. *app/src/main/java/MainActivity.java*

The code folding outline is useful when you are editing large source files; folding certain blocks of code can help to better show the structure of the program (and sometimes, it can also help you hunt down some missing curly braces). Code folding can be enabled or disabled in "Settings" (Windows and Linux) or "Preferences" (macOS) window. To go to the "Settings" window, press Ctrl + Alt + S. To go to the "Preferences" window press Command + , (comma)

Table 4-4. *Keyboard Shortcuts for Code Folding*

Task	Windows or Linux	macOS
Open Settings or Preferences dialog	Ctrl + Alt + S	⌘ + ',' (comma)
Expand code block	Ctrl + Shift + '+' (plus)	⌘ + '+' (plus)
Collapse code block	Ctrl + Shift + '-' (minus)	⌘ + '-' (minus)

AS3 lets you view the program source file in a variety of modes: normal mode, presentation view, distraction free, and fullscreen mode. There are overlaps between some of the modes, so it might be best to try out all of them and see which one you prefer for yourself (see Table 4-5).

Table 4-5. View Modes

Normal mode	This is the default mode when AS3 opens. Toolbars are all visible, editor fonts are normal size, and AS3 isn't occupying the whole screen real estate
Presentation view	This is designed for delivering presentations: the toolbar disappears and the font size is bigger than usual
Fullscreen mode	AS3 will span the full screen area. In macOS, it will take the application screen to another desktop. The editor window practically remains unchanged, the font sizes are of normal size, and the toolbars are visible
Distraction free mode	It hides all the toolbars, and what remains is just the editor. This won't enter fullscreen mode (although you can if you want to; just activate both distraction free and fullscreen. They are not mutually exclusive)

Listing 4-2 shows the full code for MainActivity.java and highlights some parts of it.

Listing 4-2. app/src/main/java/MainActivity.java

```
package com.example.ted.hello; ❶

import android.support.v7.app.AppCompatActivity; ❷
import android.os.Bundle; ❸

public class MainActivity extends AppCompatActivity { ❹

  @Override ❺
  protected void onCreate(Bundle savedInstanceState) { ❻
    super.onCreate(savedInstanceState);
    setContentView(R.layout.activity_main); ❼
  }
}
```

❶ This package statement was taken from the wizard input screen when you created the project (company domain field); this is usually your company or personal web site written in reverse DNS notation

❷ We're importing AppCompatActivity into this source file (MainActivity.java) because we're going to use it later

❸ Same stuff as number 2; we're importing the Bundle object because we will reference it later in this source file

❹ To build an activity component, we need to inherit from android.app.Activity or one its child classes. AppCompatActivity is a child class of FragmentActivity which in turn is a child class of Activity. AppCompatActivity lets us add an ActionBar to our activity

❺ The @Override is an annotation which just helps clarify our intent that we are truly overriding the method onCreate() in AppCompatActivity. It's just one of the safeguards of the Java compiler

⊙ onCreate() is a lifecycle method of the Activity class. This method gets called by the Android runtime whenever an application has been started for the first time. The method takes in a Bundle object as argument

⊙ setContentView(R.layout.activity_main) is the method call which associates our main Java program to the layout file (*activity_main*). What this method does is to inflate the XML, which will add all the view objects (Buttons, TextView, etc.) to the activity. The runtime will parse the XML file, create all the view and viewgroup objects as defined in the XML, and add them programmatically to the activity class

Views and Layout

Now that we understand the layout and main program file a bit better, we will remove the textView object that the wizard generated for us and replace it with some controls of our own design.

Select the activity_main in the main editor (make sure you are in the design view). Select the existing "Hello World" textView by clicking it. A selected view object appears like the one in shown in Figure 4-4. Delete it.

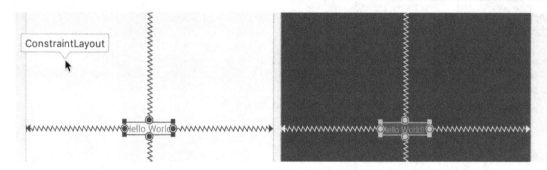

Figure 4-4. Select the "Hello World" textView

Alternatively, you can also delete a view object directly in the XML file. While layout file is selected in main editor, switch to "text" mode. Select the entire node entry of the TextView by clicking and dragging on the editor as shown in Figure 4-5. XML entries are quite finicky; if you so much as leave out or delete an extra character as shown in Figure 4-5, the XML will be malformed and AS3 won't be able to parse it properly. So you need to take care to get it right. Once it is selected, delete the selected text.

```
1     <?xml version="1.0" encoding="utf-8"?>
2  ©  <android.support.constraint.ConstraintLayout
3       xmlns:android="http://schemas.android.com/apk/res/android"
4       xmlns:app="http://schemas.android.com/apk/res-auto"
5       xmlns:tools="http://schemas.android.com/tools"
6       android:layout_width="match_parent"
7       android:layout_height="match_parent"
8       tools:context="com.example.ted.hello.MainActivity"
9       tools:layout_editor_absoluteY="81dp"
10      tools:layout_editor_absoluteX="0dp">
11
12      <TextView
13        android:layout_width="wrap_content"
14        android:layout_height="wrap_content"
15        android:text="Hello World!"
16        tools:layout_editor_absoluteY="247dp"
17        tools:layout_editor_absoluteX="154dp"
18        android:id="@+id/textView"
19        app:layout_constraintTop_toTopOf="parent"
20        app:layout_constraintStart_toStartOf="parent"
21        app:layout_constraintBottom_toBottomOf="parent"
22        app:layout_constraintEnd_toEndOf="parent"/>
23
24    </android.support.constraint.ConstraintLayout>
```

Figure 4-5. Text mode of activity_main

Switch back to "design" mode so we can start adding new view objects. We will need a textView, editText, and a Button view object.

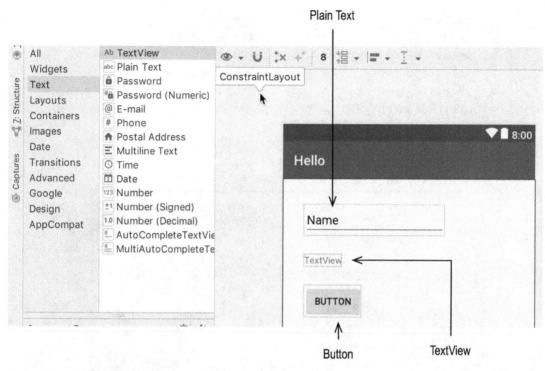

Figure 4-6. editText (PlainText), textView, and Button view objects

You can place view objects onto the layout by clicking and dragging them individually from the palette. The palette is categorized, but you can view all of them in a single list if you click the "All" option up top, as shown in Figure 4-6.

At the moment, we haven't defined any constraints for any of the new view objects we added. That will be a problem during runtime because the absence of any constraint means every view object will be positioned to location 0,0, or topmost and leftmost on the screen. See Figure 4-7.

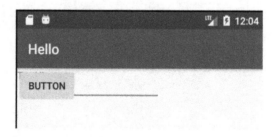

Figure 4-7. Hello app on the AVD

To remedy this, we'll put some constraints on each of the view objects.

The basic idea behind a ConstraintLayout is that you don't define absolute positions for each of the view objects but instead, define some sort of rules or guidelines for the layout and then let the Android runtime figure it out how to best arrange your widgets. It sounds like a terrible idea at first because you are relinquishing creative control and relegating it to the runtime, but it actually makes sense because it is very difficult to design for an application that may be viewed in different screen sizes, form factors, and orientation. ConstraintLayout is trying to solve this problem.

In a ConstraintLayout, each view is given some sort of rule, guide, or constraint; an example of a constraint would be always maintaining a left margin of 20dp from the container and a top margin of 40dp from whatever is on top of this view. Let's see how to do that in AS3.

In the main editor, click the editText view to select it. Notice that when a view object is selected, you can see both the sizing handles and the constraint handles (see Figure 4-8). You can experiment on the sizing handles, but our concern right now is the constraint handle.

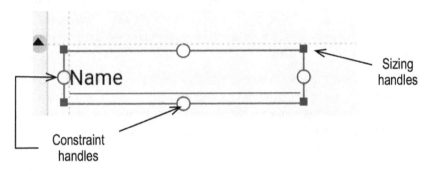

Figure 4-8. Constraint handles and sizing handles

To define a left and top margin constraint for our object, do the following.

1. Make sure that the "Autoconnect" inspector is not turned off (Figure 4-9)

Figure 4-9. Autoconnect inspector

2. Click the top constraint handle and drag it all the way to the top of the container. An arrow pointing upward will appear from the top constraint handle; keep dragging it until it sticks to the top of the container as shown in Figure 4-10

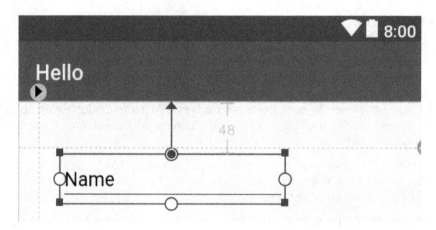

Figure 4-10. Edit Text with constraints

3. Do the same thing for the left constraint handle: click and drag it up until it sticks to the left side of the container. Don't worry too much about grayed out numbers on the margin; you can fix that to precise values in the properties inspector

4. You can change the values of the margin constraints in the attributes inspector as shown in Figure 4-11. Click the constraint values, which will become editable. You can choose any value from the drop-down or simply type the precise amount of margin (in dp) and then press ↵ (Enter)

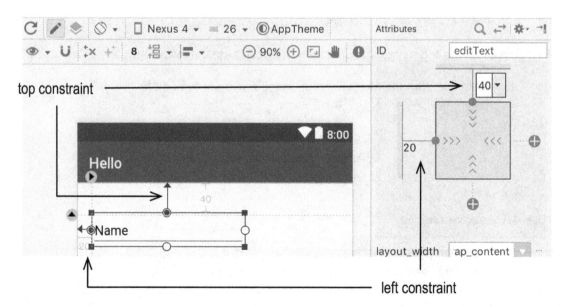

Figure 4-11. Attributes inspector

> **Note**   *dp* stands for device-independent pixel. It varies based on screen density. In a 160dpi screen, 1 dp = 1 pixel. dp is a commonly used unit of measurement in AS3

You can do this for the remaining two view objects in our layout. But as you will soon find out, layout work can be as time-consuming—if not more—than writing codes. Alternatively, instead of defining constraints for each of the component, you can let AS3 do all the work and define the constraints for you. To do that, follow these steps.

1. Remove all the constraints by clicking the "Clear constraints button" (see Figure 4-12)

2. Move view objects roughly to the positions you want them to be, relative to each other and relative to the container, just like playing with a paint program

3. Let AS3 define the constraints automatically by clicking the "Infer constraints" button (see Figure 4-12)

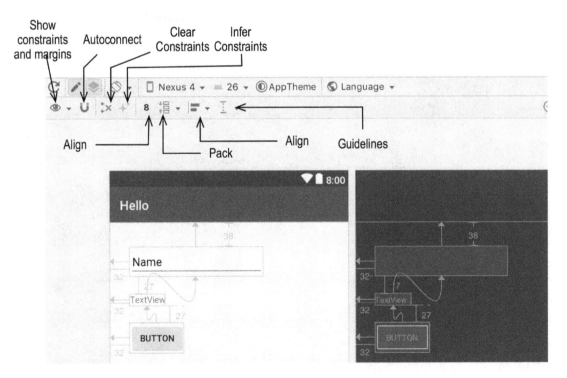

Figure 4-12. Constraint inspectors

Launch an emulator to test the app; make sure that the AVD is also API level 23 (Marshmallow) because that is the min SDK we defined for this project. Run the application from the main menu or click the "Run app" button on the toolbar. You should see something like Figure 4-13.

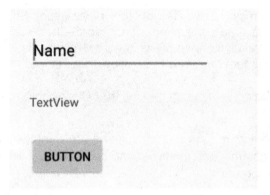

Figure 4-13. Hello app, inferred constraints

In the next chapter, we will add event handling capabilities to the Hello app.

Chapter 5

Handling Events

Event handling is basically just writing program logic in response to a user action. This program logic is written usually as part of Java methods. There are two ways you can handle events: you can do it either declaratively or programmatically. This chapter explores both ways.

Overview of Event Handling

The process of handling events declaratively can be broken down as follows.

1. Define the view object (e.g., a Button view). This can be done in either design or text mode

    ```
    <Button
      android:id="@+id/button"
      android:layout_width="wrap_content"
      android:layout_height="wrap_content"
      android:layout_marginStart="27dp"
      android:layout_marginTop="141dp"
      android:onClick="sayHello"
      android:tag="mybutton"
      android:text="Button"
      app:layout_constraintStart_toStartOf="parent"
      app:layout_constraintTop_toTopOf="parent"
      tools:layout_editor_absoluteX="27dp"
      tools:layout_editor_absoluteY="141dp"/>
    ```

2. Choose which event you want the program to respond to: for example, a click event (some view objects can respond to range of events: long-click, swipe, and so on

T. Hagos, *Learn Android Studio 3*, https://doi.org/10.1007/978-1-4842-3156-2_5

3. Associate the event with a Java method: for example, add the onClick attribute on the Button view XML element

    ```
    android:onClick="sayHello"
    ```

    Alternatively, you can associate a view object to a method in the attributes inspector

4. Implement the Java method in the main program file (MainActivity.java). The name of the method needs to be the same as the one defined in the attribute inspector

    ```
    void sayHello(View v) {
      System.out.println("Hello");
    }
    ```

To handle events programmatically, the steps can be broken down as follows.

1. Define the view object (e.g., a Button view)

2. Inside the main program, declare a variable to hold a Button view object

    ```
    Button objButton;
    ```

3. Get a programmatic reference to the Button view object defined in the layout file

    ```
    objButton = (Button) findViewById(R.layout.button)
    ```

4. Decide which event you want to respond to and specify the listener object for it (e.g., Click)

    ```
    objButton.setOnClickListener(new View.OnClickListener(){
    });
    ```

5. Override the onClick method: you can now implement the program logic here. Do what you want to do in response to the user action

    ```
    void onClick(View v) {
      // do something in here
    }
    ```

We will look at both techniques a bit closer in the following sections.

Declarative Event Handling

Open the Hello project from the last chapter, if it isn't opened yet. Open the layout file (activity_main) from the project tool window and view it in design mode.

1. Select the Button view

2. While the Button is selected, go to the Attributes inspector and find the *onClick* attribute

3. Type the text sayHello as shown in Figure 5-1

Figure 5-1. onClick attribute

Listing 5-1. app/src/main/res/layout/activity_main.xml

```
<Button
  android:id="@+id/button"
  android:layout_width="wrap_content"
  android:layout_height="wrap_content"
  android:layout_marginStart="27dp"
  android:layout_marginTop="141dp"
  android:onClick="sayHello" ❶
  android:text="Button"
  app:layout_constraintStart_toStartOf="parent"
  app:layout_constraintTop_toTopOf="parent"
  tools:layout_editor_absoluteX="27dp"
  tools:layout_editor_absoluteY="141dp"/>
```

❶ This was added automatically by AS3 when you wrote sayHello on the *onClick* attribute. The update works both ways: you could have edited this XML directly and the update would have been reflected in the attribute inspector. When you run this app, the Android runtime will look for the method sayHello in MainActivity.java; at the moment, we don't have it yet, but we will implement that method in a little while.

Filling up the entry of the onClick attribute means that you want something to happen when the Button view is clicked; the attribute entry becomes the name of a method which the Android runtime will look for when a click event happens on the Button. To implement the sayHello method, let's open the MainActivity.java in the main editor and write our method.

Listing 5-2. sayHello Method

```
void sayHello(View v) {
  System.out.println("Hello");
}
```

> **Tip**   While you are typing the code, some keywords may appear to be unrecognized. That is
> probably because you just haven't imported the proper classes yet. AS3 has a quickfix feature
> (Alt+Enter or Option+Enter). If you hover your mouse over the unrecognized keyword, AS3 will
> automatically import the necessary classes for you.

The method is simple, but there are a couple of things in it that need to be pointed out
(Table 5-1).

Table 5-1. Parts of sayHello method

Item	Code artifact	Comment
Return type	void	We don't need to return anything to our caller, so this is declared void
Method name	sayHello()	This needs to be the same as it is written in the onClick attribute of the Button
Arguments or parameters	View object	Every event handler needs to accept a View object argument. This argument is filled up by the Android runtime. If you need to know which View object was clicked, you can use this parameter

Run the application in an AVD so we can see how it behaves and we can test how our event
handler works. Once the AVD is up and running, let's open the Logcat tool window so we
can see a console dump of all the events in the emulator.

To launch the Logcat tool window, click the "Logcat" launcher; it is located somewhere in
the bottom left of the AS3 application window, as shown in Figure 5-2.

Figure 5-2. Logcat window

Go to the emulator and click the Button on our app. While you are doing that, try to watch the Logcat window (Figure 5-3).

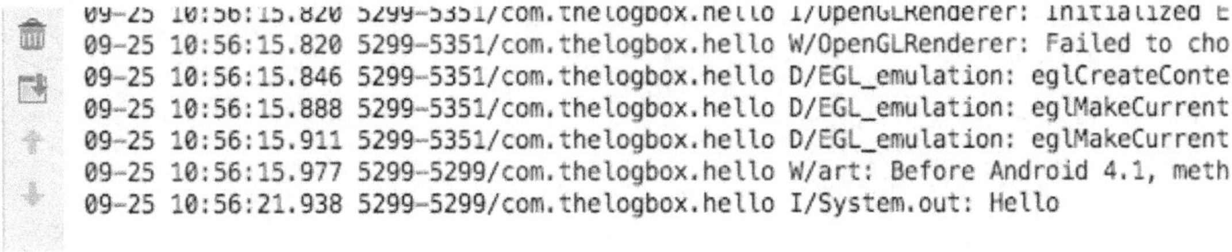

```
09-25 10:56:15.820 5299-5351/com.thelogbox.hello I/OpenGLRenderer: Initialized t
09-25 10:56:15.820 5299-5351/com.thelogbox.hello W/OpenGLRenderer: Failed to cho
09-25 10:56:15.846 5299-5351/com.thelogbox.hello D/EGL_emulation: eglCreateConte
09-25 10:56:15.888 5299-5351/com.thelogbox.hello D/EGL_emulation: eglMakeCurrent
09-25 10:56:15.911 5299-5351/com.thelogbox.hello D/EGL_emulation: eglMakeCurrent
09-25 10:56:15.977 5299-5299/com.thelogbox.hello W/art: Before Android 4.1, meth
09-25 10:56:21.938 5299-5299/com.thelogbox.hello I/System.out: Hello
```

Figure 5-3. System.out on Logcat

The output of System.out will not be on the activity; instead, it is redirected to the console Logcat window.

Programmatic Event Handling

It might be best to create a new project for this exercise, so you can keep the last project as reference. Create a new project with the information in Table 5-2.

Table 5-2. Project information for Hello2

Application name	Hello2
Company domain	Use your web site, or invent something; remember that this is in reverse DNS notation
Project location	This usually best left alone. Use the default value, but make sure to take note of this location in case the need to access it arises. Ignore the C++ and Kotlin support
Form factor	Phone and tablet only
Minimum SDK	API 23 Marshmallow
Type of activity	Empty
Activity name	If you leave the default alone it alone, this will be MainActivity, which is fine
Layout name	If you leave the default alone, this will be activity_main, which is fine

Same as for the Hello project from the last section, put editText, textView, and Button view objects in the layout file and just use the "infer constraints" to put some design semblance in your project. Your layout file should look something like Listing 5-2.

Listing 5-3. app/src/main/res/layout/activity_main.xml

```xml
<?xml version="1.0" encoding="utf-8"?>
<android.support.constraint.ConstraintLayout
  xmlns:android="http://schemas.android.com/apk/res/android"
  xmlns:app="http://schemas.android.com/apk/res-auto"
  xmlns:tools="http://schemas.android.com/tools"
  android:layout_width="match_parent"
  android:layout_height="match_parent"
  tools:context="com.example.ted.hello2.MainActivity">

  <EditText
    android:id="@+id/editText"
    android:layout_width="wrap_content"
    android:layout_height="wrap_content"
    android:ems="10"
    android:inputType="textPersonName"
    android:text="Name"
    tools:layout_editor_absoluteX="30dp"
    tools:layout_editor_absoluteY="44dp"
    app:layout_constraintTop_toTopOf="parent"
    app:layout_constraintStart_toStartOf="parent"
    android:layout_marginTop="44dp"
    android:layout_marginStart="30dp"
    android:layout_marginBottom="31dp"
    app:layout_constraintBottom_toTopOf="@+id/textView"/>

  <TextView
    android:id="@+id/textView"
    android:layout_width="0dp"
    android:layout_height="0dp"
    android:text="TextView"
    tools:layout_editor_absoluteX="30dp"
    tools:layout_editor_absoluteY="121dp"
    app:layout_constraintTop_toBottomOf="@+id/editText"
    android:layout_marginBottom="27dp"
    app:layout_constraintEnd_toEndOf="@+id/editText"
    app:layout_constraintBottom_toTopOf="@+id/button"
    app:layout_constraintStart_toStartOf="@+id/button"
    android:layout_marginEnd="1dp"/>

  <Button
    android:id="@+id/button"
    android:layout_width="wrap_content"
    android:layout_height="wrap_content"
    android:text="Button"
    tools:layout_editor_absoluteX="30dp"
    tools:layout_editor_absoluteY="170dp"
    app:layout_constraintStart_toStartOf="parent"
    app:layout_constraintBottom_toBottomOf="parent"
    android:layout_marginStart="30dp"
    app:layout_constraintTop_toBottomOf="@+id/textView"
    android:layout_marginBottom="293dp"/>
</android.support.constraint.ConstraintLayout>
```

When you handle events programmatically, you will work almost exclusively in the main program file. Open `MainActivity.java` if it isn't opened yet, so we can add some event handling codes.

Listing 5-4. Main Program File

```
public class MainActivity extends AppCompatActivity {

  @Override
  protected void onCreate(Bundle savedInstanceState) {
    super.onCreate(savedInstanceState);
    setContentView(R.layout.activity_main);

    // Write your event handling codes below this line
  }
}
```

We will add all our event handling code right after the `setContentView` method; we need this method call to complete so that all the objects in the layout file finish the inflation process. The inflation process creates all the `View` and `ViewGroup` objects as Java objects which we can then reference programmatically in the main program. The whole exercise can be summarized as follows.

1. Get a programmatic reference to the Button view

2. Set a Listener object for it

3. Override the abstract method defined on the listener object and provide program logic in response to a user action

Getting a programmatic reference to the Button view can be done with the following statement.

```
Button objButton = (Button) findViewById(R.id.button);
```

You may notice that as you type the preceding statement, AS3 tries to infer and offer some autocompletion options. Autocompletion can save you time in programming, and it gives you some confidence that you're on the right track—if things don't show up in autocompletion, it usually means you're doing something wrong because AS3 doesn't recognize it.

In Figure 5-4, as the word "Button" was being typed, there were a couple of entries in the autocompletion prompts. Whenever this prompt appears, you can use the arrow keys to choose from any of the entries. If you press the Enter key, whatever is the highlighted entry in the autocompletion popup will be put in place of the current cursor position.

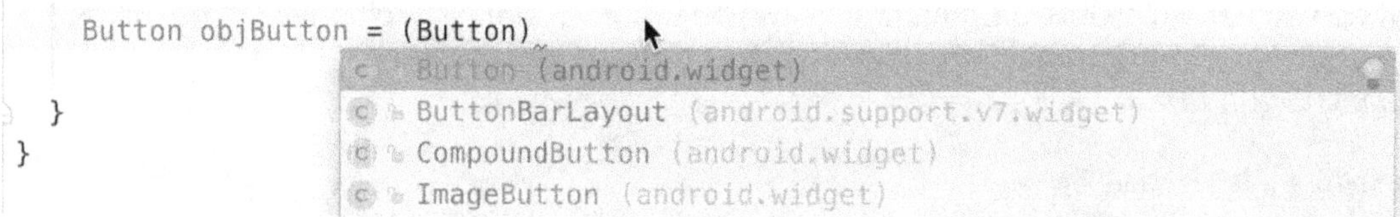

```
    Button objButton = (Button)
                          c   Button (android.widget)
 }                        c   ButtonBarLayout (android.support.v7.widget)
}                         c   CompoundButton (android.widget)
                          c   ImageButton (android.widget)
```

Figure 5-4. Autocomplete

Another thing you may have noticed is that all the instances of the word Button are in red; if you hover the mouse over "Button", AS3 will inform you via the tool tip dialog that "it cannot resolve the symbol Button" (see Figure 5-5). This error is appearing and AS3 is mildly reminding us about it because we need to import the Button definition into the current source file, and we haven't done it yet.

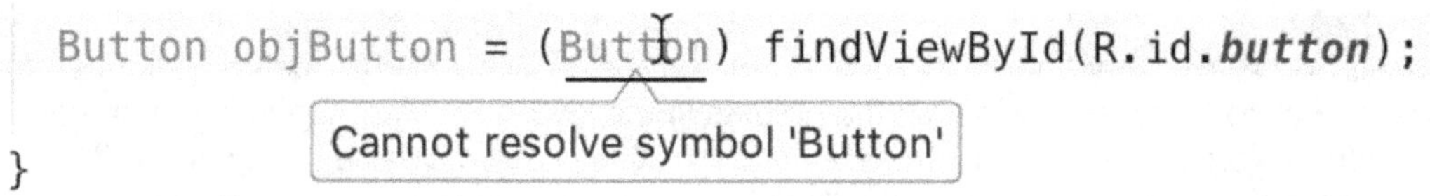

```
    Button objButton = (Button) findViewById(R.id.button);

         Cannot resolve symbol 'Button'
 }
```

Figure 5-5. AS3 warnings and errors

To resolve the error, we need to import the android.view.Button into the main program by typing the import statement anywhere in the source file before the class declaration for MainActivity. See the following example code.

```
import android.view.Button;
public class MainActivity extends AppCompatActivity {
}
```

Alternatively, you could hover the mouse over "Button" as shown in Figure 5-5, and then perform a quick fix by typing ⌥ (Option) + ↵ (Enter) if you are on macOS. If you are on Windows or Linux, the quick fix key is Alt + ↵ (Enter). Quick fixes solve a range of coding problems; missing import statements is one of them. After the quick fix, the import statement for the Button view will appear on top of the source file, together with the other import statements.

The next thing we need is to select a listener for the Button view, create a listener object for it, and finally, override the necessary abstract method defined by listener object. You can use the autocompletion facility as you type this construct.

Notice that as you type the codes (Figure 5-6), which will create the listener object, there are several possible matches for it. What we want in this case is the second entry from the top, the one with the ellipsis enclosed in a pair of curly braces. This is actually a code snippet. If we choose this, what we will get is the code in Listing 5-5.

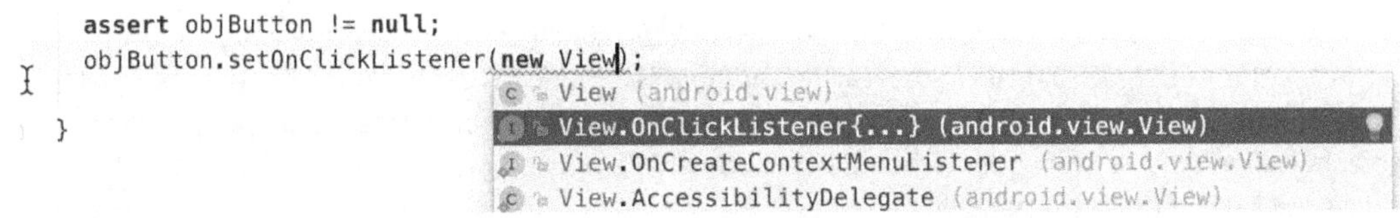

```
      assert objButton != null;
      objButton.setOnClickListener(new View);
  I
                              c ≡ View (android.view)
      }
                              i ≡ View.OnClickListener{...} (android.view.View)
                              i ≡ View.OnCreateContextMenuListener (android.view.View)
                              c ≡ View.AccessibilityDelegate (android.view.View)
```

Figure 5-6. Autocompletion for listener object

Listing 5-5. Code Snippet for View.OnClickListener

```
objButton.setOnClickListener(new View.OnClickListener() {
  @Override
  public void onClick(View view) {

  }
});
```

After this, all we need to do is write our program logic inside the body of the onClick()
method.

Listing 5-6 is the complete code listing for the main program.

Listing 5-6. MainActivity.java

```
import android.support.v7.app.AppCompatActivity;
import android.os.Bundle;
import android.view.View;
import android.widget.Button;

public class MainActivity extends AppCompatActivity {

  @Override
  protected void onCreate(Bundle savedInstanceState) {
    super.onCreate(savedInstanceState);
    setContentView(R.layout.activity_main);

    Button objButton = (Button) findViewById(R.id.button); ❶
    assert objButton != null; ❷
    objButton.setOnClickListener(new View.OnClickListener() { ❸
      @Override ❹
      public void onClick(View view) { ❺
        System.out.println("Hello World");
      }
    });
  }
}
```

❶ Get a programmatic reference to our Button object. findViewById will locate the exact Button view object for us. R.id.button is the key to finding this object. When the Android runtime inflates the layout file, it generates a class named R.java; all the Java object representations of all view objects defined in the layout file will be defined there. We are using the R.class (Resources) to locate our button programmatically

❷ This is just some defensive programming; we're trying to make sure that the findViewById method returned an actual object and that it isn't null. If you have ever encountered a NullPointerException in Java before, that may happen here. If the findViewById does not return an object, your program will crash during runtime

❸ We want to respond to a click action; that's why the method we chose is setOnClickListener. This method requires an instance of a listener object as the argument. We implemented the listener object inline and as an anonymous class—see the section "The Java Language" on anonymous classes in Appendix A

❹ @Override is an annotation; it tells the compiler that we intend to override a method in the AppCompatActivity superclass and that we're not defining a new onCreate method in MainActivity. The annotation simply clarifies our intent for the compiler

❺ onClick is an abstract method defined by the View.OnClickListener interface. It needs to be overridden for our implementation

Run the program in the emulator and open the Logcat tool window so that you can see the console dumps when you click the Button view.

> **Tip**   When you have started the emulator and deployed the app to it, you can use the "Apply changes" button to quickly update the emulator without building a new APK and pushing it to emulator (Figure 5-7). This makes for a faster workflow when you are making small code or layout changes.

Figure 5-7. Apply changes button

Working with Text and Buttons

Among the user interface elements in Android, text and button elements are probably the most common. In this section, we'll dive into a small sample application that will give us a chance to work with these two elements. The project details are as shown in Table 5-3.

Table 5-3. Project Information

Application name	NumberGuess
Project location	Leave the default
Form factor	Phone and tablet only
Minimum SDK	API 23 Marshmallow
Type of activity	Empty
Activity name	MainActivity (default)
Layout name	activity_main (default)

Figure 5-8 shows the UI for the project.

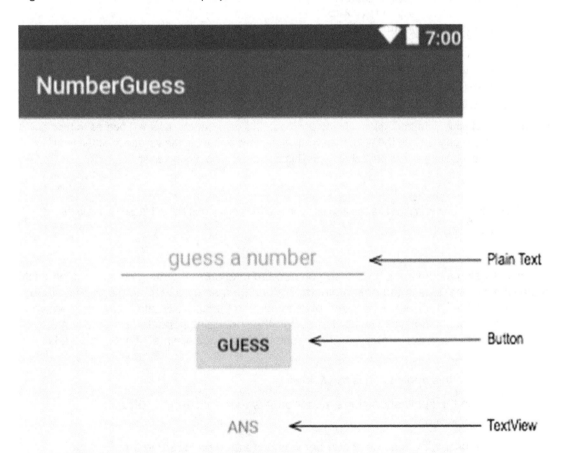

Figure 5-8. View elements for NumberGuess

There were a few cosmetic and aesthetic tweaks on the elements to make them appear a bit more pleasing to the eyes.

```
<EditText
    android:id="@+id/editText"
    android:layout_width="wrap_content"
    android:layout_height="wrap_content"
    android:layout_marginBottom="26dp"
    android:ems="10"
    android:gravity="center_vertical|center_horizontal"  ❶
    android:hint="guess a number"                        ❷
    android:inputType="number"                           ❸
    app:layout_constraintBottom_toTopOf="@+id/button"
    app:layout_constraintEnd_toEndOf="parent"
    app:layout_constraintStart_toStartOf="parent"
    tools:layout_editor_absoluteX="84dp"
    tools:layout_editor_absoluteY="106dp"/>
```

❶ This entry aligns the text inside the plain text view both vertically and horizontally

❷ The hint attribute makes the text "guess a number" appear grayed out; it's good technique to use instead of an actual label, like a text view

❸ This restricts the input to numbers. If you don't add this attribute, the user will be free to type any alphanumeric character in the field; then, you might need to handle the validation of the input using some regular expression techniques. This approach is so much easier

> **Note**   All the preceding tweaks can also be done in design mode. You can set these values in the attributes inspector.

We are still using a constraint layout, so you need to take care of putting constraints on each of the UI elements. Like in the past projects, this can be managed without much difficulty by positioning all the UI elements by hand, placing them in the approximate location where you want them to appear, and then using the tools in the constraint inspector. Use the "pack" tool to distribute them horizontally, and then use the "infer constraints". That should take care of the layout.

The basic flow of this application is the following:

1. When the application starts, a random number from 100 to 150 will be generated

2. The user will guess what number was generated by inputting that number in the text field

3. If the user's guess is higher than the random number, we will display "Guess lower" using the static text view

4. If the user's guess is lower than the random number, we will display "Guess higher" using the static text view

5. If the user guessed the number correctly, we will display the random number and a congratulatory note in the text field

Listing 5-7. MainActivity Event Handling Code (Folded Methods)

```
public class MainActivity extends AppCompatActivity
  implements View.OnClickListener {

  int numberToGuess = 0;
  EditText e;
  TextView t;

  @Override
  protected void onCreate(Bundle savedInstanceState) { ... }

  @Override
  public void onClick(View view) { ... }

  int initNumberToGuess() { ... }

}
```

You may notice that the event handling approach for this project isn't using an anonymous or an inner class; it's not that there's anything wrong with those approaches, but making MainActivity the listener object provides some convenience for this situation. The main logic of getting the user input and comparing it to the generated random number will reside in the onClick method. If this method was inside an anonymous or an inner class, then it would have necessitated that the variables holding EditText and TextView be declared final. That's just one of the Java rules about inner classes; it's okay to reference any variable on its outer class, provided it is final. And that would have made the code a bit more complicated than how it is structured as shown in Listing 5-7.

The following sections shows the code listing of onCreate, onClick, and initNumberToGuess, starting with Listing 5-8.

Listing 5-8. onCreate

```
  @Override
  protected void onCreate(Bundle savedInstanceState) {
    super.onCreate(savedInstanceState);
    setContentView(R.layout.activity_main);

    numberToGuess = initNumberToGuess();            ❶

    e = (EditText) findViewById(R.id.editText);     ❷
    t = (TextView) findViewById(R.id.textView);     ❸

    Button b = (Button) findViewById(R.id.button);
    b.setOnClickListener(this);

  }
```

❶ The numberToGuess is initialized during onCreate but it was declared as a member variable and not a local variable of onCreate. We need to reference this variable from the onClick method; that's the reason it was declared as a member variable

❷ The variable e is also initialized here but declared as a member variable as well; like numberToGuess, we need to reference this variable from the onClick method

❸ Same case as in the variable t; we also need to reference this from the onClick method

Listing 5-9. onClick

```
@Override
public void onClick(View view) {
  int number = Integer.parseInt(e.getText().toString());      ❶
  if (number == numberToGuess) {
    t.setText(number + " is the right number");
  }
  else if (number < numberToGuess) {
    t.setText("Guess higher");
  }
  else if (number > numberToGuess) {
    t.setText("Guess lower");
  }
  Log.i("Ted", numberToGuess + "");
}
```

❶ The getText method of the EditText returns anEditable object type; it's almost like text, but it's mutable, unlike a String. The Integer.parseInt, however, expects a String parameter; that's why we needed to convert the return value of getText using the toString method

Listing 5-10. initNumberToGuess

```
int initNumberToGuess() {
  Random r = new Random();               ❶
  numberToGuess = r.nextInt(100) + 50;   ❷
  Log.i("Ted", numberToGuess + "");
  return numberToGuess;
}
```

❶ The Random class is from java.util. Make sure you import this package. Alternatively, when it turns red on the main editor, hover your mouse around it and use the quick fix (Alt + Enter for Windows and Linux | opt + enter for macOS)

❷ This sets the range of the random number to be from 100 to 150

Listing 5-11 shows the full code for MainActivity, for your reference.

Listing 5-11. The Full MainActivity

```
package com.ted.numberguess;

import android.support.v7.app.AppCompatActivity;
import android.os.Bundle;
import android.util.Log;
import android.view.View;
import android.widget.Button;
import android.widget.EditText;
import android.widget.TextView;

import java.util.Random;

public class MainActivity extends AppCompatActivity
  implements View.OnClickListener {

  int numberToGuess = 0;
  EditText e;
  TextView t;

  @Override
  protected void onCreate(Bundle savedInstanceState) {
    super.onCreate(savedInstanceState);
    setContentView(R.layout.activity_main);

    numberToGuess = initNumberToGuess();

    e = (EditText) findViewById(R.id.editText);
    t = (TextView) findViewById(R.id.textView);

    Button b = (Button) findViewById(R.id.button);
    b.setOnClickListener(this);

  }

  @Override
  public void onClick(View view) {
    int number = Integer.parseInt(e.getText().toString());
    if (number == numberToGuess) {
      t.setText(number + " is the right number");
    }
    else if (number < numberToGuess) {
      t.setText("Guess higher");
    }
    else if (number > numberToGuess) {
      t.setText("Guess lower");
    }
    Log.i("Ted", numberToGuess + "");
  }
```

```
int initNumberToGuess() {
  Random r = new Random();
  numberToGuess = r.nextInt(100) + 50;
  Log.i("Ted", numberToGuess + "");
  return numberToGuess;
  }
}
```

More Event Handling Code

Using anonymous classes for event handling codes should solve a wide range of programming challenges for you, but anonymous classes are not the only way to handle events. In this section, we'll take a look at two other ways to go about this.

For this exercise, we will create a new project. Use the information in Table 5-4 to create the project.

Table 5-4. Project Information

Application name	EventHandling1
Company domain	Leave the default
Project location	Leave the default
Form factor	Phone and tablet only
Minimum SDK	API 23 Marshmallow
Type of activity	Empty
Activity name	MainActivity
Layout name	activity_main

Add three button views to the layout. In this example, they are vertically aligned to each other and are constrained to stay on the center of the screen. The easiest way to achieve this layout is to position the buttons by hand, approximating the location you want them to be at runtime. Next, select all of them by clicking and dragging around all three buttons' views, and then use the tools on the constraint inspector to fine-tune the alignment and the constraints.

You can use the "Pack" button (as shown in Figure 5-9) to distribute the views vertically. After that, use the "Infer" constraints to automatically align the views to each other and to the container.

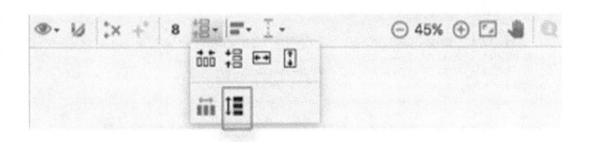

Figure 5-9. Pack vertically

Figure 5-10 shows how the layout might look.

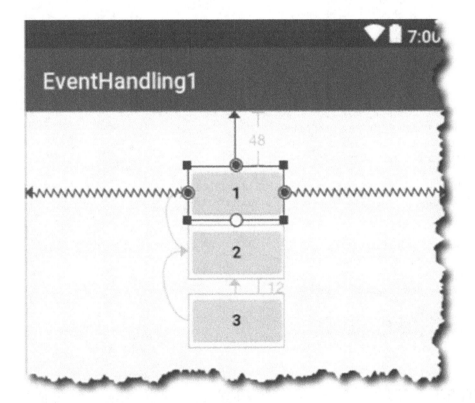

Figure 5-10. activity_main in design view for EventHandling1

The IDs of the button views have been changed to button1, button2, and button3 accordingly, so we can refer to them later in the code quite easily. You can use other names, of course; view ids are simply identifiers that you, the programmer, will ultimately decide on. But for this project, they are named like so. Listing 5-6 shows the XML code for our layout.

Listing 5-12. activity_main.xml in Text View

```xml
<?xml version="1.0" encoding="utf-8"?>
<android.support.constraint.ConstraintLayout
  xmlns:android="http://schemas.android.com/apk/res/android"
  xmlns:app="http://schemas.android.com/apk/res-auto"
  xmlns:tools="http://schemas.android.com/tools"
  android:layout_width="match_parent"
  android:layout_height="match_parent"
  tools:context="com.thelogbox.eventhandling1.MainActivity">

  <Button
    android:id="@+id/button1"
    android:layout_width="wrap_content"
    android:layout_height="wrap_content"
    android:layout_marginTop="48dp"
    android:text="1"
    app:layout_constraintEnd_toEndOf="parent"
    app:layout_constraintStart_toStartOf="parent"
    app:layout_constraintTop_toTopOf="parent"/>

  <Button
    android:id="@+id/button2"
    android:layout_width="wrap_content"
    android:layout_height="wrap_content"
    android:layout_marginTop="4dp"
    android:text="2"
    app:layout_constraintStart_toStartOf="@+id/button1"
    app:layout_constraintTop_toBottomOf="@+id/button1"/>

  <Button
    android:id="@+id/button3"
    android:layout_width="wrap_content"
    android:layout_height="wrap_content"
    android:layout_marginTop="12dp"
    android:text="3"
    app:layout_constraintStart_toStartOf="@+id/button2"
    app:layout_constraintTop_toBottomOf="@+id/button2"/>
</android.support.constraint.ConstraintLayout>
```

Using an Inner Class as a Listener

We can define another class that is nested inside `MainActivity` which can serve as our listener object (Listing 5-13). Java allows classes to be nested, so we will take advantage of this; there a few rules to observe when defining an inner class, and we'll discuss them as they become necessary.

Listing 5-13. An Inner Class Within MainActivity

```java
public class MainActivity extends AppCompatActivity {

  @Override
  protected void onCreate(Bundle savedInstanceState) { . . . }  ❶

  private class ButtonHandler implements View.OnClickListener {  ❷

  }
}
```

❶   This line shows the onCreate method in a folded mode. The code folding capabilities of AS3 are quite useful when you're working with a lot of codes; it declutters the main editor and helps you to focus

❷   Our inner class as it sits inside MainActivity. We defined it as private because it doesn't need to be visible from outside MainActivity. The same as our anonymous class in the previous sections, this too needs to implement the View.OnClickListener interface because we will use it as the listener for button clicks

> **Note**   You may see some warnings and errors on AS3 as you add the event handling code. These are most likely missing import statements; just hover your mouse on the squiggly lines and use the quick fix (Option + Enter for macOS | Alt + Enter for Windows and Linux). It is should import all the necessary packages.

Listing 5-14. ButtonHandler Implementation

```java
private class ButtonHandler implements View.OnClickListener {

  @Override
  public void onClick(View view) {  ❶
    switch (view.getId()){         ❷
      case R.id.button1:           ❸
        show("Button One");        ❹
        break;
      case R.id.button2:
        show("Button Two");
        break;
      case R.id.button3:
        show("Button Three");
        break;
      default:
        show("This should not happen");
    }
  }
}
```

❶ We're overriding the onClick method of the View.OnClickListener; when any of the three buttons are clicked, this method gets called, just like in our anonymous class code from previous sections. The runtime will populate the View parameter with the object reference of the actual button that was clicked. That is what we're going to use to identify which button exactly was clicked using the Android Toast class

❷ The getId method of the View object returns an integer value which corresponds to ID of button as it is defined in the R.class. Remember that layout files are inflated during runtime to produce the actual Java objects which correspond to View element described in the layout. The runtime generates the R.class, which we can use to programmatically refer to objects defined in the layout file

❸ We're simply checking if whatever value we got from view.getId is any one of our Buttons; in this line, we're checking if it is R.id.button1

❹ If button1 was clicked, we call a method named show() and pass a String to it. We haven't defined the show method yet

Listing 5-15. show() Method

```
void show(String message) {
  Toast.makeText(this, message, Toast.LENGTH_LONG).show(); ❶
  Log.i(getClass().getName(), message);                    ❷
}
```

❶ We are displaying a Toast message. Toast provides a small feedback in the form of a small popup. It appears as an overlay in the current activity, and the appearance is for a certain duration only so it doesn't obscure the current activity. It's an unobtrusive way to display status messages

❷ The Log class lets us create log entries pretty much like System.out.println, but it is more appropriate to use the Log class to output debugging and diagnostic messages. You can view log entries created by the Log class in the Logcat tool window

The show method (Listing 5-15) is a member of MainActivity. The ButtonHandler has access to methods (or variables) that are defined in its enclosing class. We could have defined this method inside the ButtonHandler class, and that would have been fine too.

Figure 5-11. Toast message

Complete code for MainActivity is found in Listing 5-16.

Listing 5-16. Complete Code for MainActivity

```java
package com.example.ted.eventhandling1;

import android.support.v7.app.AppCompatActivity;
import android.os.Bundle;
import android.util.Log;
import android.view.View;
import android.widget.Toast;

public class MainActivity extends AppCompatActivity {

  @Override
  protected void onCreate(Bundle savedInstanceState) {
    super.onCreate(savedInstanceState);
    setContentView(R.layout.activity_main);

    ButtonHandler bh = new ButtonHandler();
    findViewById(R.id.button1).setOnClickListener(bh);
    findViewById(R.id.button2).setOnClickListener(bh);
    findViewById(R.id.button3).setOnClickListener(bh);

  }

  private class ButtonHandler implements View.OnClickListener {

    @Override
    public void onClick(View view) {
      switch (view.getId()){
        case R.id.button1:
          show("Button One");
          break;
        case R.id.button2:
          show("Button Two");
          break;
        case R.id.button3:
          show("Button 3");
          break;
        default:
          show("This should not happen");
      }
    }
  }

  void show(String message) {
    Toast.makeText(this, message, Toast.LENGTH_LONG).show();
    Log.i(getClass().getName(), message);
  }
}
```

Using MainActivity as the Listener

Another way of handling events for the three buttons would be to use the `MainActivity` class as the listener object. We don't want to change the main program file as it stands right now; that way, we can refer to it later. We can define another class that will serve as our main program file; that way, it can be side by side with the original main program within the same project. From the main menu bar, click **File ➤ New ➤ Java** class and fill it up as shown in Figure 5-13. Alternatively, you can also right-click the folder that holds MainActivity and use the context-sensitive menu to add a class.

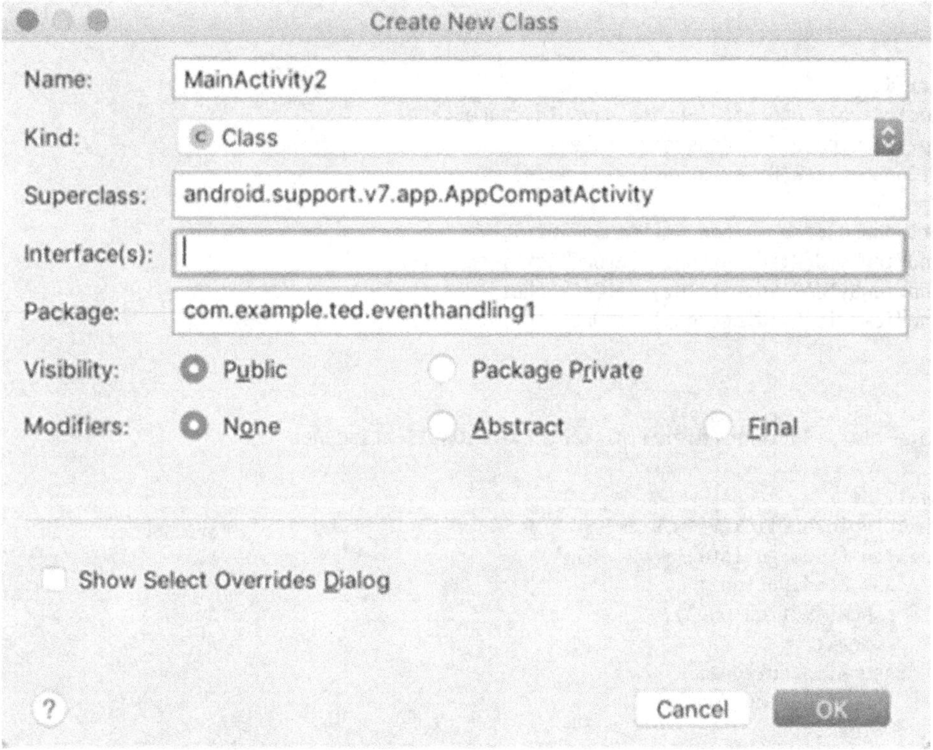

Figure 5-12. Create new class dialog

We'll name the new class `MainActivity2`. It extends the same superclass as the original main program. Leave the "interfaces" field blank, and leave the default entry on the "Package". Public visibility and no modifiers should be fine for our setting.

You might see some warnings in the editor window of the newly created program file; they are simply warning us that the new class is not registered in the AndroidManifest file (Figure 5-13).

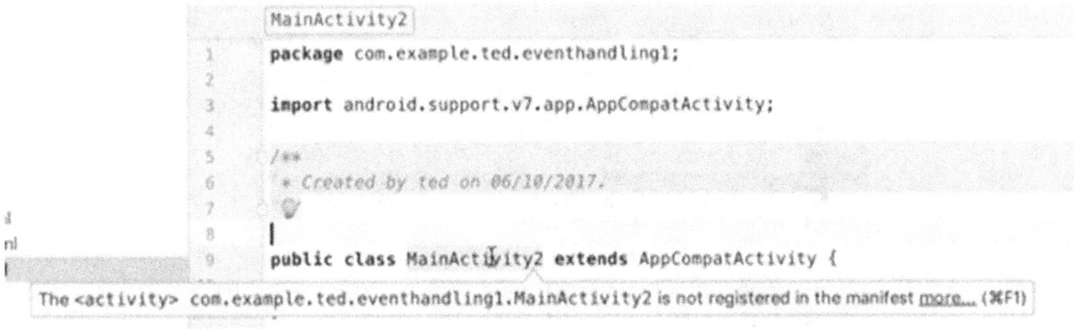

Figure 5-13. MainActivity2

Leave this for now; we will fix that later. At the moment, our new program file doesn't have everything it needs to be a proper Activity class, it doesn't override the onCreate method and it doesn't have any layout file associated with it. Let's fix that by supplying the missing code.

Listing 5-17. MainActivity2 Program File

```
public class MainActivity2 extends AppCompatActivity {

  @Override
  protected void onCreate(@Nullable Bundle savedInstanceState) {
    super.onCreate(savedInstanceState);
    setContentView(R.layout.activity_main);
  }
}
```

You could simply copy the code in Listing 5-17 into your own project, or you could try out some more AS3 tools. While you are editing MainActivity2, position the cursor somewhere inside the main class block and press Ctrl + 0 (same keyboard shortcut for Windows, Linux, and macOS). This will launch a dialog window where you can choose to override the method of a class. It's context sensitive: it knows that you're editing an AppCompatActivity class, so it shows only the methods of that class (see Figure 5-14). Alternatively, you can access the override dialog window from the main menu bar **Code ➤ Override** Methods.

Figure 5-14. Override dialog window

Using the dialog window is (sometimes) much easier than directly writing the code. If you are not quite familiar with the syntax of the method and all its attendant parameters and annotations, the dialog window will happily supply all of them. Listing 5-18 shows the (folded) MainActivity2 in its entirety.

Listing 5-18. MainActivity2

```
public class MainActivity2 extends AppCompatActivity
  implements View.OnClickListener {                                    ❶

  @Override
  protected void onCreate(@Nullable Bundle savedInstanceState) { ... } ❷

  @Override
  public void onClick(View view) { ... }                               ❸

  void show(String message) { ... }                                    ❹
}
```

❶ You need to add the implements directive on the class. What this signifies is that the MainActivity2 class is bound to behave as if it were an OnClickListener object. That's what it means to implement any interface. We basically agree to a certain object contract that whatever behaviors the interface exhibits, we will behave the same way too

❷ The onCreate method contains the same code as the one in the original main program (MainActivity.java); of course we still should add the setContentView statement and the view registrations—we'll get to that shortly. You may notice the @Nullable decorator on the Bundle parameter; this simply means that the Bundle object, in case is null, isn't a big deal and that it can be safely ignored

❸ The overridden onClick method of the OnClickListener interface is now implemented as a member method of MainActivity2

❹ This is the same implementation of the show method as we've seen in original MainActivity

Listing 5-19. View Registrations

```
@Override
protected void onCreate(Bundle savedInstanceState) {
  super.onCreate(savedInstanceState);
  setContentView(R.layout.activity_main);

  Button b1 = (Button) findViewById(R.id.button1);
  Button b2 = (Button) findViewById(R.id.button2);
  Button b3 = (Button) findViewById(R.id.button3);

  ButtonListener blistener = new ButtonListener();
  b1.setOnClickListener(blistener);
  b2.setOnClickListener(blistener);
  b3.setOnClickListener(blistener);

}
```

The onCreate method in the preceding code sample isn't that much different from our event handling codes; the only thing different is that we are using the same object to handle the events for all three buttons. None of the buttons have its own dedicated listener, as was the case with the use of anonymous classes. In this approach, the program logic is routed inside the listener object (ButtonHandler).

```
package com.example.ted.eventhandling1;

import android.os.Bundle;
import android.support.annotation.Nullable;
import android.support.v7.app.AppCompatActivity;
import android.util.Log;
import android.view.View;
import android.widget.Toast;

/**
 * Created by ted on 06/10/2017.
 */
```

```java
public class MainActivity2 extends AppCompatActivity implements View.OnClickListener {

    @Override
    protected void onCreate(@Nullable Bundle savedInstanceState) {
        super.onCreate(savedInstanceState);
        setContentView(R.layout.activity_main);
    }

    @Override
    public void onClick(View view) {
        switch (view.getId()){
            case R.id.button1:
                show("Button One");
                break;
            case R.id.button2:
                show("Button Two");
                break;
            case R.id.button3:
                show("Button Three");
                break;
            default:
                show("This should not happen");
        }
    }
    void show(String message) {
        Toast.makeText(this, message, Toast.LENGTH_LONG).show();
        Log.i(getClass().getName(), message);
    }
}
```

Listing 5-20. Complete Code for MainActivity2

```java
package com.example.ted.eventhandling1;

import android.os.Bundle;
import android.support.annotation.Nullable;
import android.support.v7.app.AppCompatActivity;
import android.util.Log;
import android.view.View;
import android.widget.Toast;

public class MainActivity2 extends AppCompatActivity
    implements View.OnClickListener {

    @Override
    protected void onCreate(@Nullable Bundle savedInstanceState) {
        super.onCreate(savedInstanceState);
        setContentView(R.layout.activity_main);
    }

    @Override
    public void onClick(View view) {
```

```
    switch (view.getId()){
      case R.id.button1:
        show("Button One");
        break;
      case R.id.button2:
        show("Button Two");
        break;
      case R.id.button3:
        show("Button Three");
        break;
      default:
        show("This should not happen");
    }
  }
  void show(String message) {
    Toast.makeText(this, message, Toast.LENGTH_LONG).show();
    Log.i(getClass().getName(), message);
  }
}
```

To test our code, we need to make a slight change in the AndroidManifest file. At the moment, the declared activity class in the manifest is MainActivity, our original main program file. When the Android runtime launches an application, it takes a look at the activity declaration in the manifest and runs that program. We need to change that entry so that the Android runtime launches MainActivity2 instead of MainActivity.

Open the AndroidManifest.xml file from the project tool window. It should be in
App ➤ manifests ➤ AndroidManifest.xml.

Listing 5-21. Activity Entry in the Manifest File

```
<?xml version="1.0" encoding="utf-8"?>
<manifest package="com.example.ted.eventhandling1"
          xmlns:android="http://schemas.android.com/apk/res/android">

  <application
    android:allowBackup="true"
    android:icon="@mipmap/ic_launcher"
    android:label="@string/app_name"
    android:roundIcon="@mipmap/ic_launcher_round"
    android:supportsRtl="true"
    android:theme="@style/AppTheme">
    <activity android:name=".MainActivity2">   ❶
      <intent-filter>
        <action android:name="android.intent.action.MAIN"/>

        <category android:name="android.intent.category.LAUNCHER"/>
      </intent-filter>
    </activity>
  </application>
</manifest>
```

❶ This entry is what tells the Android runtime which java file is the main program or the startup file for the application. Change the value of the activity element to ".MainActivity2", as shown in Listing 5-13

Now you can run it in the emulator.

Working with Multiple Activities

In this chapter, we will take a look at some ways on how to work with multiple screens. Some applications may not need more than one Activity but some apps may require several. You will soon, no doubt, encounter the need to work with multiple Activities. It's not particularly difficult to work with multiscreen applications, but we need to backtrack a little bit to consider how Android applications are architected.

Component Activation

The Android platform is gung-ho on loose coupling. An application is nothing more than a collection of components held together by a manifest file, and each of these components can be activated by sending a message to it. If you want to show (activate) an Activity, you need to create a message, send it to the runtime, and let the runtime activate it for you. You cannot deal with a component directly. Listing 6-1 shows a pseudocode on how other platforms might show a second screen—many developers are quite familiar with this idiom, but unfortunately, it won't work in Android.

Listing 6-1. FirstActivity.java

```
class FirstActivity extends AppCompatActivity
  implements View.OnClickListener {

  public void onClick(View v) {
    SecondActivity second = new SecondActivity(); // WON'T WORK
  }
}

class SecondActivity extends AppCompatActivity {
}
```

© Ted Hagos 2018
T. Hagos, *Learn Android Studio 3*, https://doi.org/10.1007/978-1-4842-3156-2_6

To activate a component, like an Activity, we need to do the following.

1. Create an Intent object

2. Specify what we want to do or maybe even how to do it

3. Send the Intent object to the runtime and let it take care of component activation

Intents can activate components in the Android platform; they're a message passing mechanism that you can use if you want to work with an activity, service, content provider, or broadcast receiver.

Intents have a very crucial role in the Android platform, and their capabilities go beyond just launching another Activity. Some of the capabilities of Intents may be a bit advanced for a beginner book and hence will not be discussed here. But in this chapter, we'll take a look at a couple of interesting things about intents and activities. For example:

- Launching another Activity using an explicit intent

- Passing data from one activity to another

- Returning data from a second activity to the main activity

- Life cycle methods of activities

- A little bit of Fragments

An implicit intent is like asking someone (in our case, this is the Android runtime) to buy some sugar. It doesn't really matter where he gets it: he could go to convenience store nearby or buy it from a superstore across town. We don't really care as long as we get the sugar. An explicit intent, on the other hand, is asking somebody to get us some sugar, and he needs to buy on a 7/11 3 blocks away.

Going back to our pseudocode (Listing 6-1), if we know that we want to launch a specific activity (SecondActivity), we can use an explicit intent. The following pseudocode shows how to accomplish this.

```
// FirstActivity.java
class FirstActivity extends AppCompatActivity
  implements View.OnClickListener {

  public void onClick(View v) {
    Intent intent = new Intent(this, SecondActivity.class);
    startActivity(intent);
  }
}

// SecondActivity.java
class SecondActivity extends AppCompatActivity {

}
```

The next few sections will go into some details illustrating how to work with activities and intents.

Launching a Specific Activity

When you want to launch another activity (or any component), you will need to use explicit intents. This intent object is created and launched (usually) in the activity that wants to initiate the activation; this a two-step process. Firstly, we must create the intent object.

```
Intent intent = new Intent(<Context>, <Target>);
```

The Context object is simply a reference to the state of the component that wants to initiate or launch the intent: this is usually the *this* keyword, or, if you are creating the intent from within an inner class, it will be *ActivityName.this* (where ActivityName is the name of your Activity, e.g., MainActivity).

The `Target` is the name of the `Activity` that you want to launch; this is usually written *NameOfActivity.class*.

After the intent object has been created, it can now be launched with the following command:

```
startActivity(intent);
```

If, for example, we want to launch an activity named `SecondActivity` from `MainActivity.java`, we can manage this with the following code:

```
Intent intent = new Intent(MainActivity.this, SecondActivity.class);
startActivity(intent);
```

At this point, The Android runtime would have resolved the intent, and if it finds SecondActivity.class, it will be opened. The `MainActivity` will go out of focus and won't be visible to the user because SecondActivity will occupy the whole device screen. The user will only be able to navigate back to MainActivity if (1) the user uses the back button, (2) SecondActivity is terminated, or (3) a return button is coded in the SecondActivity that calls MainActivity using another Intent object (which we won't do in this project).

Let's put all these things together in a demo project.

Demo Project

In this section we'll take a look at one of the fundamental uses of an Intent object. We will launch a subactivity (second activity) from the main activity.

1. Create a new project

2. Remove the generated `textView` from `activity_main` and place a Button view instead. We will use the button to launch the second activity, we will refer to it as subactivity

3.   Create a new empty Activity from the AS3 File menu

4.   Place a button in the second activity layout. We will use this button to shut down or close the activity

5.   Go to main activity, create the handler, create the intent, fire up the AVD, launch the second activity

6.   Go to second activity

7.   Create a button, create a handler, implement the function (finish())

Create a new project using the following information (see Table 6-1).

Table 6-1. Project Details for FirstIntent

Application Name	FirstIntent
Company domain	Use your web site, or invent something; remember that this is in reverse DNS notation
Project location	Leave the default value. Ignore the C++ and Kotlin support
Form factor	Phone and tablet only
Minimum SDK	API 23 Marshmallow
Type of activity	Empty
Activity name	MainActivity
Layout name	activity_main

Go to `actvity_main.xml` on the main editor window and remove the generated `textView` (`Hello`) object. Place a Button view into the layout by clicking and dragging the Button view from the palette. Place the Button anywhere you like and click "Infer constraints" on the constraint inspector as shown in Figure 6-1.

infer constraints

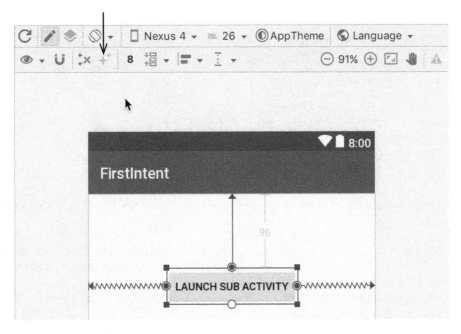

Figure 6-1. *activity_main with Button view*

Change the text (label) of the Button: you can do this either by editing the activity_main. xml directly or by changing the text attribute of the Button on the attribute inspector (see Figure 6-2).

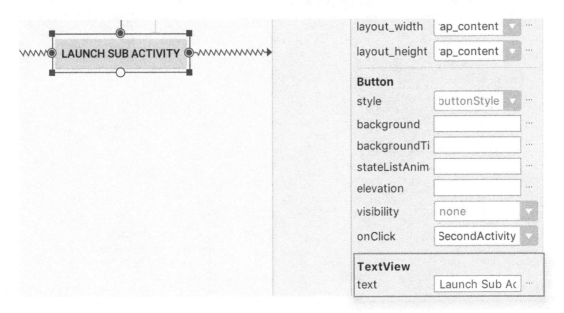

Figure 6-2. *Attributes inspector*

Alternatively, you may switch to "text mode" and edit the layout file directly as shown in Listing 6-2.

Listing 6-2. Editing the Label of the Button View

```
<Button
    android:id="@+id/button"
    android:layout_width="wrap_content"
    android:layout_height="wrap_content"
    android:text="Launch Sub Activity" ❶
    app:layout_constraintLeft_toLeftOf="parent"
    app:layout_constraintRight_toRightOf="parent"
    tools:layout_editor_absoluteY="201dp"/>
```

❶   The android:text attribute is the label of the Button view. This is what the user will see written on the Button

The next thing is to create another activity component. You can do this by selecting the "app" folder in the project tool window (as shown in Figure 6-3), then **New ➤ Activity ➤ Empty Activity**. Similarly, you can also achieve the same thing by going to the main menu bar **File ➤ Activity ➤ Empty Activity**; just make sure that in either case, you have selected the "app" folder in the project tool window.

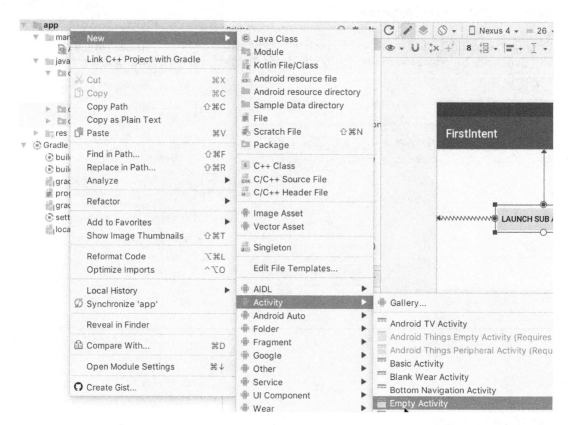

Figure 6-3. New Activity

Figure 6-4 shows the creation dialog for the second activity component. Change the name to SecondActivity and the name of the layout to activity_second; we will accept the default for the package name because we want it on the same package as the main activity.

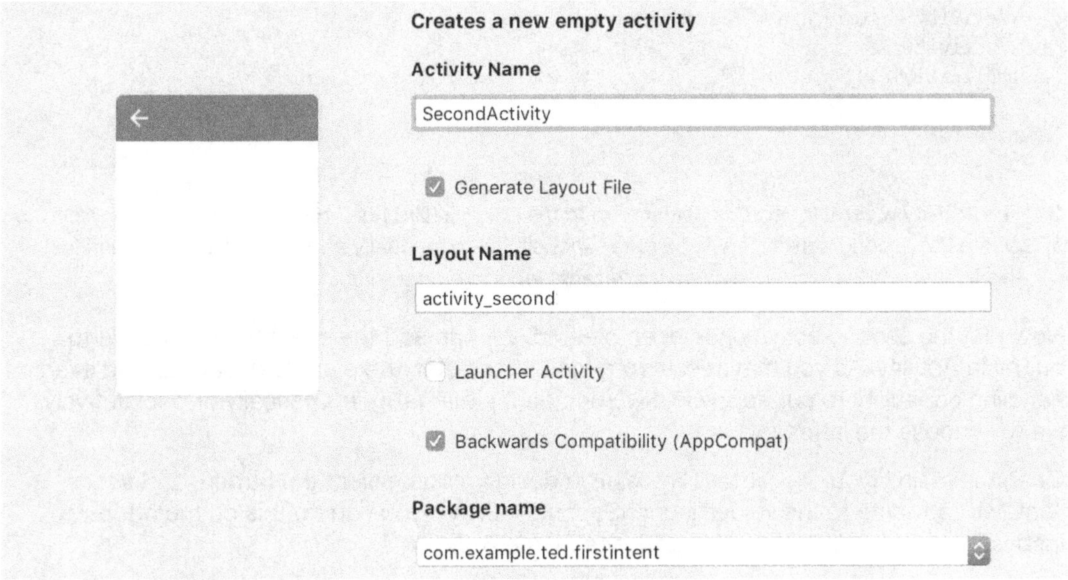

Creates a new empty activity

Activity Name

SecondActivity

☑ Generate Layout File

Layout Name

activity_second

◯ Launcher Activity

☑ Backwards Compatibility (AppCompat)

Package name

com.example.ted.firstintent

Figure 6-4. Second Activity

Note   All activity components in an application <u>must</u> be registered in the AndroidManifest file. One of the advantages of using the Activity wizard is that it also automatically updates the AndroidManifest file, thus adding a declaration for the newly created Activity. You can view the AndroidManifest.xml at app/manifests/AndroidManifest.xml.

Listing 6-3. Entry of SecondActivity on the AndroidManifest

```
<manifest package="com.example.ted.firstintent"
         xmlns:android="http://schemas.android.com/apk/res/android">

  <application
    android:allowBackup="true"
    android:icon="@mipmap/ic_launcher"
    android:label="@string/app_name"
    android:roundIcon="@mipmap/ic_launcher_round"
    android:supportsRtl="true"
    android:theme="@style/AppTheme">
    <activity android:name=".MainActivity">
```

```
        <intent-filter>
          <action android:name="android.intent.action.MAIN"/>
          <category android:name="android.intent.category.LAUNCHER"/>
        </intent-filter>
      </activity>
      <activity android:name=".SecondActivity">  ❶
      </activity>
    </application>

</manifest>
```

❶ The Activity wizard added this declaration to the AndroidManifest. Had we not used the wizard to
    create the second activity, it will be our responsibility to manually add this entry to the manifest:
    this is one good reason to always use wizards when one is available

Now that the second activity has been created, we can add the event handling code to
our main Activity. As you may recall from the last chapter, there are two ways to add event
handling capability to our app; while we can do it either programmatically or declaratively,
we will choose the latter.

Open the main layout file (activity_main) in design mode, select the button, and set its
"onClick" attribute to the value "launchSecondActivity" (you can do this on the attribute
inspector while the button is selected: see Figure 6-5).

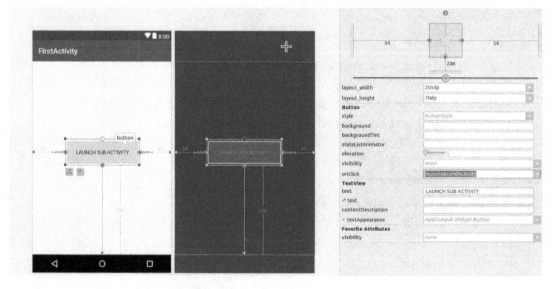

Figure 6-5. *FirstActivity, attributes inspector*

Listing 6-4. *activity_main with the onClick Handler*

```
<Button
    android:id="@+id/button"
    android:layout_width="wrap_content"
    android:layout_height="wrap_content"
```

```
android:layout_marginTop="96dp"
android:onClick="launchSecondActivity" ❶
android:text="Launch Sub Activity"
app:layout_constraintLeft_toLeftOf="parent"
app:layout_constraintRight_toRightOf="parent"
app:layout_constraintTop_toTopOf="parent"
tools:layout_editor_absoluteY="96dp"/>
```

❶   When you set the onClick attribute of the Button view on the inspector, the layout file will be
automatically updated. Conversely, you can go directly to this layout file and add the onClick
attribute as seen on this code example

The next step is to actually implement the launchSecondActivity method on the associated
activity file (MainActivity.java).

TWO PARTS OF AN ACTIVITY

Remember that an Activity component has two parts, a layout file (xml) and a program file (Java). Now that we
have two activity components, we have a total of four files to work with:

Layout file	Program file
activity_main.xml	MainActivity.java
activity_second.xml	SecondActivity.java

If there is any action that you want to happen as a result of a user-generated event on activity_main, you
should code that in MainActivity.java. Similarly, if the event is triggered from activity_second, that
code goes into SecondActivity.java.

Listing 6-5. Event Handling Code for launchSecondActivity

```
package com.example.ted.firstintent;

import android.content.Intent;
import android.support.v7.app.AppCompatActivity;
import android.os.Bundle;
import android.view.View;
import android.widget.Button;

public class MainActivity extends AppCompatActivity {

  @Override
  protected void onCreate(Bundle savedInstanceState) {
    super.onCreate(savedInstanceState);
    setContentView(R.layout.activity_main);
```

```
    Button objButton = (Button) findViewById(R.id.button);
  }

  public void launchSecondActivity(View v) { ❶
    Intent i = new Intent(this, SecondActivity.class); ❷ ❸ ❹
    startActivity(i); ❺
  }
}
```

❶   Like in the last chapter, make sure that the name of the method is spelled exactly as it written on
     onClick attribute of the Button view. Also, make sure that the method takes in a View argument

❷   An Intent object is created and assigned to a variable. The intent constructor takes in two
     arguments

❸   The first argument is a context object; generally it is referring to the object that wants to start or
     launch the intent. The this keyword is used because we want to launch the intent from within
     the MainActivity, and since the event handling method (launchSecondActivity) is a member of
     the MainActivity, we can simply use the this keyword—if you want to be precise, you could
     substitute the this keyword with the more verbose and explicit MainActivity.this

❹   The second argument of the intent constructor is the component class of the activity which you
     actually want to launch. This is generally constructed as the name of the program file appended
     with .class, which references the Java byte code (compiled) version of the class; hence in this
     case, it is SecondActivity.class. This is an example of an explicit intent because the exact name
     of the intent's target activity is hard-coded. Implicit intents, by contrast, do not specify the exact
     activity it wants to launch; instead, it relies on the Android runtime to resolve the intent so that it
     can launch the component that best matches it

❺   To finally launch the second activity, we call the startActivity method passing the intent as
     the argument. You cannot simply create an instance of the SecondActivity class to launch it.
     Remember that an Android application is a bunch of loosely coupled components that are
     held together by at least two things, namely, the AndroidManifest and Intents. The startActivity
     method simply tells the Android runtime that we want to activate another component and that
     we are using an intent object to help the runtime resolve the request

If we run this application right now, what we will see is the main activity with a single button;
when the button is clicked, the screen will change and display the second activity. That
behavior should be fine but to really complete the exercise, we will add a button to the
second activity which will function as a "close" button. When it is clicked, it should shut
down and kill the second activity, which will remove it on the screen stack, thus making our
main activity visible to the user again.

Go to the layout file of the second activity (activity_second.xml) and add a Button view to it
(see Figure 6-5). Like our main activity, keep it simple; place the button where you want it to
appear and use the "Infer constraints" on the constraint inspector for an easy and automatic
layout.

Set the text attribute of the Button to "Close" (Figure 6-6) but leave the onClick handler
blank. We'll handle the event programmatically in the associated Java file.

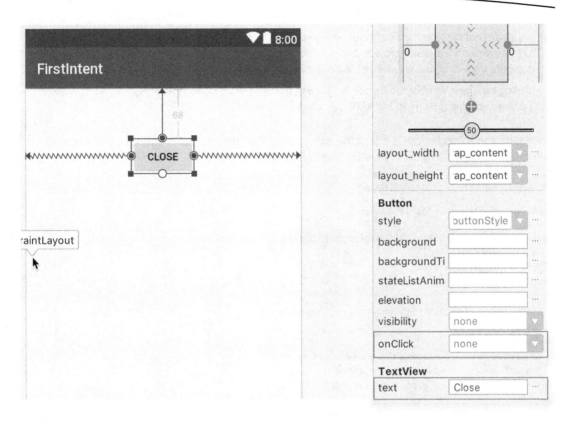

Figure 6-6. activity_second with the Close button

Listing 6-6. Button on activity_second

```xml
<?xml version="1.0" encoding="utf-8"?>
<android.support.constraint.ConstraintLayout
  xmlns:android="http://schemas.android.com/apk/res/android"
  xmlns:app="http://schemas.android.com/apk/res-auto"
  xmlns:tools="http://schemas.android.com/tools"
  android:layout_width="match_parent"
  android:layout_height="match_parent"
  tools:context="com.example.ted.firstintent.SecondActivity">

  <Button
    android:id="@+id/button2" ❶
    android:layout_width="wrap_content"
    android:layout_height="wrap_content"
    android:layout_marginTop="68dp"
    android:text="Close" ❷
    app:layout_constraintLeft_toLeftOf="parent"
    app:layout_constraintRight_toRightOf="parent"
    app:layout_constraintTop_toTopOf="parent"
    tools:layout_editor_absoluteY="68dp"/>
</android.support.constraint.ConstraintLayout>
```

❶   If you did not change the id attribute of the Button, it will be *button2*, since this is the second
    Button view on the entire project. You can change this value either here on the layout file or in the
    attribute inspector, but we will just leave it as the default; button2 should be fine

❷   Change the text label of the Button to "Close" to make it a bit descriptive. Again, this can be
    done either directly here in the XML file or in the attribute inspector (See Figure 6-5)

The last thing to do before we test the app is to implement some event handling code in
response to the button click. See Listing 6-7 for the full code of SecondActivity.java.

Listing 6-7. Full Code of SecondActivity.java

```
package com.example.ted.firstintent;

import android.support.v7.app.AppCompatActivity;
import android.os.Bundle;
import android.view.View;
import android.widget.Button;

public class SecondActivity extends AppCompatActivity {

  @Override
  protected void onCreate(Bundle savedInstanceState) {
    super.onCreate(savedInstanceState);
    setContentView(R.layout.activity_second); ❶

    Button secondButton = (Button) findViewById(R.id.button2); ❷
    assert secondButton != null; ❸
    secondButton.setOnClickListener(new View.OnClickListener() {
      @Override
      public void onClick(View view) {
        finish(); ❹
      }
    });
  }
}
```

❶   We already know what this does; this is the glue code that associates this Java file to a layout
    file. The runtime will inflate the XML layout file, update the R.class, and create the actual Java
    objects which represent the view objects of the layout file, thus in turn making these Java objects
    available for us to reference in our code. It comprises the "screen" for the Activity object

❷   findViewById is a locator method; it tries to find the Java object that was created during the
    inflation process. If it is found, the address of that object will be stored in the variable named
    secondButton

❸   This is just defensive coding; we're just making sure that secondButton actually contains the
    address of an object, and that it isn't null or empty

❹   This is the important code. When the finish method is called against an Activity object, it
    effectively destroys the activity and closes it. Destroying the Activity removes it from memory

Pass Data to Another Activity

In this section, we will explore how to pass data from the main activity to a second activity. While we're doing this, we'll practice a little bit of math programming. We will try to calculate the GCF (greatest common factor) of two numbers. We will create two activities (MainActivity and Calculate). The MainActivity will do the following

1. Wait for user input (two numbers), so we'll create two plain text view objects

2. Restrict the inputs to only digits; it doesn't make sense to accept alphanumeric inputs

3. Check if the text fields are empty; we only want to proceed if they are properly filled with numbers

4. Create an intent, and then we'll piggyback on that it so we can get the two inputted numbers to the Calculate activity

The second activity (Calculate) is the workhorse. It will be the one to do the number-crunching. Here's a breakdown of its tasks:

1. Get the intent that was passed from MainActivity

2. Check if there's some data piggybacking on it

3. If there's data, we will extract it so we can use it for calculation

4. When the calculation is done, we will display the results in a text view object

About the GCF Algorithm

There are quite a few ways on how to calculate GCF, but the most well-known is probably Euclid's algorithm. We will implement it this way.

1. Get the input of two numbers

2. Find the larger number

3. Divide the larger number using the smaller number

   ▪ If the remainder of step no. 3 is zero, then the GCF is the smaller number

   ▪ On the other hand, if the remainder is not zero, do the following:

      ▪ Assign the value of the smaller number to the larger number, then assign the value of the remainder to the smaller number

      ▪ Repeat step no. 3 (until the remainder is zero)

Let's create a new project for the GCF exercise; see Table 6-2 for details.

Table 6-2. *GCF Project Details*

Application name	GCF
Company domain	Use your web site, or invent something; remember that this is in reverse DNS notation
Project location	Leave the default
Form factor	Phone and tablet only
Minimum SDK	API 23 Marshmallow
Type of activity	Empty
Activity name	MainActivity (default)
Layout name	activity_main (default)

This project will have a second activity. When the project has done creating the activity and gradle is done on the build, add the second activity. On the project tool window, right-click **app ➤ Activity ➤ Empty activity**. Use the details in Table 6-3 for the newly created activity.

Table 6-3. *Second Activity*

Activity name	Calculate
Layout name	activity_calculate

Figures 6-7 and 6-8 show the layout of files for activity_main and activity_calculate.

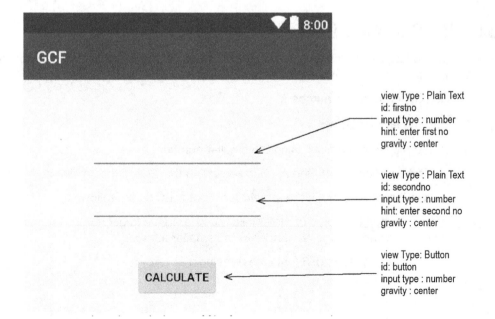

Figure 6-7. *activity_main layout*

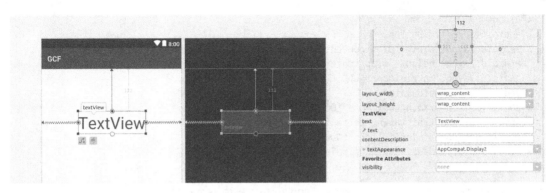

Figure 6-8. activity_calculate layout

Listing 6-8. activity_main.xml

```xml
<?xml version="1.0" encoding="utf-8"?>
<android.support.constraint.ConstraintLayout
  xmlns:android="http://schemas.android.com/apk/res/android"
  xmlns:app="http://schemas.android.com/apk/res-auto"
  xmlns:tools="http://schemas.android.com/tools"
  android:layout_width="match_parent"
  android:layout_height="match_parent"
  tools:context="com.example.ted.gcf.MainActivity">

  <EditText
    android:id="@+id/firstno"
    android:layout_width="wrap_content"
    android:layout_height="wrap_content"
    android:layout_marginTop="63dp"
    android:ems="10"
    android:gravity="center_vertical|center_horizontal"      ❶
    android:inputType="number"                                ❷
    app:layout_constraintLeft_toLeftOf="parent"
    app:layout_constraintRight_toRightOf="parent"
    app:layout_constraintTop_toTopOf="parent"/>

  <EditText
    android:id="@+id/secondno"
    android:layout_width="wrap_content"
    android:layout_height="wrap_content"
    android:layout_marginTop="28dp"
    android:ems="10"
    android:gravity="center"
    android:inputType="number"
    app:layout_constraintLeft_toLeftOf="parent"
    app:layout_constraintRight_toRightOf="parent"
    app:layout_constraintTop_toBottomOf="@+id/firstno"/>
```

```
<Button
    android:id="@+id/button"
    android:layout_width="wrap_content"
    android:layout_height="wrap_content"
    android:layout_marginTop="29dp"
    android:text="calculate"
    app:layout_constraintLeft_toLeftOf="parent"
    app:layout_constraintRight_toRightOf="parent"
    app:layout_constraintTop_toBottomOf="@+id/secondno"/>
</android.support.constraint.ConstraintLayout>
```

❶ Set the gravity attribute to center vertical and horizontal to center align the text inside

❷ This restricts the input to numbers only

Tip

1. You can set the `gravity` attribute of the `EditText` in the attributes inspector. While the `EditText` is selected in the design mode editor, click the "View all attributes" button in the inspector, as shown in Figure 6-9

2. You can set the input type of the `EditText` on the attributes inspector by clicking the ellipsis (…) beside "input type". The choices for input types will be visible on a popup (see Figure 6-10)

Figure 6-9. View all attributes in the inspector

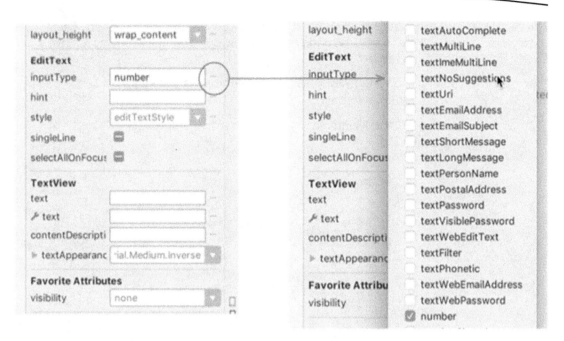

Figure 6-10. Input type attribute on the inspector

We can now move on to the layout details of `activity_calculate`. The UI elements of the second activity are very simple; there is only one `TextView` element in. The XML file of the `activity_calculate` is shown in Listing 6-9.

Listing 6-9. Layout File of Calculate Activity

```xml
<?xml version="1.0" encoding="utf-8"?>
<android.support.constraint.ConstraintLayout
  xmlns:android="http://schemas.android.com/apk/res/android"
  xmlns:app="http://schemas.android.com/apk/res-auto"
  xmlns:tools="http://schemas.android.com/tools"
  android:layout_width="match_parent"
  android:layout_height="match_parent"
  tools:context="com.example.ted.gcf.Calculate">

  <TextView
    android:id="@+id/textView"
    android:layout_width="176dp"
    android:layout_height="76dp"
    android:layout_marginTop="113dp"
    android:gravity="center"
    android:text="TextView"
    app:layout_constraintLeft_toLeftOf="parent"
    app:layout_constraintRight_toRightOf="parent"
    app:layout_constraintTop_toTopOf="parent"/>
</android.support.constraint.ConstraintLayout>
```

The details on how to set the constraints will be left to you already. We've already seen detailed examples on how to work with the constraint layout. The quickest way to have a decent layout is to do the following:

1. Drag and position each view object to the approximate location where you want them to show

2. Use the "pack" and "align" tools in the constraint inspector (see Figure 6-11)

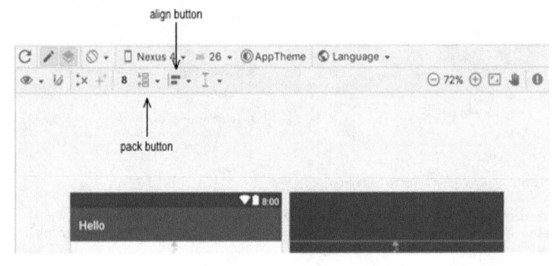

Figure 6-11. Constraint inspector

Now that we have a basic UI design, let's take a look at how we can write codes that accessed these user interface elements.

Listing 6-10. MainActivity.java

```java
public class MainActivity extends AppCompatActivity implements View.OnClickListener {

    private EditText fno;
    private EditText sno;
    private Button btn;

    @Override
    protected void onCreate(Bundle savedInstanceState) { ... }

    @Override
    protected void onStart() { ... }

    public void onClick(View v) { ... }

}
```

The preceding listing shows the skeleton structure of the MainActivity. The variables fno, sno are defined as class members because we will reference them from both the onClick and onCreate methods. The MainActivity is the listener object; that's why the onClick method is overridden in the body of the MainActivity.

> **Note** As you begin to write the codes, AS3 might indicate that there are warnings and errors by displaying some bulb icons and squiggly lines. These are most likely because of missing import statements and method (yet) to be overridden. Use the quick fix to solve these warnings and errors: (Alt + Enter for Windows and Linux I Option + Enter for macOS)

Listing 6-11. onCreate Method

```
@Override
protected void onCreate(Bundle savedInstanceState) {
  super.onCreate(savedInstanceState);
  setContentView(R.layout.activity_main);
  fno = (EditText) findViewById(R.id.firstno);
  sno = (EditText) findViewById(R.id.secondno);
  btn = (Button) findViewById(R.id.button);
  btn.setOnClickListener(this);
}
```

This is very typical code for the onCreate method. Most of our code samples will look almost identical to this.

Listing 6-12. onClick Method

```
public void onClick(View v) {

  boolean a = TextUtils.isEmpty(fno.getText());              ❶
  boolean b = TextUtils.isEmpty(sno.getText());

  if (!a & !b) {                                              ❷

    int firstnumber = Integer.parseInt(fno.getText().toString());    ❸
    int secondnumber = Integer.parseInt(sno.getText().toString());

    Intent intent = new Intent(this, Calculate.class);       ❹
    Bundle bundle = new Bundle();                            ❺
    bundle.putInt("fno", firstnumber);                      ❻
    bundle.putInt("sno", secondnumber);
    intent.putExtra("gcfdata", bundle);                     ❼
    startActivity(intent);                                   ❽

  }
}
```

❶   TextUtils can check if a TextView object doesn't have any text inside it. You can check for an
      empty text field some other way by extracting the string inside it and checking if the length is
      greater than zero, but TextUtils is a more succinct way to do it

❷   Let's make sure that both text fields are not empty. If one of them is empty, all the codes inside
      this block will simply be sidestepped, so no harm no foul. The app will dutifully wait for user
      input

❸   The getText() method returns an Editable object, which is not compatible with the parseInt
      method of the Integer class. The toString method should convert the Editable object to a
      regular String

❹   This line creates an Intent object. The first argument to the Intent constructor is a context object.
      The intent needs to know from where it is being launched, hence the this keyword; we are
      launching the intent from ourselves (MainActivity). The second argument to the constructor is
      the target activity that we want to launch

❺   We are going to piggyback some data into the intent object, so we will need a container for this
      data. A Bundle object is like a dictionary; it stores data in key/value pairs

❻   The Bundle object supports a bunch of put methods that take care of populating the bundle. The
      Bundle can store a variety of data, not only integers. If we wanted to put a string into the Bundle,
      we could say bundle.putString() or bundle.putBoolean() if we wanted to store boolean data

❼   After we've populated the Bundle object, we can now piggyback on the Intent object by calling
      the putExtra method. Similar to Bundle object, the Intent also uses the key/value pair for
      populating and accessing the extras. In this case, "gcfdata". We need to use the same key later
      (in the second activity) to retrieve the bundle

❽   This statement will launch the Activity

Listing 6-13. onStart Method

```
@Override
protected void onStart() {
  super.onStart();
  fno.setText("");
  sno.setText("");
}
```

The onStart method of MainActivity may be called many times over in the life cycle of the
application. It will be called for the first time when we launch the application (after onCreate),
and subsequently every time another activity grabs the focus and then the user navigates
back to MainActivity. Every time that happens, we're simply clearing out the contents of the
text fields. Listing 6-14 shows the full code for MainActivity.

Listing 6-14. MainActivity

```
package com.example.ted.gcf;

import android.content.Intent;
import android.support.v7.app.AppCompatActivity;
import android.os.Bundle;
```

```java
import android.text.TextUtils;
import android.view.View;
import android.widget.Button;
import android.widget.EditText;

public class MainActivity extends AppCompatActivity implements View.OnClickListener {

  private EditText fno;
  private EditText sno;
  private Button btn;

  @Override
  protected void onCreate(Bundle savedInstanceState) {
    super.onCreate(savedInstanceState);
    setContentView(R.layout.activity_main);
    fno = (EditText) findViewById(R.id.firstno);
    sno = (EditText) findViewById(R.id.secondno);
    btn = (Button) findViewById(R.id.button);
    btn.setOnClickListener(this);
  }

  @Override
  protected void onStart() {
    super.onStart();
    fno.setText("");
    sno.setText("");
  }

  public void onClick(View v) {

    boolean a = TextUtils.isEmpty(fno.getText());
    boolean b = TextUtils.isEmpty(sno.getText());

    if (!a & !b) {

      int firstnumber = Integer.parseInt(fno.getText().toString());
      int secondnumber = Integer.parseInt(sno.getText().toString());

      Intent intent = new Intent(this, Calculate.class);
      Bundle bundle = new Bundle();
      bundle.putInt("fno", firstnumber);
      bundle.putInt("sno", secondnumber);
      intent.putExtra("gcfdata", bundle);
      startActivity(intent);

    }
  }
}
```

MainActivity.java is mostly boilerplate code. It only takes care of the input and launching the second activity. The real work of the GCF happens inside the Calculate activity. Let's walk through the code of Calculate.java.

After MainActivity passes some data using the Intent and Bundle objects, the first few things we should take care of inside the Calculate activity is to extract that bundle data and eventually extract the key/value pairs of data inside the bundle.

```
Intent intent = getIntent();                          ❶
Bundle bundle = intent.getBundleExtra("gcfdata");     ❷
```

❶   This code will be called inside the onCreate method of the Calculate activity; the getIntent statement here will return whatever was the intent object that was used to launch this activity

❷   The getBundleExtra returns the bundle object which we passed to the intent object in MainActivity. Remember that when we inserted the bundle object in MainActivity, we used the key "gcfdata"; hence, we need to use the same key here in extracting the bundle

Once we have successfully extracted the bundle, we can get the two integer values that we stashed in it earlier.

```
int first = bundle.getInt("fno", 1);
int second = bundle.getInt("sno", 1);
```

The first parameter of the getInt method is simply the key. This has to be the same key that we used in the putInt method (back in MainActivity). The optional second parameter is simply a default value, in case the key is not found in the bundle. The next steps will be to start calculating the GCF.

Listing 6-15. GCF Logic

```
    int bigno, smallno = 0;
    int rem = 1;

    if (first > second ) {          ❶
      bigno = first;
      smallno = second;
    }
    else {
      bigno = second;
      smallno = first;
    }

    while ((rem = bigno % smallno) != 0) { ❷
      bigno = smallno;
      smallno = rem;
    }
    gcftext.setText(String.format("GCF = %d", smallno)); ❸
```

❶ Were trying to find out which is the larger number, a simple if statement and some assignments to bigno and smallno variable should take care of it

❷ There are two things going on in this statement. First, we are dividing bigno with smallno and we are assigning the remainder to the rem variable. Next, this whole expression is being tested to determine if the result is zero, because if it is, we should exit the while loop. It means we have already found the GCF. If it is not equal to zero, change the values of bigno and smallno according to Euclid's algorithm

❸ Once we found the GCF, we will set its value as the text of the TextView object

Listing 6-16. Full Code for Calculate.java

```java
package com.example.ted.gcf;

import android.content.Intent;
import android.support.v7.app.AppCompatActivity;
import android.os.Bundle;
import android.widget.TextView;

public class Calculate extends AppCompatActivity {

  @Override
  protected void onCreate(Bundle savedInstanceState) {
    super.onCreate(savedInstanceState);
    setContentView(R.layout.activity_calculate);

    int bigno, smallno = 0;
    int rem = 1;

    TextView gcftext = (TextView) findViewById(R.id.textView);
    Intent intent = getIntent();
    Bundle bundle = intent.getBundleExtra("gcfdata");

    if ((bundle != null) & !bundle.isEmpty()) {

      int first = bundle.getInt("fno", 1);
      int second = bundle.getInt("sno", 1);

      if (first > second ) {
        bigno = first;
        smallno = second;
      }
      else {
        bigno = second;
        smallno = first;
      }
```

```
    while ((rem = bigno % smallno) != 0) {
      bigno = smallno;
      smallno = rem;
    }
    gcftext.setText(String.format("GCF = %d", smallno));
  }


 }
}
```

Figures 6-12 and 6-13 show the GCF application in action.

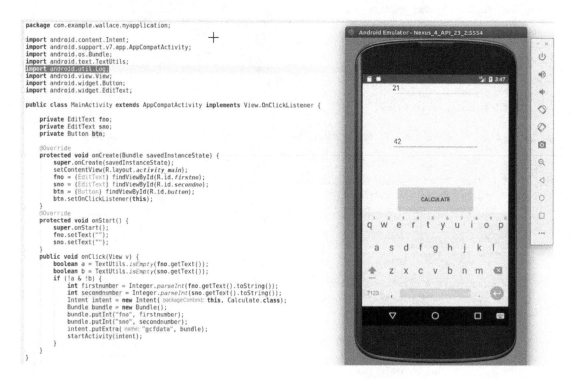

Figure 6-12. GCF MainActivity

```
package com.example.wallace.myapplication;

import android.content.Intent;
import android.support.v7.app.AppCompatActivity;
import android.os.Bundle;
import android.text.TextUtils;
import android.util.Log;
import android.view.View;
import android.widget.Button;
import android.widget.EditText;

public class MainActivity extends AppCompatActivity implements View.OnClickListener {

    private EditText fno;
    private EditText sno;
    private Button btn;

    @Override
    protected void onCreate(Bundle savedInstanceState) {
        super.onCreate(savedInstanceState);
        setContentView(R.layout.activity_main);
        fno = (EditText) findViewById(R.id.firstno);
        sno = (EditText) findViewById(R.id.secondno);
        btn = (Button) findViewById(R.id.button);
        btn.setOnClickListener(this);
    }
    @Override
    protected void onStart() {
        super.onStart();
        fno.setText("");
        sno.setText("");
    }
    public void onClick(View v) {
        boolean a = TextUtils.isEmpty(fno.getText());
        boolean b = TextUtils.isEmpty(sno.getText());
        if (!a & !b) {
            int firstnumber = Integer.parseInt(fno.getText().toString());
            int secondnumber = Integer.parseInt(sno.getText().toString());
            Intent intent = new Intent( packageContext: this, Calculate.class);
            Bundle bundle = new Bundle();
            bundle.putInt("fno", firstnumber);
            bundle.putInt("sno", secondnumber);
            intent.putExtra( name: "gcfdata", bundle);
            startActivity(intent);
        }
    }
}
```

Figure 6-13. GCF Result

Returning Results from Other Activities

In the previous section, we launched a subactivity and we passed it some data. In this section, we'll take a look at how to return data from a subactivity. Figure 6-14 shows the sequence of events on how to go about this.

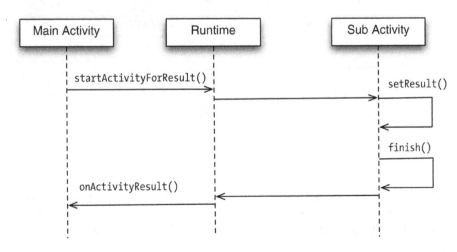

Figure 6-14. Sequence of events

We will launch a subactivity from the `MainActivity`. This can be managed by creating an explicit intent object and calling `startActivityForResult`. An activity may launch multiple other activities, and each of them could return some results. When these results come back, they will all be inside the `onActivityResult` method, so we need to know from which activity each result is coming from; the `REQUEST_CODE` will help us out with that.

```
Intent intent = new Intent(MainActivity.this, SubActivity.class);
startActivityForResult(intent, REQUEST_CODE)
```

When the runtime resolves the intent, the `SubActivity` gets created and will become visible. By then, it will be able to create its own data, perhaps via a user input. If it wants to return data back to `MainActivity`, it needs to create an intent object send the data back to `MainActivity` by piggybacking on the intent object.

```
String data = "Data to send back";
intent.putExtra("key", data);
setResult(Activity.RESULT_OK, intent);
finish();
```

When `SubActivity` calls the finish method, it will be destroyed, and `MainActivity` will then go back to the top of the activity stack. The runtime will call `MainActivity`'s `onActivityResult`; this is where we can extract the data that `SubActivity` sent back.

Let's set up a demo project so that we can explore these concepts and see what they look like in code.

Project Setup

Create a new project using the details in Table 6-4.

Table 6-4. Details for GetResultsSubActivity

Application name	GetResultsSubActivity
Project location	Leave the default
Form factor	Phone and tablet only
Minimum SDK	API 23 Marshmallow
Type of activity	Empty
Activity name	MainActivity (default)
Layout name	activity_main (default)

This project will have a second activity. When the project has finished creating the activity and gradle is done on the build, add the second activity. On the project tool window, right-click **app ➤ Activity ➤ Empty activity**. Use the details in Table 6-5 to create the new activity.

Table 6-5. *SecondActivity*

Activity name	SecondActivity
Layout name	activity_second

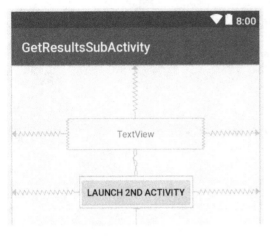
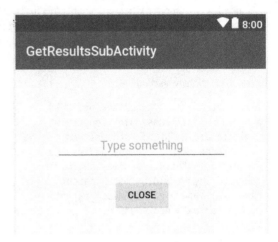

activity_main   activity_second

Figure 6-15. UI elements of the activities

Listing 6-17. activity_main

```
<?xml version="1.0" encoding="utf-8"?>
<android.support.constraint.ConstraintLayout
  xmlns:android="http://schemas.android.com/apk/res/android"
  xmlns:app="http://schemas.android.com/apk/res-auto"
  xmlns:tools="http://schemas.android.com/tools"
  android:layout_width="match_parent"
  android:layout_height="match_parent"
  tools:context="com.example.ted.getresultssubactivity.MainActivity">

  <Button
    android:id="@+id/button"
    android:layout_width="wrap_content"
    android:layout_height="wrap_content"
    android:layout_marginBottom="296dp"
    android:gravity="center"
    android:text="Launch 2nd Activity"
    app:layout_constraintBottom_toBottomOf="parent"
    app:layout_constraintLeft_toLeftOf="parent"
    app:layout_constraintRight_toRightOf="parent"
    app:layout_constraintTop_toBottomOf="@+id/textView"/>

  <TextView
    android:id="@+id/textView"
    android:layout_width="211dp"
```

```
      android:layout_height="0dp"
      android:layout_marginBottom="40dp"
      android:layout_marginTop="80dp"
      android:gravity="center"
      android:text="TextView"
      app:layout_constraintBottom_toTopOf="@+id/button"
      app:layout_constraintLeft_toLeftOf="parent"
      app:layout_constraintRight_toRightOf="parent"
      app:layout_constraintTop_toTopOf="parent"/>
</android.support.constraint.ConstraintLayout>
```

Listing 6-18. activity_second

```
<?xml version="1.0" encoding="utf-8"?>
<android.support.constraint.ConstraintLayout
  xmlns:android="http://schemas.android.com/apk/res/android"
  xmlns:app="http://schemas.android.com/apk/res-auto"
  xmlns:tools="http://schemas.android.com/tools"
  android:layout_width="match_parent"
  android:layout_height="match_parent"
  tools:context="com.example.ted.getresultssubactivity.SeconActivity">

  <EditText
    android:id="@+id/editText"
    android:layout_width="262dp"
    android:layout_height="0dp"
    android:layout_marginBottom="27dp"
    android:layout_marginTop="90dp"
    android:ems="10"
    android:gravity="center"
    android:hint="Type something"
    android:inputType="text"
    app:layout_constraintBottom_toTopOf="@+id/button2"
    app:layout_constraintLeft_toLeftOf="parent"
    app:layout_constraintRight_toRightOf="parent"
    app:layout_constraintTop_toTopOf="parent"/>

  <Button
    android:id="@+id/button2"
    android:layout_width="wrap_content"
    android:layout_height="wrap_content"
    android:layout_marginBottom="301dp"
    android:gravity="center"
    android:text="Close"
    app:layout_constraintBottom_toBottomOf="parent"
    app:layout_constraintLeft_toLeftOf="parent"
    app:layout_constraintRight_toRightOf="parent"
    app:layout_constraintTop_toBottomOf="@+id/editText"/>
</android.support.constraint.ConstraintLayout>
```

Program Files

Listing 6-19. MainActivity

```
public class MainActivity extends AppCompatActivity
  implements View.OnClickListener{

  private static final int REQUEST_CODE = 1000; ❶
  Button b;
  TextView t;

  @Override
  protected void onCreate(Bundle savedInstanceState) { ... } ❷

  public void onClick(View v) { ... } ❸

  @Override
  protected void onActivityResult(int requestCode, int resultCode, Intent data) { ... }
}
```

❶ The request code can be any value; we just need to mark each activity that will send data back to us

❷ This will contain all our initialization codes, as usual

❸ When the button is clicked, we will launch SecondActivity

Listing 6-20. onClick Method

```
@Override
public void onClick(View v) {
  Intent intent = new Intent(this, SecondActivity.class); ❶
  startActivityForResult(intent, REQUEST_CODE); ❷
}
```

❶ This creates just the usual explicit intent object

❷ The startActivity method will simply launch another screen; we are using the startActivityForResult method because we expect the target activity to return some data to us. The request code will serve as a marker that we can use later when the result comes back to us, and we can use that value to route program logic, in case our application starts several activities

We go over to SecondActivity, where an edit text awaits input. When the button is clicked, we'll just retrieve the contents of text field and inject it to an Intent object. Listing 6-21 shows the code for that.

Listing 6-21. SecondActivity

```
b.setOnClickListener(new View.OnClickListener() {
  @Override
  public void onClick(View view) {
    Intent intent = new Intent();
    EditText e = (EditText) findViewById(R.id.editText);
    String data = e.getText().toString();  //
    intent.putExtra("secondactivity", data); ❶
    setResult(Activity.RESULT_OK, intent); ❷
    finish(); ❸
  }
});
```

❶   We inject the contents of the data variable into the intent object using the putExtra method. We're
     assigning it a key of "secondactivity", and we need to use the same key when we retrieve it later

❷   This will prepare the data we are about to return

❸   This will kill SecondActivity. As soon as it dies, the runtime will call MainActivity's onActivityResult

We now scoot back over to MainActivity after SecondActivity is killed. Because
SecondActivity set the result code and has pushed some data back to MainActivity, the
onActivityResult is called by the runtime. Listing 6-22 walks through the code.

Listing 6-22. When the Result Comes Back

```
@Override
protected void onActivityResult(int requestCode, int resultCode, Intent data) {
  super.onActivityResult(requestCode, resultCode, data);

  if((requestCode == REQUEST_CODE) &&
     (resultCode == Activity.RESULT_OK)) {   ❶

    t.setText(data.getStringExtra("secondactivity"));  ❷

  }
}
```

❶   We check if the request code is from an activity we're interested in. Also, we need to check if the
     result code is RESULT_OK, which means the operation has succeeded. Otherwise, you might
     need to add, at the very least, some logging codes here

❷   We pull the data using the key "secondactivity"; this is the same key that we used back in
     SecondActivity, when we injected the data into the intent

Listing 6-23. Complete Code for MainActivity

```
package com.example.ted.getresultssubactivity;

import android.app.Activity;
import android.content.Intent;
import android.support.v7.app.AppCompatActivity;
import android.os.Bundle;
import android.view.View;
import android.widget.Button;
import android.widget.TextView;

public class MainActivity extends AppCompatActivity
  implements View.OnClickListener{

  private static final int REQUEST_CODE = 1000;
  Button b;
  TextView t;

  @Override
  protected void onCreate(Bundle savedInstanceState) {
    super.onCreate(savedInstanceState);
    setContentView(R.layout.activity_main);

    b = (Button) findViewById(R.id.button);
    t = (TextView) findViewById(R.id.textView);
    b.setOnClickListener(this);
  }

  @Override
  public void onClick(View v) {
    Intent intent = new Intent(this, SecondActivity.class);
    startActivityForResult(intent, REQUEST_CODE);
  }

  @Override
  protected void onActivityResult(int requestCode, int resultCode, Intent data) {
    super.onActivityResult(requestCode, resultCode, data);

    if((requestCode == REQUEST_CODE) &&
       (resultCode == Activity.RESULT_OK)) {

      t.setText(data.getStringExtra("secondactivity"));

    }
  }
}
```

Listing 6-24. Complete Code for SecondActivity

```
package com.example.ted.getresultssubactivity;

import android.app.Activity;
import android.content.Intent;
import android.support.v7.app.AppCompatActivity;
import android.os.Bundle;
import android.view.View;
import android.widget.Button;
import android.widget.EditText;

public class SecondActivity extends AppCompatActivity {

  @Override
  protected void onCreate(Bundle savedInstanceState) {
    super.onCreate(savedInstanceState);
    setContentView(R.layout.activity_second);

    Button b = (Button) findViewById(R.id.button2);
    b.setOnClickListener(new View.OnClickListener() {
      @Override
      public void onClick(View view) {
        Intent intent = new Intent();
        EditText e = (EditText) findViewById(R.id.editText);
        String data = e.getText().toString();
        intent.putExtra("secondactivity", data);
        setResult(Activity.RESULT_OK, intent);
        finish();
      }
    });
  }
}
```

Implicit Intents

Android's approach to program interactivity is quite unique because it's very user-centric. It gives the user a lot of power to make choices on how they manipulate and create data. Let's take a common usage scenario for an Android device. A user opens the "Contacts" application and chooses the contact detail of John Doe, for example. This contact could have an e-mail address, a mobile phone, and a Twitter name, for example. The user could tap on each and every one of John's contact points, and each time, Android will launch a different application, the default e-mail client, a dialer, and a downloaded Twitter app. The user probably doesn't care which application was launched or how many applications are currently open; he just wants to send a message. If this user doesn't like the e-mail app or the default Twitter app, he could delete these apps and replace them with something else, and he should be back in business.

For this kind of program interaction to happen, Android needed to architect the platform focusing heavily on loose coupling and plugability. A component (like the contacts app) should not know any specific detail about what app it should use when an e-mail address or a mobile phone number is tapped. The resolution for what kind of app to use for a specific kind of data should not be hardwired into the contacts app; otherwise, the user won't be able to use his choice of e-mail or `Twitter` app.

This is where intents come in; the basic idea is that when a component has data or information that is beyond its capability to service, it can go out to the Android platform— using intents— and ask around if there's any application that can (or wants to) do that.

Intents allow us to utilize the capabilities of other application simply by creating and launching the intent, without specifying the target component— if you specify the target component, that will become an explicit intent. The general syntax for creating implicit intents is as follows:

```
Intent intent = new Intent();   ❶
intent.setAction(ACTION);       ❷
intent.setData(DATA);           ❸
startActivity(intent);          ❹
```

❶   Create the intent object

❷   Specify the action. These actions are constants of the Intent class: for example, Intent.ACTION_ VIEW

❸   Specify the data, if there's any

❹   Launch the activity

Let's explore implicit intents in a demo project and see how these things come together in code.

Demo Project

Let's create a demo project, Table 6-6 shows the details for this project.

Table 6-6. ImplicitIntents Project Details

Application name	ImplicitIntents
Project location	Leave the default value. Ignore the C++ and Kotlin support
Form factor	Phone and tablet only
Minimum SDK	API 23 Marshmallow
Type of activity	Empty
Activity name	MainActivity (default)
Layout name	activity_main (default)

You can refer to Listing 6-25 and Figure 6-16 for the UI details.

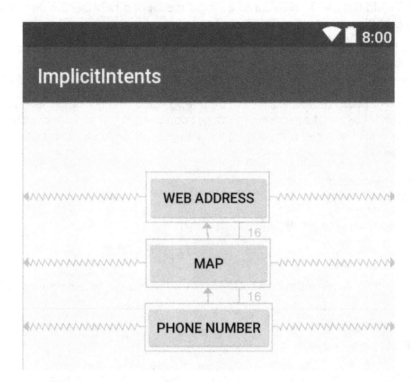

Figure 6-16. *Implicit Intents*

Listing 6-25. *activity_layout*

```xml
<?xml version="1.0" encoding="utf-8"?>
<android.support.constraint.ConstraintLayout
  xmlns:android="http://schemas.android.com/apk/res/android"
  xmlns:app="http://schemas.android.com/apk/res-auto"
  xmlns:tools="http://schemas.android.com/tools"
  android:layout_width="match_parent"
  android:layout_height="match_parent"
  tools:context="com.example.ted.implicitintents.MainActivity">

  <Button
    android:id="@+id/btnwebaddress"
    android:layout_width="126dp"
    android:layout_height="0dp"
    android:layout_marginBottom="80dp"
    android:layout_marginTop="69dp"
    android:text="Web address"
    app:layout_constraintBottom_toTopOf="@+id/btnphonenumber"
    app:layout_constraintLeft_toLeftOf="parent"
    app:layout_constraintRight_toRightOf="parent"
    app:layout_constraintTop_toTopOf="parent"/>
```

```
<Button
   android:id="@+id/btnmap"
   android:layout_width="127dp"
   android:layout_height="48dp"
   android:layout_marginTop="24dp"
   android:text="Map"
   app:layout_constraintLeft_toLeftOf="parent"
   app:layout_constraintRight_toRightOf="parent"
   app:layout_constraintTop_toBottomOf="@+id/btnwebaddress"/>

<Button
   android:id="@+id/btnphonenumber"
   android:layout_width="wrap_content"
   android:layout_height="wrap_content"
   android:layout_marginBottom="264dp"
   android:layout_marginTop="24dp"
   android:text="Phone Number"
   app:layout_constraintBottom_toBottomOf="parent"
   app:layout_constraintLeft_toLeftOf="parent"
   app:layout_constraintRight_toRightOf="parent"
   app:layout_constraintTop_toBottomOf="@+id/btnmap"/>
</android.support.constraint.ConstraintLayout>
```

Listing 6-26. Skeleton of MainActivity

```
public class MainActivity extends AppCompatActivity
   implements View.OnClickListener{

   @Override
   protected void onCreate(Bundle savedInstanceState) { ... }

   @Override
   public void onClick(View v) { ... }

}
```

This is a very basic structure for the main program. We will use MainActivity as the listener object and then we'll implement onClick as an overridden member method. There are three buttons in the application. The "web address" button tries to resolve an http request, the "map" button tries to resolve a geo code, and the "phone number" button tries to resolve a telephone number.

Opening an http Request

To handle an http request, like what our "web address" button will try to do, we need to do a couple of things. Firstly, we'll need a URI object; this can be managed by the following code

```
Uri uri = Uri.parse("http://www.apress.com");
```

The parse method of the Uri object should be able to take a String object specifying a web URL and return a proper URI object to us. The next step is to create an intent. We can use the no-arg constructor of the Intent to do this.

```
Intent intent = new Intent();
```

After the intent is created, we can now set its action using the following code.

```
intent.setAction(Intent.ACTION_VIEW);
```

Setting the action of the intent helps the Android runtime to choose which application within our device can best handle the request;ACTION _VIEW is one of the constants defined in Intent class, and it's what you might use if you want to handle a web URL. You can find more information about some of the most common Intent actions from the official Android web site (see Figure 6-17).

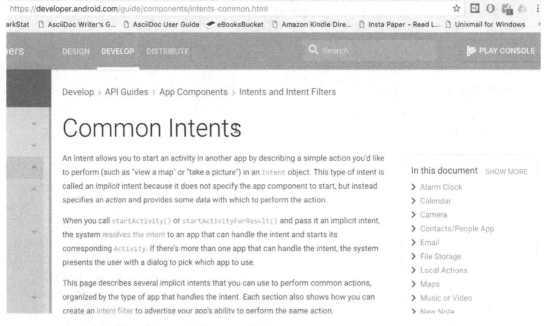

Figure 6-17. Common Intents documentation from the official Android site

After setting the action of the Intent, we should now set its data, so it knows where to go when it launches the browser. This can be done with the following code.

```
intent.setData(uri);
```

Lastly, we need to launch the intent object.

```
startActivity(intent);
```

We can shorten the code by passing the Uri and the action to the Intent constructor.

```
Uri uri = Uri.parse("http://www.apress.com");
Intent intent = new Intent(Intent.ACTION_VIEW, uri);
startActivity(intent);
```

Listing 6-27. Complete Code for MainActivity

```
package com.example.ted.implicitintents;

import android.content.Intent;
import android.net.Uri;
import android.support.v7.app.AppCompatActivity;
import android.os.Bundle;
import android.util.Log;
import android.view.View;

public class MainActivity extends AppCompatActivity
  implements View.OnClickListener{

  @Override
  protected void onCreate(Bundle savedInstanceState) {
    super.onCreate(savedInstanceState);
    setContentView(R.layout.activity_main);

    findViewById(R.id.btnwebaddress).setOnClickListener(this);
    findViewById(R.id.btnmap).setOnClickListener(this);
    findViewById(R.id.btnphonenumber).setOnClickListener(this);

  }

  @Override
  public void onClick(View v) {

    Uri uri = null;
    Intent intent = null;

    switch(v.getId()) {
      case R.id.btnwebaddress:
        uri = Uri.parse("http://www.apress.com");
        intent = new Intent(Intent.ACTION_VIEW,uri);      ❶
        startActivity(intent);
        break;
      case R.id.btnmap:
        uri = Uri.parse("geo:40.7113399,-74.0263469");
        intent = new Intent(Intent.ACTION_VIEW, uri);     ❷
        startActivity(intent);
        break;
      case R.id.btnphonenumber:
        uri = Uri.parse("tel:639285083333");
        intent = new Intent(Intent.ACTION_DIAL, uri);     ❸
        startActivity(intent);
        break;
```

```
        default:
          Log.i(getClass().getName(), "Cannot resolve button click");
      }
    }
}
```

❶   Launches a browser and grabs the web site www.apress.com (see Figure 6-18)

❷   Opens Google Maps and shows the location of the specified geo code (see Figure 6-18)

❸   Launches the dialer app (see Figure 6-18)

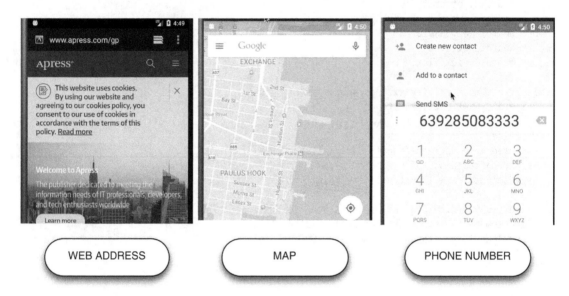

Figure 6-18. Output of the application

Activity Life Cycle

Mobile apps aren't really desktop apps running on a smaller screen. We don't use mobile apps the way we use desktop apps. When we use a desktop app, it usually stays open and active for quite some time because we are focused on the task at hand. Mobile apps, on the other hand, have a shorter life span. We usually take it out of the pocket, do something quick, and then put it back. Sometimes even, when we are using a particular app, we might get interrupted by another app (e.g., a phone call), so the original app we were looking at would be eclipsed by the interrupting app. All the activation and juggling of these apps are managed by the Android runtime.

As a developer, you are not in control of the life cycle of the app; the user is. You cannot assume that the user will not be interrupted in the middle of inputting data to your app. You also cannot assume that your app will always exit gracefully; it could get killed without getting the chance to properly shut down. You need to be defensive in designing your code and consider that these things can happen. Fortunately, the Android runtime notifies us whenever something happens to our components (like the activity). This section explores the various events that can happen to an activity throughout its life cycle, from the point of creation to its eventual destruction. Figure 6-19 show the activity life cycle.

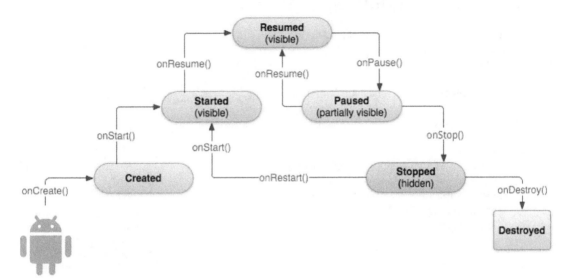

Figure 6-19. Activity Life cycle

Table 6-7. Callback Methods

Event	Description
onCreate	Called when the activity is first created; you can put your initialization codes here
onRestart	When the activity has been stopped and restarted again. This is always followed by onStart
onStart	When the activity is starting to become visible to the user
onResume	The activity is ready to interact with the user, at this point; the activity is at the top of the activity stack, and it occupies the whole screen
onPause	When the activity is about to go to the background; this can happen when another activity grabs the focus
onStop	When the activity is no longer visible to the user
onDestroy	Called when the activity is destroyed. For the application to come back, it needs to be created again

Listing 6-28 shows the overridden life-cycle methods for an Activity.

Listing 6-28. MainActivity, Life-Cycle Methods

```java
package com.example.ted.activitylifecycle;

import android.support.v7.app.AppCompatActivity;
import android.os.Bundle;
import android.util.Log;

public class MainActivity extends AppCompatActivity {

  private String TAG;

  @Override
  protected void onCreate(Bundle savedInstanceState) {
    super.onCreate(savedInstanceState);
    setContentView(R.layout.activity_main);
    TAG = getClass().getSimpleName();
    Log.i(TAG, "onCreate");
  }

  @Override
  protected void onStart() {
    super.onStart();
    Log.i(TAG, "onStart");
  }

  @Override
  protected void onResume() {
    super.onResume();
    Log.i(TAG, "onResume");

  }

  @Override
  protected void onPause() {
    super.onPause();
    Log.i(TAG, "onPause");

  }

  @Override
  protected void onStop() {
    super.onStop();
    Log.i(TAG, "onStop");

  }
```

```
@Override
protected void onDestroy() {
  super.onDestroy();
  Log.i(TAG, "onDestroy");

}
}
```

You can view the log messages in the Logcat tool window.

Figure 6-20. Recent apps button

> **Tip**   If you want to see the onDestroy message, you can use the "Recent apps" button of the
> device (if it has one) to see all the running apps (Figure 6-20). You can kill the application from
> there.

Chapter 7

UI Elements

UI Elements

As of this writing, there are 3.3 million apps in the Google play store. That's a lot of apps and lot of developers to compete with.

If you're going to publish your app in the store, we need to at least make sure that the app can stand toe to toe with professionally done applications. It needs to have a little bit of polish.

Google has published a set of guidelines for UI approach; it's called material design, and you can read more about it in their web site `https://material.io`. It's a big topic and we don't intend to cover it here. But in this chapter, we will discuss three things that can get you started and point you in the direction for further investigation. These are the themes and colors, the AppBar, and Fragments.

Themes and Colors

When AS3 creates a project with an empty activity, it does quite a few things for you, and we've seen some of those affordances in the past couple of sample applications we've worked on. In this chapter, we'll focus a little bit on aesthetics. We won't do a deep dive into UI design because it's a big area, and quite beyond the scope of this book—and my expertise; I haven't been a UI guy. But we'll look at some quick and easy things to make our apps look decent.

Let's create a new project with an empty activity and name it `StylesAndThemes`; leave the default form factor to "Phone and Tablets".

> **Note** A style is a collection of attributes that specify the look and format for an individual view object; a style refers to height, color, font, and so on. A theme, on the other hand, is a style applied to entire Activity or application

T. Hagos, *Learn Android Studio 3*, https://doi.org/10.1007/978-1-4842-3156-2_7

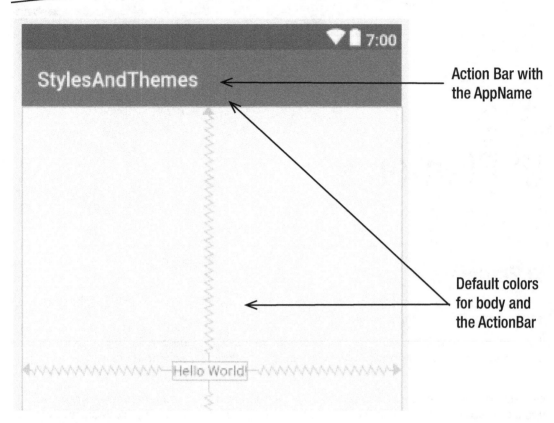

Action Bar with the AppName

Default colors for body and the ActionBar

Figure 7-1. activity_main

We've never messed around with these colors in our past applications; we simply let AS3 decide for us how our app would look (Figure 7-1 shows the default theme for an app), at least as far as color is concerned. If you want to do a bit of branding and give your application some identity, we can start by customizing the color and the theme.

Colors

While it's possible to specify the color for every part of the application, that may prove to be tedious and time-consuming. An easier way would be to work with themes. The overall theme for an application is controlled by the AndroidManifest (you can open the manifest file from the project tool window, **app ➤ manifests ➤ AndroidManifest**).

Android makes heavy use of XML, as you can probably tell by now. Also, the practice of referencing values, whether string, color, style, or something else, is very prevalent—you will find it everywhere. Let's look at two entries in the manifest file (see Listing 7-1).

Listing 7-1. AndroidManifest

```xml
<?xml version="1.0" encoding="utf-8"?>
<manifest package="com.ted.stylesandthemes"
          xmlns:android="http://schemas.android.com/apk/res/android">

  <application
    android:allowBackup="true"
    android:icon="@mipmap/ic_launcher"
    android:label="@string/app_name"               ❶
    android:roundIcon="@mipmap/ic_launcher_round"
    android:supportsRtl="true"
    android:theme="@style/AppTheme">                ❷
    <activity android:name=".MainActivity">
      <intent-filter>
        <action android:name="android.intent.action.MAIN"/>

        <category android:name="android.intent.category.LAUNCHER"/>
      </intent-filter>
    </activity>
  </application>

</manifest>
```

❶   The @string notation means we are referencing this value from app/res/values/strings.xml.
     This is the preferred way of defining strings in your app. Writing the strings in a resource affords
     us the ability to manage the string resources from a central location; it facilitates ease of change
     and localization as well. The strings and styles resources can be opened from the project tool
     window (see Figure 7-2).

     app/res/values/strings.xml

     ```xml
     <resources>

       <string name="app_name">StylesAndThemes</string>

     </resources>
     ```

❷   The @style notation means we are referencing this entry from the app/res/values/styles.xml
     file. Inside that file, there should be a definition for AppTheme

In Listing 7-2, the AppTheme value which is referenced from the manifest file is defined. Firstly,
it wasn't built from scratch; it is inheriting from the DarkActionBar theme, but it allows us to
customize a couple of colors. There are three colors defined in the styles, but you can add
more if you want to. We will just work with these three for now.

> **Note**   In previous versions of Android Studio, you may have needed to create /res/styles.xml file.
> In AS3, when we created the empty activity, the styles resource file was automatically generated.

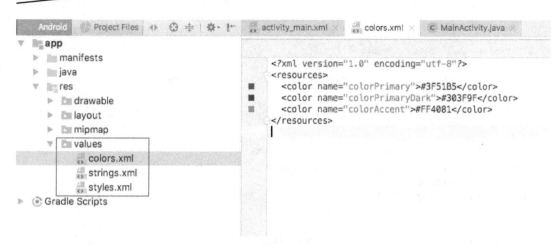

Figure 7-2. colors.xml

Listing 7-2. /app/res/values/colors.xml

```
<resources>

  <!-- Base application theme. -->
  <style name="AppTheme" parent="Theme.AppCompat.Light.DarkActionBar">
    <!-- Customize your theme here. -->
    <item name="colorPrimary">@color/colorPrimary</item>
    <item name="colorPrimaryDark">@color/colorPrimaryDark</item>
    <item name="colorAccent">@color/colorAccent</item>
  </style>

</resources>
```

colorPrimary, colorPrimaryDark, and colorAccent are not (really) defined in styles.xml; instead, we find another indirection referring us to yet another resource file. It can get annoying sometimes, but these indirections are necessary all in the name of manageability. So, you need to get used to it.

Listing 7-3. /app/res/values/colors.xml

```
<?xml version="1.0" encoding="utf-8"?>
<resources>
  <color name="colorPrimary">#3F51B5</color>
  <color name="colorPrimaryDark">#303F9F</color>
  <color name="colorAccent">#FF4081</color>
</resources>
```

If you open colors.xml, we can finally see the hex values of the colors. AS3 shows you the colors in the gutter of the editor; the color changes immediately when you change the hex values (Figure 7-3). If you want to change the tint of the app, you can start by making changes to this file.

```xml
<?xml version="1.0" encoding="utf-8"?>
<resources>
    <color name="colorPrimary">#3F51B5</color>
    <color name="colorPrimaryDark">#303F9F</color>
    <color name="colorAccent">#FF4081</color>
</resources>
```

Figure 7-3. colors.xml in the main editor

If you need help the with the hex values of colors, there are plenty of web resources for that; colorhexa.com is one such site (www.color.hexa.com), showing you related colors and gradients of specific colors, so it's good to use when you want to work with color hex values. Color scheming, however, is a big area, and there are quite a few principles and guidelines involved. Another good resource for colors is Materialpalette (www.materialpalette.com, shown in Figure 7-4).

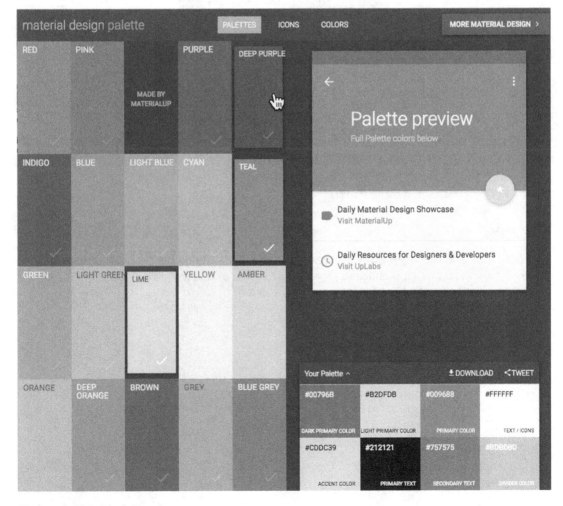

Figure 7-4. Materialpalette.com

Materialpalette is geared toward Android design, specifically material design. The basic idea is to choose two colors and the site builds a palette for you. Now we can simply copy the hex values of primary, dark primary, accent, and light primary colors.

Listing 7-4. Customized colors.xml

```xml
<?xml version="1.0" encoding="utf-8"?>
<resources>
  <color name="colorPrimary">#009688</color>
  <color name="colorPrimaryDark">#00796B</color>
  <color name="colorAccent">#CDDC39</color>
  <color name="colorPrimaryLight">#B2DFDB</color>
</resources>
```

Switch the main editor to the activity_main tab to see the new look of our app (Figure 7-5).

Figure 7-5. activity_main with customized colors

Themes

Android's look and feel have evolved throughout the years. As newer devices and newer Android versions came in, this also ushered in new look and feel for the apps. Figure 7-6 shows some snapshots of the themes over the years.

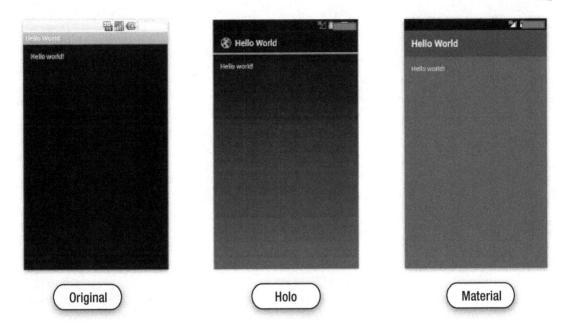

| Original | Holo | Material |

Figure 7-6. Various Android themes

Table 7-1 lists some of the more important and milestone themes of Android.

Table 7-1. Android Themes

Theme	Description
Theme.Light	This was used by Android versions 2 and below (API 10 and below); e.g., Gingerbread
Theme.Holo.Light	Android 3 (API 11 and above)
Theme.Holo.DarkActionBar	API 14 onward
Theme.AppCompat	API 7
android:Theme.Material	API 21 (Lollipop) onward

The default theme for the past couple of projects we've created is Theme.AppCompat.Light.DarkActionBar. It's a decent theme, and if your needs are quite simple, there may be no need to do further work on this theme. But if you want to tweak the look and feel of your app, you can start trying out various themes. You can do this by editing the parent theme in styles.xml (as shown in Figure 7-7).

Figure 7-7. Edit themes

Try changing the theme a couple of times and then go back to `activity_main` (design mode) so you can explore the various Android themes.

AppBar

Menus are very important in UI design, and they are indispensable tools in the programmer's arsenal. Menu systems allow the user to get to an app's functionality. Traditionally, menu systems are organized hierarchically and intro groups. Android's menu system, at some point in time, has behaved exactly like that—grouped and hierarchical. But that was in the past. Android's approach to menus has changed dramatically over the course of its lifetime.

Before API 11 (Honeycomb), Android menus relied on hardware buttons (like the ones you see in Figure 7-8). Developers could rely on the home buttons (plus some others, like the option button) always being there. And we built our apps per those assumptions, because those assumptions were reasonable at the time. Of course, times have changed. Screen resolutions have increased dramatically, and the hardware buttons have disappeared. Fortunately, Android's approach to menus has also changed and kept up with the state of hardware capabilities.

Figure 7-8. API 10 (Gingerbread)

A new kind of menu system has been added to Android starting from API 11. Apps that are built with a min SDK of 11 can use the ActionBar (see an example in Figure 7-9).

Figure 7-9. ActionBar

The ActionBar is a dedicated area at the top of the screen and is persistent throughout the app. It's a lot like the main menu bar of AS3 if you think about it. You can generally use the ActionBar to display the most important features of your app and make them accessible in a predictable way; for instance, putting a permanent Search widget on top, and so forth. It creates a cleaner look by removing clutter in your menus; if not all items in the menu can be accommodated on the screen, the ActionBar will display an overflow icon—this is the vertical ellipsis, three dots arranged vertically, which is always found on the far right of the bar. It also displays the name of the application, so it reinforces the brand identity of the app.

Nowadays, the ActionBar has fallen a bit out of fashion and has been eclipsed by the Toolbar, the new kid on the block. The Toolbar is a bit more versatile because it's not permanently clipped on top of the screen, you can place it anywhere you want and it has a few more capabilities. The ActionBar, however, remains a viable solution for simple menu systems. In fact, nothing stops you from using both the ActionBar and the Toolbar; just work with the best tools you have.

Demo App

Create a new project with the following details (Table 7-2).

Table 7-2. ActionBar Project Details

Application name	ActionBar
Project location	Use the default
Form factor	Phone and tablet only
Minimum SDK	API 23 Marshmallow
Type of activity	Empty
Activity name	MainActivity (default)
Layout name	activity_main (default)

To use the ActionBar, the minimum SDK should be set to API 11; this makes Honeycomb a cut-off. If a project has a minimum SDK of 11 or above, it means it can handle the ActionBar.

After creating the project, make sure that the theme is set to "AppTheme". After that, create a **menu** folder under the **res** folder. In the project tool window, right-click the res folder **New ➤ Android Resource Directory** (see Figure 7-10).

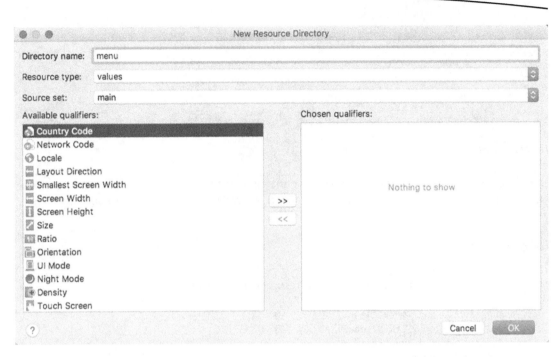

Figure 7-10. Create a new resource directory

Create a menu file under the newly created menu directory. Right-click the menu folder, **New ➤ Menu Resource File** (see Figure 7-11).

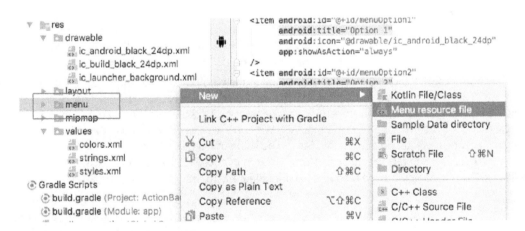

Figure 7-11. Create a menu folder

Name the new resource file as "main_menu", as shown in Figure 7-12.

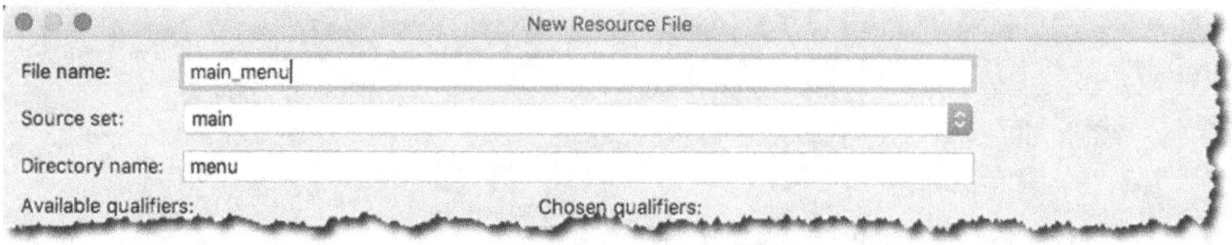

Figure 7-12. New à Menu resource file

Double-click the `main_menu` resource file from the project tool window. Let's add some menu items as shown in Listing 7-5. The `main_menu.xml` file will be created in the folder `/app/res/values/menu/main_menu.xml`.

Listing 7-5. main_menu.xml

```
<?xml version="1.0" encoding="utf-8"?>
<menu xmlns:android="http://schemas.android.com/apk/res/android">

    <item android:id="@+id/menuFile"                  ❶
          android:title="@string/menuFile"/>          ❷
    <item android:id="@+id/menuEdit"
          android:title="@string/menuEdit"/>
    <item android:id="@+id/menuHelp"
          android:title="@string/menuHelp"/>
    <item android:id="@+id/menuExit"
          android:title="@string/menuExit"/>
</menu>
```

❶   The `@id+` notation means that we would like create an ID for this item; this is the same ID that we'll use later when we reference it from our program using the `findViewById` method

❷   The `title` attribute is the one that will be displayed on the menu. We could write it just a simple string here, but that would be tantamount to hard-coding that value in this file. That's generally a bad idea. The `@string` notations means we are referencing the title from the `/app/res/values/strings.xml` file. The first time you type title, AS3 will show it as an error because the string resource is not yet created in strings.xml. Select the value of the title attribute (`@string/menuFile`) and use the quick fix (**Alt + Enter** in Windows/Linux | **Option + Enter** in macOS) so you can create the resource file. See Figure 7-13

```
    menu   item
1   <?xml version="1.0" encoding="utf-8"?>
2   <menu xmlns:android="http://schemas.android.com/apk/res/android">
3     <item android:id="@+id/menuFile"
4           android:title="@string/menuFile"
5       />                              ⬩ Create string value resource 'menuFile'   ▶
6     <item android:id="@+id/menuEdit"   ⮫ Override Resource in Other Configuration... ▶
7           android:title="@string/men   ⮫ Inject language or reference              ▶
8       />
9     <item android:id="@+id/menuHelp"
10          android:title="@string/menuHelp"
11      />
12    <item android:id="@+id/menuExit"
```

Figure 7-13. Create a new String resource item

Switch over to `MainActivity` so we can add the newly created `main_menu` to the AppBar. To do this, we need to override the `onCreateOptions` method of the `MainActivity`. You can use the override methods facility of AS3 to do this, from the main menu bar, **Code → Override Methods**.

```
@Override
public boolean onCreateOptionsMenu(Menu menu) {
  MenuInflater inflater = getMenuInflater();
  inflater.inflate(R.menu.main_menu, menu);
  return true;
}
```

If you run the application on the emulator, you will see something that looks like Figure 7-14.

Figure 7-14. Menu items in ActionBar (when the action overflow is clicked)

Let's use some images on the menu. AS3 comes with a lot of images that you can use for a wide range of applications. Before we can use any image, we should add it to our resources folder. You can use either rasterized (bitmapped) or vector assets for images. In this example, we'll use vector assets.

On the project tool window, right-click /app/res ➤ **New** ➤ **Vector** asset (Figure 7-15).

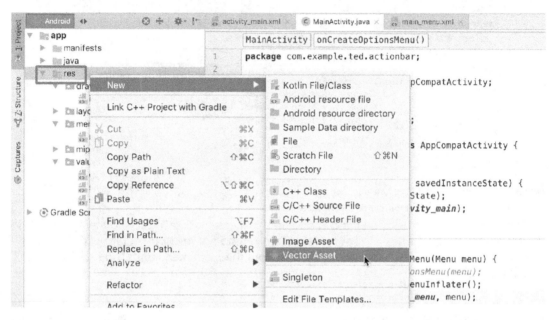

Figure 7-15. Add a vector asset to the project

Click the icon so you can find images that will suit your needs (Figure 7-16).

Figure 7-16. Configure vector asset dialog

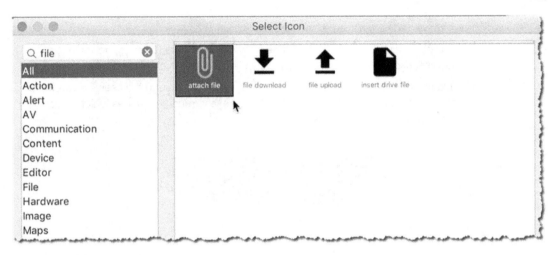

Figure 7-17. Select icon dialog

To use the images in the app, we need to associate them with each item on main_menu resource file. See Listing 7-6 on how to do this.

Listing 7-6. New main_menu.xml

```
<?xml version="1.0" encoding="utf-8"?>
<menu xmlns:app="http://schemas.android.com/apk/res-auto"
      xmlns:android="http://schemas.android.com/apk/res/android">
  <item android:id="@+id/menuFile"
        android:title="@string/menuFile"
        android:icon="@drawable/ic_attach_file_black_24dp"     ❶
        app:showAsAction="ifRoom"/>                            ❷
  <item android:id="@+id/menuEdit"
        android:title="@string/menuEdit"
        android:icon="@drawable/ic_edit_black_24dp"
        app:showAsAction="always"/>                            ❸
  <item android:id="@+id/menuHelp"
        android:title="@string/menuHelp"
        android:icon="@drawable/ic_help_black_24dp"
        app:showAsAction="ifRoom"/>
  <item android:id="@+id/menuExit"
        android:title="@string/menuExit"
        android:icon="@drawable/ic_power_settings_new_black_24dp"
        app:showAsAction="always"/>
</menu>
```

❶ The vector assets we added were saved in /app/res/drawable

❷ If showAsAction attribute is ifRoom, the icon will be shown only if there is enough room in the ActionBar; otherwise, users will only see it when they click the action overflow button

❸ If showAsAction attribute is set to always, the icon will always be visible to the user. Be careful to use this sparingly; if all your icons are specified as "always" the runtime decides which of your icons will be shown, and they may not be all visible.

Figure 7-18. Icons on the ActionBar

To handle the events for each menu item, we can either use the android:onClick attribute on each item or override the onOptionsItemSelected method in MainActivity.

If you want to go the onClick route, add the onClick attribute to an item in main_menu, like the following:

```
<item android:id="@+id/menuEdit"
      android:title="@string/menuEdit"
      android:icon="@drawable/ic_edit_black_24dp"
      app:showAsAction="always"
      android:onClick="mnuEdit"/>
```

Then, in MainActivity, implement the mnuEdit method:

```
public void mnuEdit(MenuItem item) {
  Toast.makeText(this, "Edit", Toast.LENGTH_SHORT).show();
}
```

The other way of handling events for menu items is to override the onOptionItemSelected in MainActivity.

```
public boolean onOptionsItemSelected(MenuItem item) {

  switch(item.getItemId()){      ❶
    case R.id.menuFile:          ❷
      showMessage("File");
      break;
    case R.id.menuEdit:
      showMessage("Edit");
      break;
    case R.id.menuHelp:
      showMessage("Help");
      break;
    case R.id.menuExit:
      showMessage("Exit");
      break;
    default:
      showMessage("Default");
  }
  return true;
}
```

❶   getItemId returns which among the menu item was clicked. We will use this to route program
     logic inside the switch structure

❷   We're comparing the value of getItemId with each menu item

Listing 7-7. Complete Code for MainActivity

```
package com.example.ted.actionbar;

import android.support.v7.app.AppCompatActivity;
import android.os.Bundle;
import android.view.Menu;
import android.view.MenuInflater;
import android.view.MenuItem;
import android.widget.Toast;

public class MainActivity extends AppCompatActivity {

  @Override
  protected void onCreate(Bundle savedInstanceState) {
    super.onCreate(savedInstanceState);
    setContentView(R.layout.activity_main);
  }

  @Override
  public boolean onCreateOptionsMenu(Menu menu) {
    // return super.onCreateOptionsMenu(menu);
    MenuInflater inflater = getMenuInflater();
    inflater.inflate(R.menu.main_menu, menu);
    return true;
  }
```

```
@Override
public boolean onOptionsItemSelected(MenuItem item) {
  //return super.onOptionsItemSelected(item);
  switch(item.getItemId()){
    case R.id.menuFile:
      showMessage("File");
      break;
    case R.id.menuEdit:
      showMessage("Edit");
      break;
    case R.id.menuHelp:
      showMessage("Help");
      break;
    case R.id.menuExit:
      showMessage("Exit");
      break;
    default:
      showMessage("Default");
  }
  return true;
}

private void showMessage(String msg) {
  Toast.makeText(this, msg, Toast.LENGTH_SHORT).show();
}
}
```

Fragments

In the early days of Android, when it ran only on phones and there weren't any high-resolution screens, activities were sufficient as a way of composing the UI and interacting with the user. Then came the tablets and high-resolution screens; it became increasingly difficult to create applications that can run (well) on both phone and tablets. Developers were faced with hard choices. Either we create the applications choosing the least capable hardware as the target, making it like the least common denominator approach; or we craft the application to adapt to a range of form factors by removing and adding UI elements in response to the device's capability (which proved very difficult to do manually). Android's solution to this problem was Fragments; this was introduced sometime in 2011 when API 11 was released (Honeycomb).

Fragments are quite an advanced concept, and beginning programmers may approach it with trepidation, but the basic concept behind it is quite simple. If we think of an activity as a composition unit for our UI, think of a fragment as a miniactivity—it's a smaller composition unit. You will usually show (and hide) fragments during runtime in response to something that a user did; for example, tilting the device, switching from portrait to landscape orientation and thus making more screen space available. You may even use fragments as a strategy to adapt to device form factors; when the app is running on smaller screen, you will show only some of the fragments.

A fragment, like an activity, is comprised of two parts—a Java program and a layout file. The idea is almost the same: define the UI elements in an XML file and then inflate the XML file in the Java program so that all the view objects in the XML will become a Java object. After that, we can reference each view object in the XML using the R.class. Once we've wrapped our brains around that concept, just think of a fragment as an ordinary view object that we can drag and drop on the main layout file—except, of course, fragments aren't ordinary views (but they are views).

The following workflow summarizes the steps on how to get started using Fragments. We will explore them in more detail in the demo project.

1. Create an Activity

2. Create a Fragment class (Java file) and a fragment layout resource (XML file)

3. In the fragment layout resource, compose the UI by dragging and dropping view elements in it—like how we do it in an activity resource file

4. In the Fragment class, override the onCreateView method and inflate the XML file

5. To add the fragment to the activity statically, add a fragment element to activity_main and associate this element to Fragment class

6. To add the fragment during runtime;

    a. In the activity_main layout file, insert a ViewGroup object that will act as a placeholder for the fragment

    b. In MainActivity.java, create an instance of the Fragment class

    c. Get a FragmentManager object; the getManager() method of the Activity class should do that

    d. Get a FragmentTransaction object by calling the beginTransaction() method of the fragment manager

    e. Add the fragment to the activity by calling the add() method of the transaction object

> **Note**   The transaction object is what you will use to manage the availability and visibility of fragments. Use the add and remove methods to attach and detach fragments to/from the activity.

The topic of fragments is a big one, but we will try to cover at least the basic techniques of composition both at design time and during runtime.

Project Setup

Let's create a project to demonstrate fragments:

1. Create a new project with the following details (Table 7-3).

Table 7-3. *Fragments App, Project Details*

Application name	Fragments
Project location	Use the default
Form factor	Phone and tablet only
Minimum SDK	API 23 Marshmallow
Type of activity	Empty
Activity name	MainActivity (default)
Layout name	activity_main (default)

2. Create a new class, from the main menu bar, **File ➤ New ➤ Java class**. Name it FragmentA and extend the Fragment class. Make sure it is on the same package as the MainActivity class.

```
package com.example.ted.fragments;
import android.app.Fragment;

public class FragmentA extends Fragment {

}
```

> **Note**   As you type the code snippet extends Fragment, AS3 will suggest two possible packages for it. One is android.app.Fragment (this is the one we want), and the other is android.support.v4.app.Fragment (we don't need this). The latter package is just in case you intend to run this application on Android versions below API 11, but our app's min SDK is API 23, so we don't need the support library for v4.

3. Create a new layout file; this will be the layout file for the Fragment class. You can do this from project tool window. Right-click the res folder, **New ➤ Layout Resource file.** Name the new file fragment_a, leave the default root element, and make sure it is on the "layout" directory (see Figures 7-19 and 7-20).

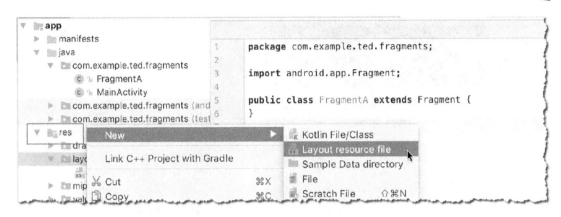

Figure 7-19. *Create a new layout resource file*

New Resource File	
File name:	fragment_a
Root element:	android.support.constraint.ConstraintLayout
Source set:	main
Directory name:	layout

Figure 7-20. *New layout resource file dialog for fragment_a*

4. Put a TextView object on fragment_a. A fragment resource file is not that much different from the resource file of our MainActivity. They are both Viewgroups, and as such, they are meant to contain other view objects. So, all the techniques we've learned on how to compose view objects in a layout resource file apply to fragments as well. The fragment is using a constraint layout (same as activity_main), so you can use the constraint inspector and the attributes inspector to customize the look of the fragment. The appearance of the TextView has been tweaked a little bit in this example. Listing 7-1 shows the XML code for the fragment resource, and Figure 7-21 shows how it looks on design mode

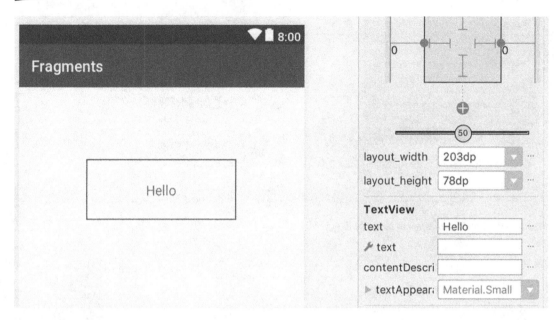

Figure 7-21. fragment_a layout file

Listing 7-8. /app/res/layout/fragment_a

```xml
<?xml version="1.0" encoding="utf-8"?>
<android.support.constraint.ConstraintLayout
  xmlns:android="http://schemas.android.com/apk/res/android"
  xmlns:app="http://schemas.android.com/apk/res-auto"
  xmlns:tools="http://schemas.android.com/tools"
  android:layout_width="match_parent"
  android:layout_height="match_parent">

  <TextView
    android:id="@+id/textView"
    android:layout_width="203dp"
    android:layout_height="78dp"
    android:layout_marginTop="94dp"
    android:gravity="center"
    android:text="Hello"
    android:textSize="18sp"
    app:layout_constraintLeft_toLeftOf="parent"
    app:layout_constraintRight_toRightOf="parent"
    app:layout_constraintTop_toTopOf="parent"/>
</android.support.constraint.ConstraintLayout>
```

5. Associate the fragment layout file with the Fragment class. In
    FragmentA.java, we will override the onCreateViewMethod and inflate
    the fragment resource file.

Listing 7-9. onCreateView Method of FragmentA

```
public View onCreateView(LayoutInflater inflater, @Nullable ViewGroup container, Bundle
savedInstanceState) {

  View v = inflater.inflate(R.layout.fragment_a,container,attachToRoot:false);
  return v;

}
```

Like the setContentView method of the Activity, inflate reads the XML resource file (1st parameter), creates the actual Java objects so that we can reference them later in the R.class, and then attaches the created Java objects to the wherever the fragment is embedded (2nd parameter)—in this case, the container object is our Activity. The last statement in the callback is to simply return the View object which the inflater has created.

6. We will put the fragment resource file inside the activity_main layout file, just like it is another view object (e.g., TextView or Button). Open activity_main in design mode. From the palette, go to **Layouts ➤ <fragment>** (Figure 7-22).

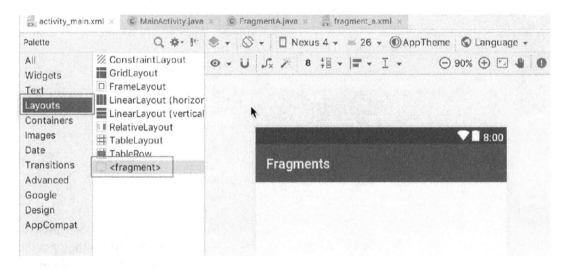

Figure 7-22. Embed the fragment layout file in activity_main

7. Choose the Fragment we created from the dialog window (Figure 7-23).

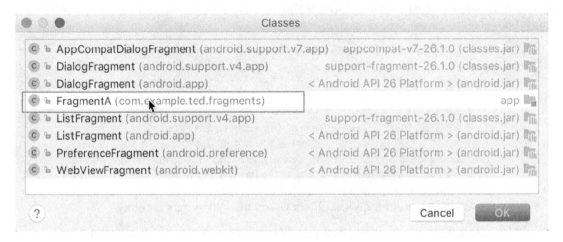

Figure 7-23. Choose the fragment

8. The fragment is a ViewGroup object, which means it's just another view object. You can move it around in `activity_main` just like any other widget. Move it to its approximate position and use the tools in the constraint inspector to fix its position (Figure 7-24).

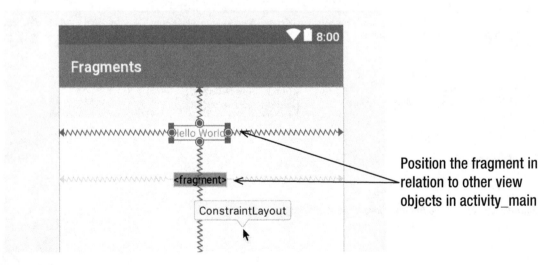

Figure 7-24. activity_main with the fragment layout file

If you run the app, you should see something like Figure 7-25.

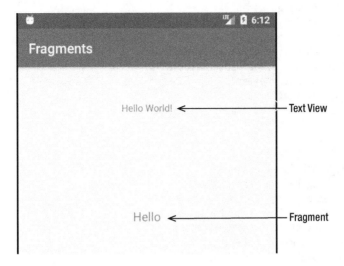

Figure 7-25. Fragments app, running

The complete code listings for FragmentA, activity_main.xml, and MainActivity are shown in Listings 7-10, 7-11, and 7-12, respectively. The complete code listing for fragment_a is shown in Listing 7-10.

Listing 7-10. Complete Code Listing for FragmentA.java

```java
package com.example.ted.fragments;

import android.app.Fragment;
import android.os.Bundle;
import android.support.annotation.Nullable;
import android.view.LayoutInflater;
import android.view.View;
import android.view.ViewGroup;

public class FragmentA extends Fragment {

  @Nullable
  @Override
  public View onCreateView(LayoutInflater inflater, @Nullable ViewGroup container,
  Bundle savedInstanceState) {

    View v = inflater.inflate(R.layout.fragment_a,container,false);
    return v;

  }
}
```

Listing 7-11. Complete Code Listing for activity_main

```xml
<?xml version="1.0" encoding="utf-8"?>
<android.support.constraint.ConstraintLayout
  xmlns:android="http://schemas.android.com/apk/res/android"
  xmlns:app="http://schemas.android.com/apk/res-auto"
  xmlns:tools="http://schemas.android.com/tools"
  android:layout_width="match_parent"
  android:layout_height="match_parent"
  tools:context="com.example.ted.fragments.MainActivity">

  <TextView
    android:id="@+id/textView2"
    android:layout_width="wrap_content"
    android:layout_height="wrap_content"
    android:text="Hello World!"
    app:layout_constraintBottom_toBottomOf="parent"
    app:layout_constraintLeft_toLeftOf="parent"
    app:layout_constraintRight_toRightOf="parent"
    app:layout_constraintTop_toTopOf="parent"
    app:layout_constraintVertical_bias="0.101"/>

  <fragment
    android:id="@+id/fragment"
    android:name="com.example.ted.fragments.FragmentA"
    android:layout_width="wrap_content"
    android:layout_height="wrap_content"
    android:layout_marginTop="15dp"
    app:layout_constraintLeft_toLeftOf="parent"
    app:layout_constraintRight_toRightOf="parent"
    app:layout_constraintTop_toBottomOf="@+id/textView2"/>

</android.support.constraint.ConstraintLayout>
```

Listing 7-12. Code Listing for MainActivity.java

```java
package com.example.ted.fragments;

import android.support.v7.app.AppCompatActivity;
import android.os.Bundle;

public class MainActivity extends AppCompatActivity {

  @Override
  protected void onCreate(Bundle savedInstanceState) {
    super.onCreate(savedInstanceState);
    setContentView(R.layout.activity_main);
  }
}
```

We did not have to do anything in our `MainActivity.java` because the fragment was added statically or declaratively. What we did was to simply embed the fragment in `activity_main`, as it was just another View object.

Adding Fragments Programmatically

While we can construct UIs with Fragments during design time, adding Fragments at runtime makes our application more responsive. You can hide or show Fragments depending on the screen size of the device or its current orientation. To add fragments at runtime, we will need the `FragmentManager` and `FragmentTransaction` objects. A fragment transaction object is the one responsible for adding and removing fragments from an activity, and to get a fragment transaction, we need a fragment manager.

Let's create a new project for this exercise so that you can keep the previous project for reference. See Table 7-4 for the project details.

Table 7-4. *Fragments2 App, Project Details*

Application name	Fragments2
Project location	Use the default
Form factor	Phone and tablet only
Minimum SDK	API 23 Marshmallow
Type of activity	Empty
Activity name	MainActivity (default)
Layout name	activity_main (default)

This project will use the same files that we used in the previous project (Fragments). Before we can proceed, you need to do the following.

1. Create a fragment class, `FragmentA.java` (same as in the previous project)

2. Create a layout file for the fragment, `fragment_a` (same as in the previous project), but don't add the fragment layout in `activity_main`. Instead, we will add the fragment from with `MainActivity.java`

The codes for `fragment_a.xml`, `FragmentA.java`, and `activity_main.xml` are shown in Listings 7-13, 7-14, and 7-15, respectively.

Listing 7-13. fragment_a

```
<?xml version="1.0" encoding="utf-8"?>
<android.support.constraint.ConstraintLayout
    xmlns:android="http://schemas.android.com/apk/res/android"
    xmlns:app="http://schemas.android.com/apk/res-auto"
    xmlns:tools="http://schemas.android.com/tools"
```

```
    android:layout_width="match_parent"
    android:layout_height="match_parent">

  <TextView
    android:id="@+id/textView"
    android:layout_width="203dp"
    android:layout_height="78dp"
    android:layout_marginTop="94dp"
    android:gravity="center"
    android:text="Hello"
    android:textSize="18sp"
    app:layout_constraintLeft_toLeftOf="parent"
    app:layout_constraintRight_toRightOf="parent"
    app:layout_constraintTop_toTopOf="parent"/>
</android.support.constraint.ConstraintLayout>
```

Listing 7-14. FragmentA.java

```java
package com.example.ted.fragments;

import android.app.Fragment;
import android.os.Bundle;
import android.support.annotation.Nullable;
import android.view.LayoutInflater;
import android.view.View;
import android.view.ViewGroup;

public class FragmentA extends Fragment {

  @Nullable
  @Override
  public View onCreateView(LayoutInflater inflater, @Nullable ViewGroup container,
  Bundle savedInstanceState) {
    // return super.onCreateView(inflater, container, savedInstanceState);

    View v = inflater.inflate(R.layout.fragment_a,container,false);
    return v;

  }
}
```

Listing 7-15. activity_main

```xml
<?xml version="1.0" encoding="utf-8"?>
<android.support.constraint.ConstraintLayout
  xmlns:android="http://schemas.android.com/apk/res/android"
  xmlns:app="http://schemas.android.com/apk/res-auto"
  xmlns:tools="http://schemas.android.com/tools"
  android:layout_width="match_parent"
  android:layout_height="match_parent"
  tools:context="com.example.ted.fragments.MainActivity">
```

```
<TextView
  android:id="@+id/textView2"
  android:layout_width="wrap_content"
  android:layout_height="wrap_content"
  android:text="Hello World!"
  app:layout_constraintBottom_toBottomOf="parent"
  app:layout_constraintLeft_toLeftOf="parent"
  app:layout_constraintRight_toRightOf="parent"
  app:layout_constraintTop_toTopOf="parent"
  app:layout_constraintVertical_bias="0.101"/>

</android.support.constraint.ConstraintLayout>
```

Now that the setup is done, we can start adding the fragment to the Activity at runtime. These codes will reside in MainActivity.java.

Listing 7-16. MainActivity.java

```
public class MainActivity extends AppCompatActivity {

  @Override
  protected void onCreate(Bundle savedInstanceState) {
    super.onCreate(savedInstanceState);
    setContentView(R.layout.activity_main);

    FragmentA f = new FragmentA();                    ❶
    FragmentManager fm = getFragmentManager();        ❷
    FragmentTransaction ft = fm.beginTransaction();   ❸
    ft.add(R.id.frag_placeholder,f,s:"");             ❹
    ft.commit();                                      ❺
  }
}
```

❶   Create an instance of FragmentA

❷   Get the fragment manager for this activity (MainActivity)

❸   When a fragment manager begins a transaction, that call will return a TransactionManager object

❹   We can now add our fragment during runtime using the add method. This method takes in three parameters, but only the first two are important for us. The first parameter is a view resource ID (we haven't created that yet; we will create it in Listing 7-17), and the second parameter is the instance of our fragment class (FragmentA)

❺   We should call commit() method so that the fragment will be visible in the activity

> **Important**   When adding a fragment during runtime, the activity_main layout MUST have a view object inside it which will act as a placeholder for the fragment. In our example, this is a Frame layout view (id: frag_placeholder).

Listing 7-17. activity_main.xml

```xml
<?xml version="1.0" encoding="utf-8"?>
<android.support.constraint.ConstraintLayout
  xmlns:android="http://schemas.android.com/apk/res/android"
  xmlns:app="http://schemas.android.com/apk/res-auto"
  xmlns:tools="http://schemas.android.com/tools"
  android:layout_width="match_parent"
  android:layout_height="match_parent"
  tools:context="com.example.ted.fragments2.MainActivity">

  <TextView
    android:id="@+id/textView2"
    android:layout_width="wrap_content"
    android:layout_height="wrap_content"
    android:layout_marginBottom="245dp"
    android:text="Hello World!"
    app:layout_constraintBottom_toBottomOf="parent"
    app:layout_constraintLeft_toLeftOf="parent"
    app:layout_constraintRight_toRightOf="parent"
    app:layout_constraintTop_toBottomOf="@+id/frag_placeholder"/>

  <FrameLayout                                      ❶
    android:id="@+id/frag_placeholder"              ❷
    android:layout_width="368dp"
    android:layout_height="0dp"
    android:layout_marginBottom="8dp"
    android:layout_marginTop="8dp"
    app:layout_constraintBottom_toTopOf="@+id/textView2"
    app:layout_constraintLeft_toLeftOf="parent"
    app:layout_constraintRight_toRightOf="parent"
    app:layout_constraintTop_toTopOf="parent">

  </FrameLayout>

</android.support.constraint.ConstraintLayout>
```

❶ This will become a placeholder for our fragment. The contents of our fragments cannot be seen in design mode because the frame layout doesn't contain anything. You can see the contents of the fragment at runtime

❷ This is the ID we will use when the fragment transaction object adds the fragment

Figure 7-26 shows the Fragments2 app running.

Figure 7-26. Fragments2, running

That concludes the chapter on UI elements. We barely scratched the surface of UI design, but adding themes and colors, using the AppBar, and judicious use of Fragments should add some polish to your apps.

Chapter 8

Running in the Background

Now that we know a bit about UI elements and screens, we need to make them responsive. Responsiveness isn't really about just speed—how much work can you do in a period of time. What's it's more about is how fast the app feels. When people say that an app is responsive, most often what they mean is that the app doesn't stop them from doing what they are trying to do. It doesn't get in their way. If you've ever used an application that just froze when a certain button is clicked, you can appreciate what we're talking about. It doesn't block.

Think of blocking like calling someone on the phone. When you dial, you hear the ringing and you wait for the other person to pick up. Unless the other person picks up, the call cannot proceed. We can say that a phone call is a blocking operation because things have to happen in sequence. You dial, phone rings, the other person picks it up, then you talk. None of these things can happen at the same time. All the steps involve some form of "waiting"—or, in computing terminology, blocking. In this chapter, we will take a look at what happens when some tasks takes a long time to finish and what we can do to avoid these problems.

Long Running Tasks

Users might be able to tolerate blocking in their day-to-day life, like standing in line to renew licenses or get groceries, or waiting for somebody to pick up the phone, and so forth. But they might be less tolerant when using your app. Even the Android platform will not tolerate your app if it takes too much time in doing whatever it is its doing: the WindowManager and ActivityManager of Android are the policemen for responsiveness. When a user clicks a button, or interacts with any view that triggers an event, your application doesn't have a lot of time to finish what it's supposed to do; in fact, it has at most 5 seconds before it gets killed by the runtime. And by then, you will see the infamous ANR error (application not responding). Think of it as Android's BSOD (blue screen of death).

According to the Android guidelines, an application has anywhere from 100ms to 200ms to complete a task in an event handler—that's not a lot of time, so we really need to make sure we don't do anything too crazy inside an event handler. But that's easier said than done, and there are a couple of scenarios where we won't be in total control of the things we do inside an event handler. We can list of couple of them here.

■   When we **read a file**—Our programs need to save data or read
them at some point in time. The file IO operation can be notoriously
unpredictable sometimes; you just don't know how large that file will be.
If it's too large, it may take you more than 200ms to complete the tasks

■   When we **interact with a database**—We interact with a database by
giving it commands for reading, updating, creating, and deleting data.
Like files, sometimes, we might issue a command that will return lots of
data; it could take us a while to process these records

■   When we **interact with the network**—When we get data in and out of
network sockets, we are at the mercy of the network's condition. If it's
not congested or down, that's good for us. But it's not always up and it's
not always fast; if you write codes that deal with the network inside an
event handler, you run the risk of the ANR

■   When we **use other people's code**—We are increasingly relying on APIs
to build our applications, and for good reason: they save us time. But
we just cannot always know how these APIs are built and what kinds
of operations they have under the hood (do you really always read the
source code of all the APIs you use?)

So, what should we do so our apps don't run into an ANR? We certainly can't avoid the
things listed in the preceding because most modern (and useful) applications will need to
do one or more (or all) of these things. The answer, as it turns out, is to run things in the
background. There are a couple of ways to do this, but in this section, we'll look at running
our codes in an AsyncTask.

Demo Project

Details of the project for this chapter are as follows.

Application name	Async
Project location	Use the default
Form factor	Phone and tablet only
Minimum SDK	API 23 Marshmallow
Type of activity	Empty
Activity name	MainActivity (default)
Layout name	activity_main (default)

This project is intended to break and have performance problems. When the user clicks
"long running task", it will simulate a long running task, but all we're doing is counting from 1
to 15; each tick of the count takes 2 seconds. We are effectively holding the user hostage for
at least 30 seconds, during which he can't do much else in the app.

Figure 8-1 shows how our screen will look like, and Listing 8-1 shows the XML definition for the layout file.

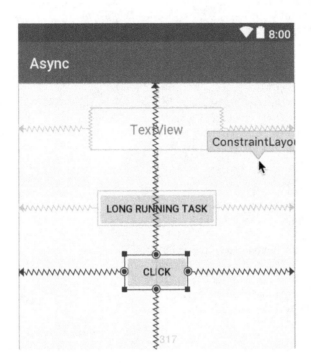

Figure 8-1. *activity_main (design mode)*

Listing 8-1. *activity_main.xml*

```xml
<?xml version="1.0" encoding="utf-8"?>
<android.support.constraint.ConstraintLayout
  xmlns:android="http://schemas.android.com/apk/res/android"
  xmlns:app="http://schemas.android.com/apk/res-auto"
  xmlns:tools="http://schemas.android.com/tools"
  android:layout_width="match_parent"
  android:layout_height="match_parent"
  tools:context="com.example.ted.async.MainActivity">

  <Button
    android:id="@+id/button"
    android:layout_width="wrap_content"
    android:layout_height="wrap_content"
    android:layout_marginBottom="317dp"
    android:gravity="center"
    android:text="Long running task"
    app:layout_constraintBottom_toBottomOf="parent"
    app:layout_constraintLeft_toLeftOf="parent"
    app:layout_constraintRight_toRightOf="parent"
    app:layout_constraintTop_toBottomOf="@+id/textView"/>
```

```
<TextView
    android:id="@+id/textView"
    android:layout_width="184dp"
    android:layout_height="0dp"
    android:layout_marginBottom="55dp"
    android:layout_marginTop="34dp"
    android:gravity="center"
    android:text="TextView"
    android:textSize="18sp"
    app:layout_constraintBottom_toTopOf="@+id/button"
    app:layout_constraintLeft_toLeftOf="parent"
    app:layout_constraintRight_toRightOf="parent"
    app:layout_constraintTop_toTopOf="parent"/>

<Button
    android:id="@+id/button2"
    android:layout_width="wrap_content"
    android:layout_height="wrap_content"
    android:text="Click"
    app:layout_constraintBottom_toBottomOf="parent"
    app:layout_constraintLeft_toLeftOf="parent"
    app:layout_constraintRight_toRightOf="parent"
    app:layout_constraintTop_toTopOf="parent"/>
</android.support.constraint.ConstraintLayout>
```

Listing 8-2. MainActivity

```
package com.example.ted.async;

import android.support.v7.app.AppCompatActivity;
import android.os.Bundle;
import android.util.Log;
import android.view.View;
import android.widget.Button;
import android.widget.TextView;

public class MainActivity extends AppCompatActivity
    implements View.OnClickListener{

    private String TAG;
    TextView tv;

    @Override
    protected void onCreate(Bundle savedInstanceState) {
        super.onCreate(savedInstanceState);
        setContentView(R.layout.activity_main);
```

```
    Button b = (Button) findViewById(R.id.button);
    Button b2 = (Button) findViewById(R.id.button2);
    tv = (TextView) findViewById(R.id.textView);
    TAG = getClass().getSimpleName();

    b.setOnClickListener(this);
    b2.setOnClickListener(new View.OnClickListener(){
      public void onClick(View v) {
        Log.i(TAG, "Clicked");
      }
    });
  }

  public void onClick(View v) { ❶
    int i = 0;
    while (i < 15) {
      try {
        Thread.sleep(2000); ❷
        tv.setText(String.format("Value of i = %d", i)); ❸
        Log.i(TAG, String.format("value of i = %d", i++ ));
      } catch (InterruptedException e) {
        e.printStackTrace();
      }
    }
  }
}
```

❶   This whole code block is designed to simulate a time-consuming activity inside an event handler

❷   This will halt execution for 10 seconds

❸   Every 10 seconds, we write the value of i to the UI

This code won't get very far. It will soon encounter an ANR error (Figure 8-2) if you click the "long running task" button and then click the other button. You will notice that you won't be able to click it because the UI thread is waiting for the "long running task to finish"—the UI is no longer responsive.

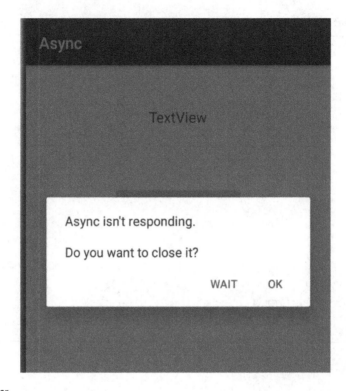

Figure 8-2. ANR error

AsyncTask

In the previous section, the problem we encountered was that when an event handler does something lengthy, the whole UI freezes and the user can't do much else—the user is blocked. AsyncTask was meant to solve these kinds of problems. It was designed to make the UI responsive, even when doing operations that takes quite some time. Figure 8-3 depicts the role of the AsyncTask in this solution.

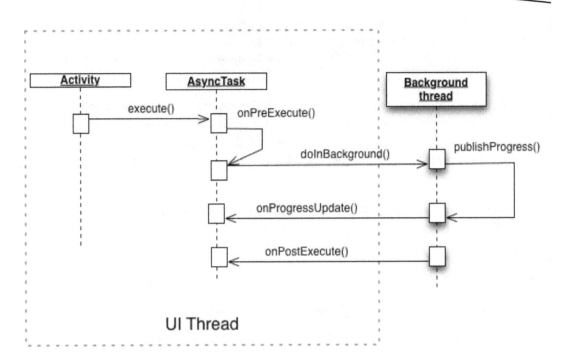

Figure 8-3. AsyncTask and MainActivity

Here's what happens in this approach.

1. MainActivity creates an AsyncTask object (we basically create a class that extends an AsyncTask)

2. Call the execute method of the AsyncTask; in this method, we will pass to the AsyncTask the object references of the UI element we want to update

3. There are various life-cycle methods of the AsyncTask, but the only mandatory callback to override is doInBackground()—we will write all the lengthy operations in here

4. At this point, AsyncTask will create a background thread, but this thread is transparent to us; we don't care about it because AsyncTask will be the one to manage it, not us

Inside the doInBackground() method, we can periodically call publishProgress(). Each time we do, the runtime will call the onProgressUpdate() method of the AsyncTask, and it will be done in thread-safe manner. It is inside this method that we can do some UI updates.

> **Note**   A thread is a sequence of instructions much like the sequence of instructions we've been writing inside methods. A thread however, is executed in a special way: it is executed in the background so that it doesn't block whatever is running in the foreground (the UI thread). This is the reason why we need to write instructions that take a long time to finish in threads.

Let's revise the AsyncTask project. Firstly, we need to create a new class that extends from AsyncTask.

Listing 8-3. Worker.java (Shell)

```
package com.example.ted.async;
import android.os.AsyncTask;
public class Worker extends AsyncTask<TextView, String, Boolean> { ❶
  @Override
  protected Boolean doInBackground(TextView... textViews) { ... } ❷
  @Override
  protected void onProgressUpdate(String... values) { ... } ❸
}
```

❶   The AsyncTask is parameterized; it's a generic type, so we need to pass arguments to it. These parameters are <Params,Progress, Result>; see Table 8-1 for more information

❷   This is the only method we are obliged to override. Inside this is where we should put the program logic, which may take some time to complete

❸   Use this method to communicate progress to the user

Table 8-1. Arguments to the AsyncTask Class

Parameter	Description
1st arg (Params)	What information do you want to pass to the background thread? This is usually the UI element(s) that you want to update. When you call execute from MainActivity, you will need to pass this parameter to the AsyncTask. This param automatically makes its way to the doInBackground method. In our example, this is a text view object. We want the background thread to have access to this UI element as it does its work
2nd arg (Progress)	What type of information do you want the background thread to pass back to onProgressUpdate method so you can specify the status of a long running operation to the user? In our case, we want to update the text attribute of the text view, so this is a String object
3rd param (Result)	What kind of data do you want to use to specify the status of doInBackground when it finishes the task? In our case, I just wanted it to return true if everything went well, so the third parameter is a Boolean

Listing 8-4. Worker Class Shell

```
public class Worker extends AsyncTask<TextView, String, Boolean> {

  private String TAG;
  private TextView tv;  ❶

  @Override
  protected Boolean doInBackground(TextView... textViews) {
    tv = textViews[0];  ❷
    TAG = getClass().getSimpleName();
    int i = 0;
    while (i++ < 15) {
      try {
        Thread.sleep(2000);
        publishProgress(String.format("Value of i = %d", i));  ❸
      } catch (InterruptedException e) {
        e.printStackTrace();
      }
    }
    return true;
  }

  @Override
  protected void onProgressUpdate(String... values) { ... }
}
```

❶   The text view is declared at the top of the class so can we access it from onProgressUpdate;
    we can't define it yet because we will only get object reference to this text view when
    doInBackground gets called

❷   Now we can define the text view; it was already passed to us when MainActivity called the
    execute() method. The parameter of this method is an array, but we know that we only passed
    one UI object (the text view), so we get only the first element of the array. We can now store that
    reference to TextView (tv) variable that we hoisted up in ❶

❸   On each tick, we will call publishProgress, so it can update the UI

Next, let's implement the onProgressUpdate method.

Listing 8-5. onProgressUpdate

```
protected void onProgressUpdate(String... values) {
  tv.setText(values[0]);
  Log.i(TAG, String.format(values[0]));

}
```

This method will catch whatever values we passed to the publishProgress method. The
parameter of this method is, again, an array. And since we passed only one string to it, we'll
only get the first element and set its value as the text attribute of the text view object.

We've basically relocated the time-consuming task in the MainActivity and put it inside the Worker class. The next step is to update the codes in MainActivity.

Listing 8-6. MainActivity

```
package com.example.ted.async;

import android.support.v7.app.AppCompatActivity;
import android.os.Bundle;
import android.util.Log;
import android.view.View;
import android.widget.Button;
import android.widget.TextView;

public class MainActivity extends AppCompatActivity
  implements View.OnClickListener{

  private String TAG;
  TextView tv;

  @Override
  protected void onCreate(Bundle savedInstanceState) { ❶
    super.onCreate(savedInstanceState);
    setContentView(R.layout.activity_main);

    Button b = (Button) findViewById(R.id.button);
    Button b2 = (Button) findViewById(R.id.button2);
    tv = (TextView) findViewById(R.id.textView);
    TAG = getClass().getSimpleName();

    b.setOnClickListener(this);
    b2.setOnClickListener(new View.OnClickListener(){
      public void onClick(View v) {
        Log.i(TAG, "Clicked");
      }
    });

  }

  public void onClick(View v) {
    Worker worker = new Worker();  ❷
    worker.execute(tv);  ❸
  }
}
```

❶   The onCreate block remains unchanged from the previous section; we just set the event handlers in here

❷   Create an instance of AsyncTask Worker class. Note that the background execution of the AsyncTask isn't started by merely creating an instance of it

❸   The execute method starts the background operation. In this method, we pass whatever we want to update to the AsyncTask. Note that you can pass more than one UI element to the execute method, since it will be passed as an array in the doInBackground method of the AsyncTask

> **Note**   The AsyncTask is not meant to run very lengthy operations, things in the order of minutes. Generally, the AsyncTask is used only for operations that last a couple of seconds. Any longer than that and WindowManager/ActivityManager may still kill the app. For long running operations, you need to use Services, but that is beyond the scope of this book.

Chapter 9

Debugging

The examples we've been working on so far haven't been very complex; this is an introductory book on Android programming using AS3 after all, but soon enough your code will grow bigger and more complex. As that happens, the chances introducing errors into your code increase and they will become harder to spot.

There are a couple of ways (and tools) to debug a program: deciding which one to use depends on what kinds of error you are trying to troubleshoot. Having said that, let's try to go over some the most common errors you will encounter.

- **Syntax errors**. These are produced by the Java compiler; it happens because you made a mistake in the code. These errors could be simple ones, like forgetting the semicolon at the end of the statement, or it could be as complex as type incompatibilities when passing parameters to a certain method. When these errors happen, AS3 gives you plenty of visual cues and textual information as to what's wrong with your code. Most of the time, it will even point you to the exact location of the problem

- **Runtime exceptions**. These are produced by the runtime. They happen because there is something in the runtime environment that you have not anticipated and your program cannot proceed; for example, if you tried to open a specific file but during runtime the file isn't where your program expected it to be. When you encounter these errors, the runtime prints out information that will be helpful in troubleshooting where the error occurred, or possibly what caused it. You will then walk through to the code and perform your analysis. You can insert various print statements in critical junctions of the code to validate and confirm your path analysis of your code, or alternatively, you can use the AS3 interactive debugger. The debugger lets you walk through your code and step through it as it executes

© Ted Hagos 2018
T. Hagos, *Learn Android Studio 3*, https://doi.org/10.1007/978-1-4842-3156-2_9

- **Logic errors.** These are probably the most difficult to solve; they're caused by you. When the program compiles and runs without problems but it isn't behaving as you expected, that is a logic error. You need to perform code analysis and then insert print statements at critical junctures of your code or use the interactive debugger (or both)

Syntax Errors

Syntax errors are the easiest to spot among the three kinds of errors, most of the time anyway; that is because AS3 has done most of the heavy lifting already when comes to spotting these kinds of errors. The main editor window gives plenty of visual cues and textual information as to what's wrong with your code.

Figure 9-1 shows how AS3 helps us spot coding errors; the code is missing semicolons on two statements. The first things you will notice when you have syntax errors are squiggly red lines in the main editor; note the squiggly lines on the spot where the semicolons are missing. AS3 gives you enough visual cues that something is not right with your code. If you hover your mouse long enough on top of the squiggly lines, AS3 will pop up useful messages in the form of tool tips.

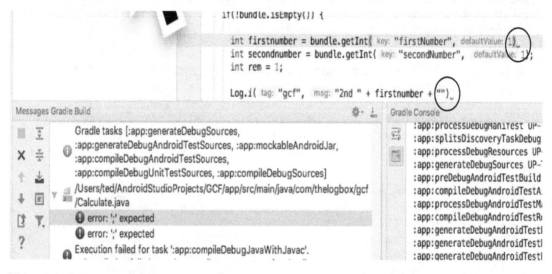

Figure 9-1. Syntax error example

If you try to "Make" or build the project, AS3 will spew out the compiler errors in the Messages tool window. If you double-click error icons (the red exclamation marks), most of the time it will take your cursor directly to the offending line in the main editor.

Syntax errors aren't always simple to solve, Figure 9-2 shows a very colorful display of AS3 while it's trying very hard to figure out what's wrong with the code, but in this case neither the squiggly lines nor the actual error messages are very helpful. What's wrong with the code is a missing opening curly brace on the if statement, but the error messages don't point to it. If you encounter these kinds of errors, you can still double-click the exclamation mark, and while it will not point you to the exact error, you can start in that general area. Usually, the error will be located prior to the location of the error message: broaden your search and practice looking at your code critically. Look for structural issues like missing parens or curly braces.

```
Intent intent = getIntent();
Bundle bundle = intent.getBundleExtra( name: "gcfdata");

if (!bundle.isEmpty()) {

    int firstnumber = bundle.getInt( key: "firstNumber", defaultValue: 1);
    int secondnumber = bundle.getInt( key: "secondNumber",  defaultValue: 1);
    int rem = 1;

    Log.i( tag: "gcf", "2nd " + firstnumber + "");
    Log.i( tag: "gcf",  msg: "2nd " + secondnumber + "");

    int bigno, smallno = 0;
    if (firstnumber > secondnumber) {
        bigno = firstnumber;
        smallno = secondnumber;
    }
    else {
        bigno = secondnumber;
        smallno = firstnumber;
    }

    while ((rem = bigno % smallno) != 0) {
        bigno = smallno;
        smallno = rem;
    }
    TextView gcf = (TextView) findViewById(R.id.textView);
    gcf.setText(smallno + "");
}
```

Messages Gradle Build

Gradle tasks [:app:generateDebugSources,
:app:generateDebugAndroidTestSources, :app:mockableAndroidJar,
:app:compileDebugAndroidTestSources,
:app:compileDebugUnitTestSources, :app:compileDebugSources]
/Users/ted/AndroidStudioProjects/GCF/app/src/main/java/com/thelogbox/gc
f/Calculate.java
  ⓘ error: variable declaration not allowed here
  ⓘ error: class, interface, or enum expected

Gradle Console

FAILED

FAILURE: Build failed with ar

* What went wrong:
Execution failed for task ':i
> Compilation failed; see the

* Try:

Figure 9-2. A more challenging syntax error

Runtime Exceptions

Runtime exceptions happen when your program runs into a condition in the environment which it doesn't expect. When this happens, the runtime prints out a message that includes the name of the exception, the line number in the program where the exception happened, and a bunch of stack trace. The stack trace includes the method that was running before the exception happened, who called that method, the method that called that method that was called, and so on and so forth. A prudent step to take is to look where in the program the error occurred and walk through your code from there.

As you walk through the codes, you will recognize some areas where you are pretty sure you know what's going on and some areas where you are less sure. In these cases, you might want to drop some print statements into the areas where you are less certain about the path your code will take; the print statements will help you validate if your path assumptions are consistent with the code's behavior at runtime. You can use either the "System.out.println" statement of Java, which is a favorite among coders, but since we are on Android, it's preferable to use the "Log" class. The Log class has five static methods that you can use for logging.

- Log.v(String, String) (verbose)

- Log.d(String, String) (debug)

- Log.i(String, String) (information)

■ Log.w(String, String) (warning)

■ Log.e(String, String) (error)

The Log methods take two string arguments. The first one is a tag, and the second is the actual message you want to log. The "tag" will be useful later when you try to filter through all the messages that the runtime outputs; it spits out everything that is happening in the Android runtime. The "tag" will help you wade through the flood of messages later on. The following code shows an example on how to use one of the Log methods.

```
private final String TAG = "My Application";
Log.i(TAG, "I got in here");
```

When you run your app, you can look at the log messages in the Logcat tool window (Figure 9-3). You can launch it either by clicking its tab in the menu strip at the bottom of the AS3 window or from the main menu bar, **View ➤ Tool Windows ➤ Logcat**.

```
Log.i( tag: "gcf",  msg: "second activity");

Intent intent = getIntent();
Bundle bundle = intent.getBundleExtra( name: "gcfdata");

if(!bundle.isEmpty()) {

  int firstnumber = bundle.getInt( key: "firstNumber", defaultValue: 1);
  int secondnumber = bundle.getInt( key: "secondNumber",  defaultValue: 1);
  int rem = 1;

  Log.i( tag: "gcf",  msg: "2nd " + firstnumber + "");
  Log.i( tag: "gcf",  msg: "2nd " + secondnumber + "");
```

```
id 6.0, API 23 ◆     com.thelogbox.gcf (3208)                     ◆   Verbose  ◆  Q▾  ☑ Regex

m.thelogbox.gcf W/art: Before Android 4.1, method android.graphics.PorterDuffColorFilter android.support.graphi
m.thelogbox.gcf I/gcf: onResume()
m.thelogbox.gcf D/OpenGLRenderer: Use EGL_SWAP_BEHAVIOR_PRESERVED: true
m.thelogbox.gcf I/OpenGLRenderer: Initialized EGL, version 1.4
m.thelogbox.gcf W/OpenGLRenderer: Failed to choose config with EGL_SWAP_BEHAVIOR_PRESERVED, retrying without...
m.thelogbox.gcf D/EGL_emulation: eglCreateContext: 0xae4a3720: maj 2 min 0 rcv 2
m.thelogbox.gcf D/EGL_emulation: eglMakeCurrent: 0xae4a3720: ver 2 0 (tinfo 0xae492990)
m.thelogbox.gcf D/EGL_emulation: eglMakeCurrent: 0xae4a3720: ver 2 0 (tinfo 0xae492990)
m.thelogbox.gcf W/art: Before Android 4.1, method int android.support.v7.widget.ListViewCompat.lookForSelectabl
m.thelogbox.gcf I/gcf: 12
m.thelogbox.gcf I/gcf: second activity
m.thelogbox.gcf I/gcf: 2nd 12
m.thelogbox.gcf I/gcf: 2nd 13
m.thelogbox.gcf D/EGL_emulation: eglMakeCurrent: 0xae4a3720: ver 2 0 (tinfo 0xae492990)
```

Figure 9-3. Logcat messages

The Logcat window shows all the messages (default setting) in the Android runtime (Figure 9-4). You can adjust the log level to either "verbose" (default) which shows all the messages, or any of the other four levels: "debug", "info", "warning", "error", or "assert".

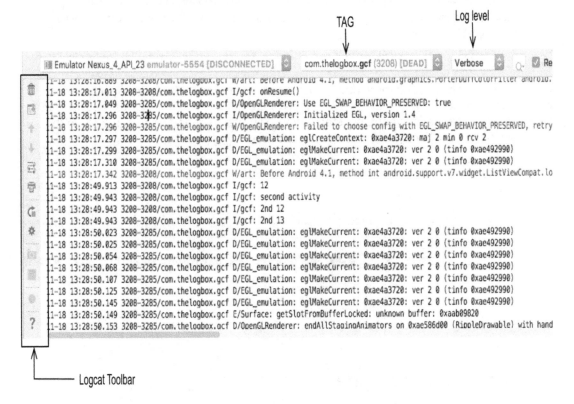

Figure 9-4. *Logcat tool window*

Logic Errors

Logic errors are the hardest to find, because neither the compiler nor the runtime can give you information as to what's going wrong. The only way you can tell that there is something wrong is because the program is not behaving as it should. As you progress in your programming career, you will run into the concept, and hopefully the practice, of unit testing; this is usually the first line of defense against these kinds of errors, but unfortunately, unit testing is not within the scope of this book. However, we will discuss a technique that can also help you solve logic errors.

AS3 includes an interactive debugger which allows you to walk and step through your code as it is running. To get started on interactive debugging, stop your app if it is currently running. From the main menu bar, click **Run ➤ Debug App**.

> **Note**   Running the app in debug mode isn't the only way to debug the app. You can also attach the debugger process in a currently running application. There are situations where this second technique is useful; for example, when the bug you are trying to solve occurs on very specific conditions, you may want to run the app for a while, and when you think you are close to the point of error, you can then attach the debugger.

After the app is started in debug mode, you can now set breakpoints. Breakpoints are created by clicking the gutter along the margin of the editor (Figure 9-5). Breakpoints can be set on lines that have executable statements. You can start adding breakpoints in those areas of your code where you aren't sure what's happening.

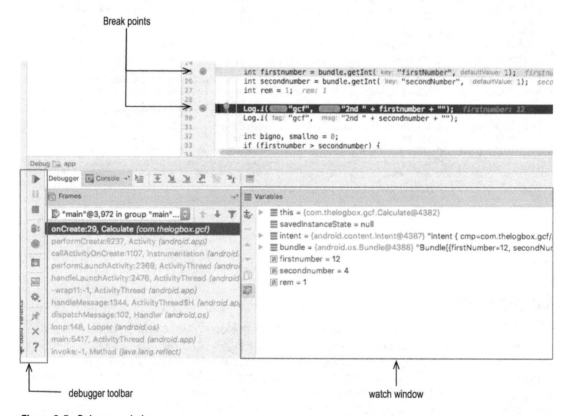

Figure 9-5. Debugger window

When you set a breakpoint, there will be a pink circle icon in the gutter, and the whole line is lit in pink. At this point, your app is already running, and when the execution comes to a line where you set a breakpoint, the line where the breakpoint is set turns to blue. At this point, the debugger window opens, the execution of the program is halted, and AS3 enters the interactive debugging mode. While you are in this state, the state of the application is displayed in the Debug tool window. During this time, you can inspect values of variables and even see the threads running in the app.

In the watch window (or variables view, shown in Figure 9-5), you can add a variable, or an expression, to watch by clicking the plus sign with the spectacles icon. There will be a text field where you can enter any valid java expression. When you press Enter, the expression will be evaluated and you will be able to see the result of the expression. To remove a watch expression, select the expression and click the minus sign icon on the watch window.

To resume program execution, you can click the "Resume program" button at the top of debugger toolbar, alternatively; you can do it also from the main menu bar, **Run ➤ Resume Program**. If you want to halt the program before it finishes naturally, you can click the "Stop app" button on the debugger toolbar: it's the red square icon. Alternatively, you can do this also from the main menu bar, **Run ➤ Stop app**.

Chapter 10

Data Persistence

When applications create or capture data from user inputs, those data will only be available during the lifetime of the application. You only have access to that data as long as the application is not yet killed by the runtime. When the application is shut down, all the data that has been created while the application was running will be lost. Android offers a variety of ways for us to persist data so that it can outlive the application lifetime and allow us access to the same data across application life cycles. The storage options available to use are listed in Table 10-1.

Table 10-1. *Storage options*

SharedPreferences	This is the simplest form of storage. It's just a dictionary object that uses the key/value pair idiom. This is useful if your data is simple enough to be structured as a dictionary object (key/value pairs). Android stores these files internally as XML files. SharedPrefs only stores simple data types (e.g., String and primitive data types). It cannot store more complex data
Internal or external storage	Stores data in the device storage (internal) or media storage like SDCARD (external). If you need to store data that is more complex in structure than a dictionary can afford (e.g., audio, video files), you may want to consider using this type of persistence mechanism
SQLite database	This one uses a relational database. If you have worked with other databases before—MS SQL server, MySQL, PostgreSQL, or any other relational database—this is essentially the same. Data is stored in tables, and you need to use SQL statements to create, read, update, and delete data
Network	If you can assume that your users will always have Internet access and you have a database server that is hosted on the Internet, then you can use this option. This setup can get a bit complicated because you will need to host the database somewhere (Amazon, Google, any other cloud provider), provide a REST interface for the data, and use an HTTP library as a client in the Android app. We won't cover this topic in this book

(continued)

Table 10-1. (*continued*)

Content Providers	Content Provider is another component on the Android platform; it's right up there with Activities, Services, and Broadcast receivers. This component makes data available to applications other than itself. Think of it like a database that has public HTTP API layer. Any application that communicates over HTTP can read and write data to it

In this chapter, we will look at using the shared preferences and internal storage.

SharedPreferences

SharedPreferences is the simplest and fastest way to persist data in Android. The creation and retrieval of data uses the dictionary idiom of key/value pair. There are other things in Android that use this idiom in managing data; some of them you've already seen in the past projects we worked on (e.g., Intents and Bundles). Working with SharedPreferences should feel very familiar to us.

To create a SharedPreferences file, we need to use the getPreferences method while inside an Activity class and then specify the mode of access for the file.

```
SharedPreferences sp = getPreferences(CONTEXT.MODE_PRIVATE);
```

As per Android documentation, Context.MODE_PRIVATE is what we are supposed to use because the public mode has already been deprecated since API level 17. Next, we need an `Editor` object so we can start modifying data in the newly created file.

```
SharedPreferences.Editor editor = sp.edit();
```

Now we can start putting in some data.

```
edit.putString("name","Gandalf the Grey");
edit.putInt("age", 2019);
```

The first parameter to the put commands is always the key, and the second parameter is the value. In the preceding example, "name" and "age" are the keys and "Gandalf the Grey" and 2019 are values, respectively. The put commands, by themselves, do not save the data to the file, so we need to use either the `apply` or the `commit` method.

```
editor.apply(); // or
editor.commit();
```

Either the commit or apply method will save the information and persist it in an XML file; there are only slight differences between these two methods.

- commit—this is synchronous and returns a boolean value, it returns true if the write operation succeeded

- apply—this also saves the data but does not return any value. It is executed asynchronously

> **Note**   You don't need to specify a file name for the shared preferences file; the Android runtime will automatically assign a name for the newly created file. By convention, the newly created file follows the name of the activity class from where getPreferences was called from; for example, if you called getPreferences from MainActivity.java, the name of the shared preferences file will be MainActivity.xml

Retrieving data from a shared preferences file is just as easy as creating it. To access the created shared preferences file, we use the same syntax when we created the file in the first place.

```
SharedPreferences sp = getPreferences(CONTEXT.MODE_PRIVATE);
```

The getPreferences method returns an instance of a SharedPreferences object. The first time this method is called, it will look for an XML file bearing the same name as the activity from which the method was called; if it doesn't find that file, it will be created, but if the file already exist, it will be used instead. Since we already created the file the first time we called getPreferences, Android won't be creating a new file, nor will it overwrite what we created before.

Once we have a shared preferences object, we can extract data from it.

```
sp.getString("name", "default value");
sp.getInt("age", 0);
```

Demo Project

The project details are as follows.

Table 10-2. Project details for SharedPreferences

Application name	SharedPreferences
Company domain	Use your web site, or invent something; remember that this is in reverse DNS notation
Project location	Use the default
Form factor	Phone and tablet only
Minimum SDK	API 23 Marshmallow
Type of activity	Empty
Activity name	MainActivity (default)
Layout name	activity_main (default)

The UI details for the main layout file are shown in Figure 10-1.

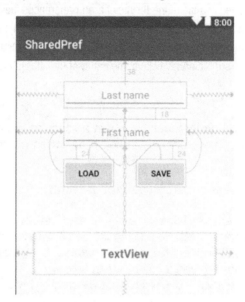

Figure 10-1. activity_main layout file

The corresponding XML definition is shown in Listing 10-1.

Listing 10-1. activity_main.xml

```xml
<?xml version="1.0" encoding="utf-8"?>
<android.support.constraint.ConstraintLayout
  xmlns:android="http://schemas.android.com/apk/res/android"
  xmlns:app="http://schemas.android.com/apk/res-auto"
  xmlns:tools="http://schemas.android.com/tools"
  android:layout_width="match_parent"
  android:layout_height="match_parent"
  tools:context="com.example.ted.sharedpref.MainActivity"
  tools:layout_editor_absoluteY="81dp">

  <Button
    android:id="@+id/btnload"
    android:layout_width="wrap_content"
    android:layout_height="wrap_content"
    android:layout_marginTop="24dp"
    android:text="load"
    app:layout_constraintStart_toStartOf="@+id/etlastname"
    app:layout_constraintTop_toBottomOf="@+id/etlastname"/>

  <Button
    android:id="@+id/btnsave"
    android:layout_width="wrap_content"
    android:layout_height="wrap_content"
```

```xml
    android:layout_marginTop="24dp"
    android:text="save"
    app:layout_constraintEnd_toEndOf="@+id/etlastname"
    app:layout_constraintTop_toBottomOf="@+id/etlastname"/>

  <EditText
    android:id="@+id/etfirstname"
    android:layout_width="wrap_content"
    android:layout_height="wrap_content"
    android:layout_marginBottom="212dp"
    android:layout_marginTop="36dp"
    android:ems="10"
    android:gravity="center"
    android:hint="Last name"
    android:inputType="textPersonName"
    app:layout_constraintBottom_toTopOf="@+id/textView"
    app:layout_constraintLeft_toLeftOf="parent"
    app:layout_constraintRight_toRightOf="parent"
    app:layout_constraintTop_toTopOf="parent"/>

  <EditText
    android:id="@+id/etlastname"
    android:layout_width="wrap_content"
    android:layout_height="wrap_content"
    android:layout_marginTop="18dp"
    android:ems="10"
    android:gravity="center"
    android:hint="First name"
    android:inputType="textPersonName"
    app:layout_constraintLeft_toLeftOf="parent"
    app:layout_constraintRight_toRightOf="parent"
    app:layout_constraintTop_toBottomOf="@+id/etfirstname"/>

  <TextView
    android:id="@+id/textView"
    android:layout_width="320dp"
    android:layout_height="0dp"
    android:layout_marginBottom="146dp"
    android:gravity="center"
    android:text="TextView"
    android:textSize="20sp"
    android:textStyle="bold"
    app:layout_constraintBottom_toBottomOf="parent"
    app:layout_constraintLeft_toLeftOf="parent"
    app:layout_constraintRight_toRightOf="parent"
    app:layout_constraintTop_toBottomOf="@+id/etfirstname"/>
</android.support.constraint.ConstraintLayout>
```

The basic workflow for this app is as follows:

1. Type the last name and first name information in the two text fields
    (Figure 10-1)

2. When the "SAVE" button is clicked, extract the string values from the
    text fields

    ▨ Create a shared preferences files (if one does not exist yet)

    ▨ Push the last name and first name data into the shared pref file by using one
        of the put methods of editor object

    ▨ Save the changes

3. When the "LOAD" button is clicked

    ▨ Retrieve the shared preferences file using the same syntax as when it was
        created

    ▨ Retrieve the data on the file using one of the get methods

    ▨ Show the retrieved data by setting the text attribute of a TextView object

Listing 10-2 shows the MainActivity class with the folded event handlers.

Listing 10-2. MainActivity with Folded Event Handlers

```
public class MainActivity extends AppCompatActivity {

  @Override
  protected void onCreate(Bundle savedInstanceState) {

    super.onCreate(savedInstanceState);
    setContentView(R.layout.activity_main);

    Button btnsave = (Button) findViewById(R.id.btnsave);
    Button btnload = (Button) findViewById(R.id.btnload);

    final EditText etlastname = (EditText) findViewById(R.id.etlastname);
    final EditText etfirstname = (EditText) findViewById(R.id.etfirstname);
    final TextView tv = (TextView) findViewById(R.id.textView);

    btnsave.setOnClickListener(new View.OnClickListener() { ... });

    btnload.setOnClickListener(new View.OnClickListener(){ ... });

  }
}
```

The object references for the view objects (EditText, TextView, and Button) are all defined
within the onCreate method. We can do this because the event handlers for both our buttons
are created using inner (anonymous classes). This is also the reason why the two EditTexts
and the TextView are declared final. Whenever an inner class will use a member variable of
its enclosing class, that variable needs to be declared final.

Listing 10-3. Save Button

```
btnsave.setOnClickListener(new View.OnClickListener() {
  @Override
  public void onClick(View view) {

    SharedPreferences sp = getPreferences(Context.MODE_PRIVATE);   ❶
    SharedPreferences.Editor edit = sp.edit();                     ❷

    String lname = etlastname.getText().toString();                ❸
    String fname = etfirstname.getText().toString();

    edit.putString("lname", lname);                                ❹
    edit.putString("fname", fname);
    edit.apply();                                                  ❺

    Toast.makeText(MainActivity.this, "Saved it", Toast.LENGTH_SHORT).show();
  }
});
```

❶   Creates the shared preferences file, if one doesn't exist yet

❷   We can't save data to the shared preferences file (yet); we need an interface object for it. The editor objects will do that job

❸   Retrieve whatever the user has typed on the EditText objects and assign them to String variables

❹   Use the editor object to persist data into the shared preferences file

❺   Commit the changes to the file

Listing 10-4. Load Button

```
btnload.setOnClickListener(new View.OnClickListener(){
@Override
public void onClick(View view)  {
  SharedPreferences sp = getPreferences(Context.MODE_PRIVATE);   ❶
  String lname = sp.getString("lname", "na");                    ❷
  String fname = sp.getString("fname", "na");
  tv.setText(String.format("%s , %s", lname, fname));            ❸
}
});
```

❶   Retrieve the shared preferences object by getting a reference to it. The syntax for creating a shared preferences object is the same as that for retrieving it. Android is clever enough to figure out that if the file doesn't exist, you want to create, and if it does exist, you want to retrieve it

❷   Get the data out of the shared pref file using one of the get methods; store it in a String variable

❸   Set the text of the TextView object using the retrieved data from the shared pref file

Listing 10-5. Complete Code for MainActivity

```java
package com.example.ted.sharedpref;

import android.content.Context;
import android.content.SharedPreferences;
import android.support.v7.app.AppCompatActivity;
import android.os.Bundle;
import android.view.View;
import android.widget.Button;
import android.widget.EditText;
import android.widget.TextView;
import android.widget.Toast;

import org.w3c.dom.Text;

public class MainActivity extends AppCompatActivity {

  @Override
  protected void onCreate(Bundle savedInstanceState) {
    super.onCreate(savedInstanceState);
    setContentView(R.layout.activity_main);

    Button btnsave = (Button) findViewById(R.id.btnsave);
    Button btnload = (Button) findViewById(R.id.btnload);

    final EditText etlastname = (EditText) findViewById(R.id.etlastname);
    final EditText etfirstname = (EditText) findViewById(R.id.etfirstname);
    final TextView tv = (TextView) findViewById(R.id.textView);

    btnsave.setOnClickListener(new View.OnClickListener() {
      @Override
      public void onClick(View view) {

        SharedPreferences sp = getPreferences(Context.MODE_PRIVATE);
        SharedPreferences.Editor edit = sp.edit();

        String lname = etlastname.getText().toString();
        String fname = etfirstname.getText().toString();

        edit.putString("lname", lname);
        edit.putString("fname", fname);
        edit.apply();

        Toast.makeText(MainActivity.this, "Saved it", Toast.LENGTH_SHORT).show();
      }
    });
```

```
btnload.setOnClickListener(new View.OnClickListener(){

    @Override
    public void onClick(View view) {
        SharedPreferences sp = getPreferences(Context.MODE_PRIVATE);
        String lname = sp.getString("lname", "na");
        String fname = sp.getString("fname", "na");
        tv.setText(String.format("%s , %s", lname, fname));
    }
});

    }
}
```

The XML file that was created is safely tucked away in the internal storage of the Android device.

Verifying the File

If you want to peek and verify this file, you can use the "Android Device Monitor" tool. You can launch it from the main menu bar **Tools ➤ Android ➤ Android Device Monitor** (shown in Figure 10-2).

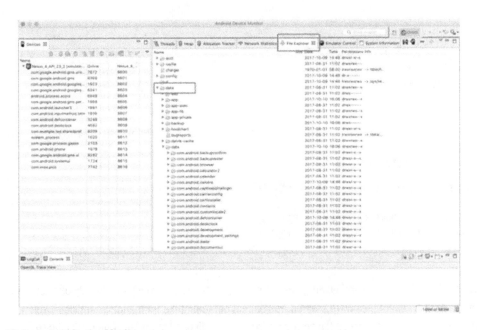

Figure 10-2. Android Device Monitor

The Android Device Monitor is used as a debugging and analysis tool, but we will use it to take a peek at the preferences file we just created. Go to the File Explorer. From there, drill down to the folder **data ➤ data ➤** fully qualified name of the project, which in my case is "com.ted.example.sharedpref". Inside that folder, you will find a folder named "shared_prefs". There you will find the file "MainActivity.xml", which was created by the application. You cannot open the xml file from within Android Device Monitor, but you can download it to your computer by pulling the file from the device (see Figure 10-3).

> **Note**   On the Windows platform, if you encounter some problems launching the `Android Device Monitor`, you can shut down AS3 and then launch it again as Administrator.

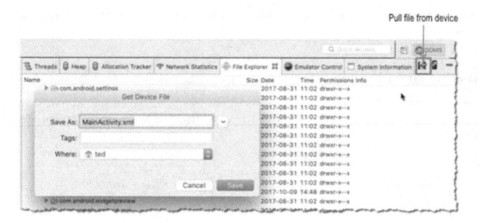

Pull file from device

Figure 10-3. Download a file to your PC

After downloading the file, you can use whatever XML editing tool you wish to open the file.

Listing 10-6. Contents of the XML File

```
<?xml version='1.0' encoding='utf-8' standalone='yes' ?>
<map>
    <string name="fname">James</string>
    <string name="lname">Gosling</string>
</map>
```

> **Note**   Files that are created using getPreferences(Context.MODE_PRIVATE) can only be accessed by the Activity where they were created. You cannot get to that file from another activity. If you need to share the preferences file across activities, you will need to create "Application Level SharedPreferences".

Application Level SharedPreferences

It's not difficult to make the shared preferences file available to other activities; the code needed to accomplish this isn't very different from our previous example.

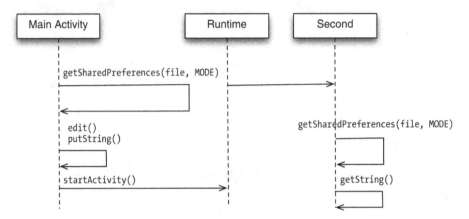

Figure 10-4. *Sequence of events*

In Figure 10-4, we use the getSharedPreferences method instead of getPreferences (as in the previous section). The method requires two parameters: the first is the file name and the second is the mode of access. This method looks for a file name as specified by the first parameter. If it doesn't find the file, it will be created for the first time.

```
SharedPreferences sp = getSharedPreferences(filename, Context.MODE);
```

Next, we get an editor object using the shared preferences object and start putting some data to the file using some variation of the put command. After that, we can save the file.

```
Editor edit = sp.edit();
edit.putString("name", "Gandalf the grey");
edit.apply();
```

At this point, we launch a second activity by creating an explicit intent and calling startActivity.

When the second activity is created, we can open the shared preferences file to start the data retrieval process.

```
SharedPreferences sp = getSharedPreferences(file, Context.MODE_PRIVATE);
String lname = sp.getString("name", "na");
```

The getSharedPreferences method looks for the file name as specified in the first argument of the method. Since we've already created this file back in the MainActivity, instead of creating a new one, the existing file will be opened.

We can explore this further on a demo project. We could create an entirely new project but since the difference of the new project from the previous project will be very small, you might want to just make a copy of the previous project and do some minor edits. Follow the next step to copy the previous project.

1. Close any open project in AS3; from the main menu bar **File ➤ Close project**

2. Use the file manager of your OS (Finder for macOS, Explorer for Windows) and copy the folder SharedPref to SharedPref2. If you need the location of the project file, AS3 displays the location in the **Project tool window** (Figure 10-5)

Project location in file manager

Figure 10-5. Project location

3. Open the project from the main menu bar **File ➤ Open**. You may see some warnings like those shown in Figure 10-6. Click OK

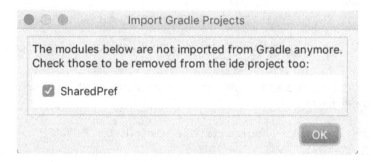

Figure 10-6. Warning

4.   You will need to change some identifiers in the new project; at the very least, change the package name to sharedpref2. Let's use the refactoring facilities of AS3 to facilitate this change. Highlight the package name as shown in Figure 10-7: right-click **Refactor ➤ Rename**

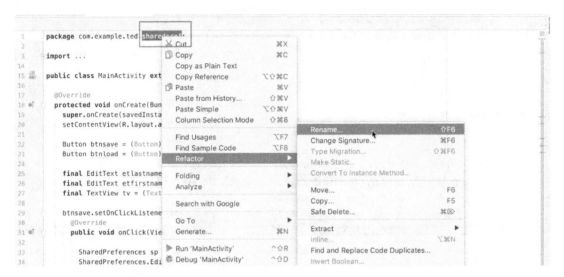

Figure 10-7. Refactor

5.   Some warnings will be shown by AS3 (Figure 10-8); click **Rename package**

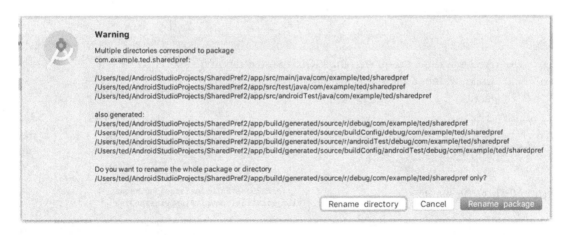

Figure 10-8. Refactor warning

6. AS3 will ask for the new name of the package We want to rename it to sharedpref2 (Figure 10-9). Type in the new name and click **Refactor**

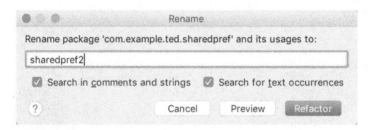

Figure 10-9. Refactor to new name

7. Some more warnings will appear from AS3 before doing the refactor (Figure 10-10). Review the message, then click **Do Refactor**

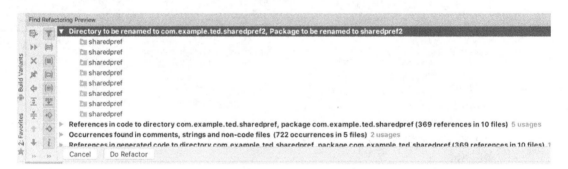

Figure 10-10. Some more warnings

8. AS3 will show some warnings. Our name change messed up the build system a bit. Click Sync Now (Figure 10-11) to fix the gradle issue

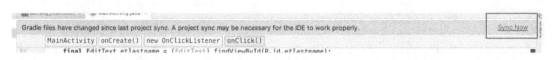

Figure 10-11. Gradle warning

9. When all the errors and warnings have settled in, we need to clean the project. From the main menu bar, click **Build ➤ Clean Project**. Then rebuild the project by clicking **Build ➤ Rebuild Project**

10. The next step is to run the project in the emulator. We need to be sure that it's still running before we make any changes to it

11. Create a second, empty activity for this project (Table 10-3)

Table 10-3. Details of New Activity

Activity name	Second
Layout name	activity_second (default)

Listing 10-7 shows the layout file for the app.

Listing 10-7. activity_second.xml

```
<?xml version="1.0" encoding="utf-8"?>
<android.support.constraint.ConstraintLayout
  xmlns:android="http://schemas.android.com/apk/res/android"
  xmlns:app="http://schemas.android.com/apk/res-auto"
  xmlns:tools="http://schemas.android.com/tools"
  android:layout_width="match_parent"
  android:layout_height="match_parent"
  tools:context="com.example.ted.sharedpref2.Second">

  <TextView
    android:id="@+id/textView2"
    android:layout_width="305dp"
    android:layout_height="65dp"
    android:gravity="center"
    android:text="TextView"
    android:textSize="20sp"
    app:layout_constraintLeft_toLeftOf="parent"
    app:layout_constraintRight_toRightOf="parent"
    tools:layout_editor_absoluteY="97dp"/>
</android.support.constraint.ConstraintLayout>
```

Figure 10-12 shows the UI.

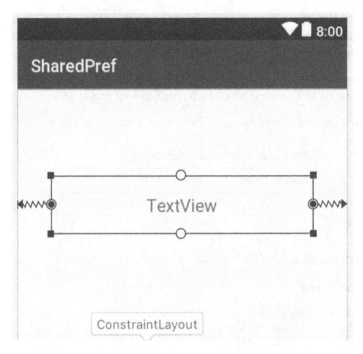

Figure 10-12. activity_second

The only view object in the Second Activity is a TextView. We will use this to display the contents of the shared preferences xml file.

Let's take a look at how to create the shared file from MainActivity.java.

Listing 10-8. Creation of SharedPref File (SAVE Button)

```
btnsave.setOnClickListener(new View.OnClickListener() {
  @Override
  public void onClick(View view) {

    String file = getPackageName() + "myFile"; ❶
    SharedPreferences sp = getSharedPreferences(file, Context.MODE_PRIVATE); ❷
    SharedPreferences.Editor edit = sp.edit();

    String lname = etlastname.getText().toString();
    String fname = etfirstname.getText().toString();

    edit.putString("lname", lname);
    edit.putString("fname", fname);
    edit.apply();

    Toast.makeText(MainActivity.this, "Saved it", Toast.LENGTH_SHORT).show();
  }
});
```

❶ The file name for a sharedpref should ideally be <package name of project> + <filename>. The getPackage() method should return the package name

❷ Pass the file name and the mode to the getSharedPreferences method in order to create the file

Let's change the for the LOAD button. Instead of opening the shared pref file, let's open the Second Activity.

Listing 10-9. Code for LOAD Button

```
btnload.setOnClickListener(new View.OnClickListener(){

  @Override
  public void onClick(View view) {
    Intent intent = new Intent(MainActivity.this, Second.class);
    startActivity(intent);
  }
});
```

We will open the shared pref file from within the second activity, and we'll do it with the onCreate method.

Listing 10-10. Complete Code for Second Activity

```
package com.example.ted.sharedpref2;

import android.content.Context;
import android.content.SharedPreferences;
import android.support.v7.app.AppCompatActivity;
import android.os.Bundle;
import android.widget.TextView;

public class Second extends AppCompatActivity {

  @Override
  protected void onCreate(Bundle savedInstanceState) {
    super.onCreate(savedInstanceState);
    setContentView(R.layout.activity_second);

    TextView tv = (TextView) findViewById(R.id.textView2);
    String file = getPackageName() + "myFile";
    SharedPreferences sp = getSharedPreferences(file, Context.MODE_PRIVATE);

    String lname = sp.getString("lname", "na");
    String fname = sp.getString("fname", "na");
    tv.setText(String.format("%s , %s", lname, fname)) ;

  }
}
```

The complete code listing for MainActivity is shown in Listing 10-11 for your reference.

Listing 10-11. Complete Code for MainActivity

```
package com.example.ted.sharedpref2;

import android.content.Context;
import android.content.Intent;
import android.content.SharedPreferences;
import android.support.v7.app.AppCompatActivity;
import android.os.Bundle;
import android.view.View;
import android.widget.Button;
import android.widget.EditText;
import android.widget.TextView;
import android.widget.Toast;

public class MainActivity extends AppCompatActivity {

  @Override
  protected void onCreate(Bundle savedInstanceState) {
    super.onCreate(savedInstanceState);
    setContentView(R.layout.activity_main);

    Button btnsave = (Button) findViewById(R.id.btnsave);
    Button btnload = (Button) findViewById(R.id.btnload);

    final EditText etlastname = (EditText) findViewById(R.id.etlastname);
    final EditText etfirstname = (EditText) findViewById(R.id.etfirstname);
    final TextView tv = (TextView) findViewById(R.id.textView);

    btnsave.setOnClickListener(new View.OnClickListener() {
      @Override
      public void onClick(View view) {

        String file = getPackageName() + "myFile";
        SharedPreferences sp = getSharedPreferences(file, Context.MODE_PRIVATE);
        SharedPreferences.Editor edit = sp.edit();

        String lname = etlastname.getText().toString();
        String fname = etfirstname.getText().toString();

        edit.putString("lname", lname);
        edit.putString("fname", fname);
        edit.apply();

        Toast.makeText(MainActivity.this, "Saved it", Toast.LENGTH_SHORT).show();
      }
    });

    btnload.setOnClickListener (new View.OnClickListener(){

      @Override
      public void onClick(View view) {
```

```
    /*
    SharedPreferences sp = getPreferences(Context.MODE_PRIVATE);
    String lname = sp.getString("lname", "na");
    String fname = sp.getString("fname", "na");
    tv.setText(String.format("%s , %s", lname, fname));
    */
    Intent intent = new Intent(MainActivity.this, Second.class);
    startActivity(intent);
    }
  });

  }
}
```

Using shared preferences is the easiest and quickest way to save application data, but it has some limitations. You can only save primitive types and string types; if you need to work with more complex file types (e.g., audio, video or image), you cannot accomplish that with shared preferences.

Internal Storage

When you need to work with more complex types like audio, video, or images, you can use either the internal storage (internal memory of device) or the external storage (publicly accessible memory, e.g., SDCARD).

An external storage can

- be accessed by the app that created it, other apps, and even the user

- outlive the app, even after it has been uninstalled

An internal storage

- can only be accessed by app that created it; no other app can access it

- will be deleted when the app is uninstalled

In this chapter, we will only work with internal storage.

How to Work with Internal Storage

To save data to an internal storage, we first need to create a FileInputStream object; this can be managed by the openFileInput method of the Activity class. When a file is opened for writing, all the previous contents of the file will be discarded. It is possible, however, to open a file such that we can append new contents, thus preserving the previous contents.

```
FileOutputStream fout = openFileOutput(<name of file>,  Context.MODE_APPEND);
```

If you don't want to open the file in append mode, simply pass Context.MODE_PRIVATE as the second parameter instead.

Once the file is prepared, we can write data to it.

```
fout.write(<String data>);
```

The methods openFileOutput and write may both throw Exceptions, and as such they need to be handled either by rethrowing the Exception or handling it using a try-catch construct. In our example, we used the try-catch blocks to handle the possible Exceptions.

Reading data from an internal storage is equally simple. It's a lot like the process of writing data; we simply need to prepare a FileInputStream and then read from it.

```
FileInputStream fin = openFileInput(<name of file>);
```

The file input is a stream. The basic idea is to read bytes from it a chunk at a time until we reach the end of the file.

Let's explore the details in a demo project.

Demo Project

We will show how to develop the Internal Storage Application as shown in Table 10-4.

Table 10-4. Project details for InternalStorage

Application name	InternalStorage
Project location	Use the default
Form factor	Phone and tablet only
Minimum SDK	API 23 Marshmallow
Type of activity	Empty
Activity name	MainActivity (default)
Layout name	activity_main (default)

The details for setting up the only layout file (activity_main) are shown in Figure 10-13 and Listing 10-12.

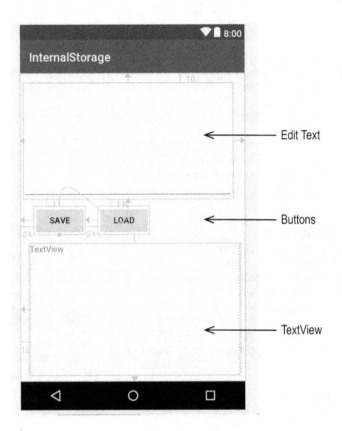

Figure 10-13. activity_main

The layout file is typical of our usual demo project, but the following needs to be pointed out.

1. The EditText is supposed to capture multiple lines of text, so you need to set its "inputType" attribute to "textMultiline". You can do this in the attribute inspector window while in design mode, or alternatively, you can write in the XML file directly, as shown in Listing 10-12.

2. We are not going to handle the click events programmatically, so we've set the values for the "onClick" attributes of both buttons

Listing 10-12. activity_main.xml

```xml
<?xml version="1.0" encoding="utf-8"?>
<android.support.constraint.ConstraintLayout
  xmlns:android="http://schemas.android.com/apk/res/android"
  xmlns:app="http://schemas.android.com/apk/res-auto"
  xmlns:tools="http://schemas.android.com/tools"
  android:layout_width="match_parent"
  android:layout_height="match_parent"
  tools:context="com.example.ted.internalstorage.MainActivity">
```

```
<EditText
    android:id="@+id/edittext"
    android:layout_width="359dp"
    android:layout_height="193dp"
    android:layout_marginEnd="16dp"
    android:layout_marginLeft="16dp"
    android:layout_marginTop="16dp"
    android:ems="10"
    android:inputType="textMultiLine"      //This makes it multiline
    app:layout_constraintEnd_toEndOf="parent"
    app:layout_constraintLeft_toLeftOf="parent"
    app:layout_constraintTop_toTopOf="parent"/>

<Button
    android:id="@+id/btnsave"
    android:layout_width="wrap_content"
    android:layout_height="wrap_content"
    android:layout_marginLeft="24dp"
    android:layout_marginTop="11dp"
    android:onClick="saveData"
    android:text="Save"
    app:layout_constraintLeft_toLeftOf="parent"
    app:layout_constraintTop_toBottomOf="@+id/edittext"/>

<Button
    android:id="@+id/btnload"
    android:layout_width="wrap_content"
    android:layout_height="wrap_content"
    android:layout_marginStart="21dp"
    android:layout_marginTop="11dp"
    android:onClick="loadData"
    android:text="Load"
    app:layout_constraintStart_toEndOf="@+id/btnsave"
    app:layout_constraintTop_toBottomOf="@+id/edittext"/>

<TextView
    android:id="@+id/textview"
    android:layout_width="360dp"
    android:layout_height="0dp"
    android:layout_marginBottom="9dp"
    android:layout_marginLeft="16dp"
    android:layout_marginTop="14dp"
    android:text="TextView"
    app:layout_constraintBottom_toBottomOf="parent"
    app:layout_constraintLeft_toLeftOf="parent"
    app:layout_constraintTop_toBottomOf="@+id/btnsave"/>
</android.support.constraint.ConstraintLayout>
```

Listing 10-13 shows the structure for MainActivity. The saveData method is associated to the "SAVE" button, and loadData is associated to the "LOAD" button.

Listing 10-13. Overview of MainActivity

```
public class MainActivity extends AppCompatActivity {

  EditText editText;       ❶
  private String filename = "myfile.txt"; ❷

  @Override
  protected void onCreate(Bundle savedInstanceState) {
    super.onCreate(savedInstanceState);
    setContentView(R.layout.activity_main);

    editText = (EditText) findViewById(R.id.edittext);

  }

  public void saveData(View v) { ... }

  public void loadData(View v) { ... }

}
```

❶ editText is defined as a member variable because we will need to reference this from both saveData and loadData

❷ File name is defined as a member variable for the same reason as in no. 1

Listing 10-14. Code for saveData

```
public void saveData(View v) {
  String str = editText.getText().toString();

  FileOutputStream out = null;
  try {
    out = openFileOutput(filename, Context.MODE_APPEND); ❶
    out.write(str.getBytes()); ❷
  } catch (FileNotFoundException e) {
    e.printStackTrace();
    // You should do more logging here
  } catch (IOException e) {
    e.printStackTrace();
  }
  finally {
    if (out != null) {       ❸
      try {
        out.close();         ❹
      } catch (IOException e) {
        e.printStackTrace();
      }
    }
  }

}
```

❶ openFileOutput gets a file ready for writing. The first argument is the name of the file to be created, and the second argument decides whether we can append to the file, or whether it will it be overwritten each time we open the file. In this case, we chose to go with the append mode so we can retain the original contents of the file. This method may throw a "FileNotFoundException"; that's why it needs to be surrounded in a try-catch block

❷ Performs the actual writing of the data to the disk. It can only work with bytes, though; that's why we needed the getBytes method. This method may throw an "IOException"; that's why we needed to specify it in the catch clause

❸ We need to know that the FileOutputStream object is not null, before we proceed any further

❹ This closes the file and releases any system resources associated with it. This method may throw an "IOException", hence the need for a nested try-catch construction

Listing 10-15. Code for loadData

```java
public void loadData(View v) {

  TextView tv = (TextView) findViewById(R.id.textview);
  FileInputStream in = null;
  StringBuilder sb = new StringBuilder();

  try {
    in = openFileInput(filename);   ❶

    int read = 0;
    while((read = in.read()) != -1) { ❷
      sb.append((char) read); ❸
    }
    tv.setText(sb.toString()); ❹

  } catch (FileNotFoundException e) {
    e.printStackTrace();
  } catch (IOException e) {
    e.printStackTrace();
  }
  finally {
    if (in != null) {
      try {
        in.close();
      } catch (IOException e) {
        e.printStackTrace();
      }
    }
  }
}
```

❶ Get the file ready for reading. This method may throw a "FileNotFoundException"; that's why it needs to be surrounded in a try-catch block, like openFileOuput

❷ The read method of the input stream reads one byte of data at a time, and when it reaches the end of the file where there's nothing more to read, it will return -1

❸ The in.read() method returns an int; we need to cast it to a char so we can use for the StringBuilder

❹ When we get to the end of the file, we can convert the StringBuilder object to String and set it as the text for Text View

You can inspect the contents of the internal storage file(s) by using the Android Device Monitor. The file is located in **data ➤ data ➤ <project package + name>**.

Chapter 11

App Distribution

At some point, you might want to distribute your application to a wide audience. Android apps can be distributed quite freely and without many restrictions: you can make it available as a download in your web site or even e-mail the app directly to the users, but many developers choose to distribute their app on a marketplace like Google or Amazon to maximize reach. Regardless of how you intend to distribute, there are certain steps you need to perform, or at least be mindful of, before you can release the app to the public.

Publishing an application can be a very involved activity, and it's not limited to the technical and procedural aspects of app distribution such as creating an account on developer. android.com, making polished icons, and signing your app. It involves creating copy and promotional text, social media activities, and many other things that are not at all technological in nature. This chapter will only focus on the technical requirements of app distribution. Log in to the Google Account that will act as the Account Owner for your Developer Account.

There are roughly two stages to publishing an application; they are briefly discussed in the following.

1. **Preparing the app for release**. In this stage, you need to clean up your application and sanitize it before release. You'll want to remove debug information, settings, and logs which were used during development. You will also need to think about icons and other visual assets for the app. During this stage, it's a good idea to test your app on an actual device; on a tablet or a phone, or on both. Most importantly, you will need to sign the application with a digital certificate

2. **Releasing the app**. During this stage, you'll need to publicize, sell, and distribute it. If you intend to release your app in the Google marketplace, you'll need to sign up for a publisher account and use the developer console of Google Play to publish

Preparing the App for Release

This section outlines and discusses some important things to consider before releasing an app for distribution. The following list gives us an idea of the things we need to consider.

1. Prepare materials and assets for release

2. Configure the app for release

3. Build a release-ready application

Prepare Materials and Assets for Release

An application is more than just the program code. You need to start thinking about application icons and other graphical assets for your app if you want to give it a bit of professional polish. An application icon helps the users identify your app as it sits on the device's home screen. This icon also appears in a couple of other areas, such as the launcher window and the downloads section; more importantly, if you are publishing your app in the Google marketplace, this icon will be displayed there too. The app icon may play a major role in creating the first impressions to your would-be users, so it is a good idea to put some work into this and to read Google's guidelines for app icons, which can be found here: **http://bit.ly/androidreleaseiconguidelines**.

Other things to consider if you will publish the app in Google's marketplace are graphical assets like screen captures and the text for promotional copy. Make sure to read Google's guidelines for graphical assets, which can be found here: **http://bit.ly/androidreleasegraphicassets**.

Configure the App for Release

Once you are ready with the application assets, you can now make changes to the app's configuration to gear it up for a proper release. The things mentioned in this section are by no means mandatory, but it's a good idea to go through them before building a release version.

Check the package name. In previous chapters, you may not have paid attention to the package name because we were building apps that were never intended to be released: those apps were our playground. That needs to change when you intend to release the app in a marketplace. The package name makes the app unique across the marketplace, and once you have decided on a package name, you will not be able to change it anymore, so give it some thought.

Remove logging and debugging information. Debugging and logging information are very useful, indispensable even, during development, but when you are about to release the app, you should strip it of all debugging and logging information. The debugging information is easy enough to deal with; you simply need to remove the android:debuggable attribute in the `<application>` tag of the Manifest file. The same cannot be said about the logging information, unfortunately. There are various approaches to the log issue: the solutions can be as simple (but tedious) as manually removing all `Log` statements or as sophisticated as writing sed or awk programs to automatically strip away the `Log` calls. Some people deal with the log issues by configuring ProGuard (which is outside the scope of this book), and some others would go as far as using a third-party library like Timber (a GitHub project) to replace Android's `Log` class. Regardless of what approach you take, just be mindful that you need to strip away the *Log* statements before you build for release.

Check the application permissions. Sometime during development, you may have experimented on some features of the application, and you may have set permissions on the manifest like permission to use the network, write to external storage, and so forth. Review the `<uses-permission>` tag on the manifest and make sure that you don't grant permissions that the application does not need.

Remote servers and URLs. If your application relies on web APIs or cloud services, make sure that the release build of the app is using production URLs and not test paths. You may have been given sandboxes and test URLs during development; you need to switch them up to the production version.

Build a Release-Ready Application

Up until this point, the way we deployed applications to either a mobile device or an emulator was very straightforward: we wrote the codes, clicked "Run", and then saw the app running on the target device. All files are packaged into an APK file and deployed without much intervention from the programmer. What you may not be aware of is that AS3 performs the important task of signing the APK with a certificate before delivering it to the target device. This certificate, however, is a debug certificate, and while it's good for purposes of testing, it's not good for production use, and most app stores, including Google, will not accept an application that is signed with a debug certificate for publishing. To distribute an app, it needs to be signed with a digital certificate, and we will use AS3 to generate it. This certificate does not need to be signed by a certificate authority like Verisign or Thawte; Android allows us to use a self-signed certificate. This section will detail the steps on how to generate a signed APK and how to create a self-signed certificate.

From the main menu, click **Build ➤ Generate Signed APK**.

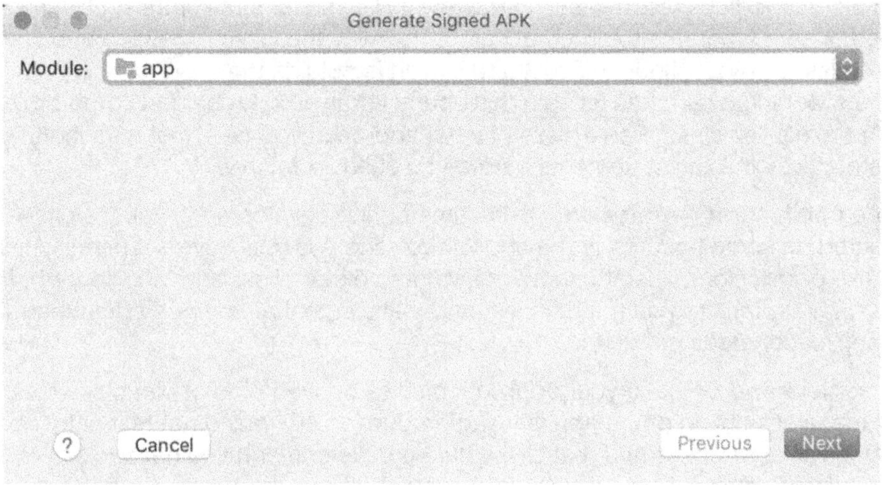

Figure 11-1. Select the module

Click "Next".

Figure 11-2. Keystore dialog

We don't have a JKS (Java key store) file yet; we will create a new one. Click the "Create new ..." button.

> **Note**   A JKS is a repository of certificates where private keys and symmetric keys are also stored. When created, this is typically a file.

In the next dialog window, provide all necessary information.

Figure 11-3. New KeyStore

Keystore

- Key store path—The location where you want to keep the keystore
- Password—This is the password for the keystore

Key

- Alias—This alias identifies the key
- Password—Password for the key; this is not the same password as the keystore's, but you can use the same password if you like

- Validity (years)—The default is 25 years; just accept this default. If you want to publish on Google Play, the certificate must be valid until the end of October 2033, so, the 25-year default value should be fine

- Other information—Only the first and last name fields are required

Click "OK" to proceed to the next dialog.

	Generate Signed APK
Key store path:	/Users/ted/Desktop/testapp.jks

Create new...   Choose existing...

Key store password:	●●●●●●●●●●●
Key alias:	testapp
Key password:	●●●●●●●●●●●

☑ Remember passwords

?   Cancel   Previous   Next

Figure 11-4. Keystore window

Now that the JKS file is created, the keystore dialog window is populated with it. Click "Next".

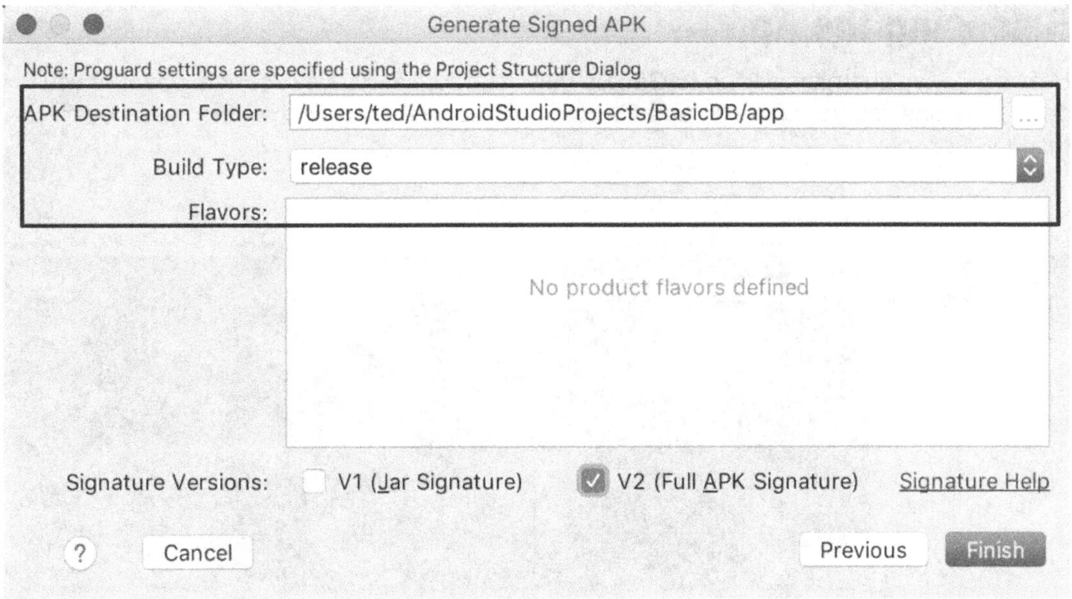

Figure 11-5. *Signed APK dialog*

Remember the APK destination folder; this is where you will find the generated and signed APK later. Also, make sure that the build type is set to "release".

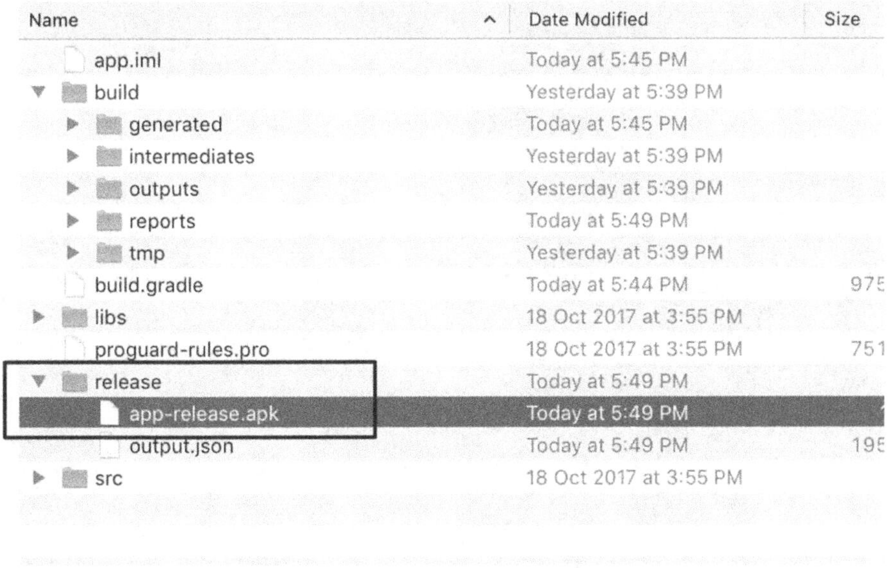

Figure 11-6. *Location of the signed APK*

At this point, you have an APK file that users can install on their devices. The file "app-release.apk" as shown in Figure 11-6 is the actual file you will submit to Google's marketplace.

Releasing the App

Before you can submit your app to Google Play, you will need a developer account. If you don't have one yet, you can sign up at `https://developer.android.com`; then head over to the Play Console.

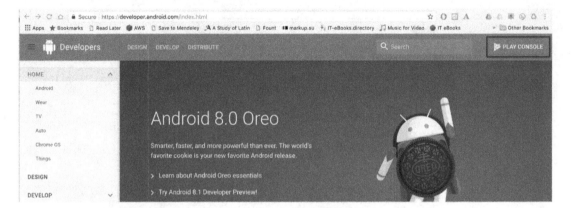

Figure 11-7. *Sign up for a developer account*

Sign in with a Google account, read and agree to the developer agreement, and finally, proceed to payment.

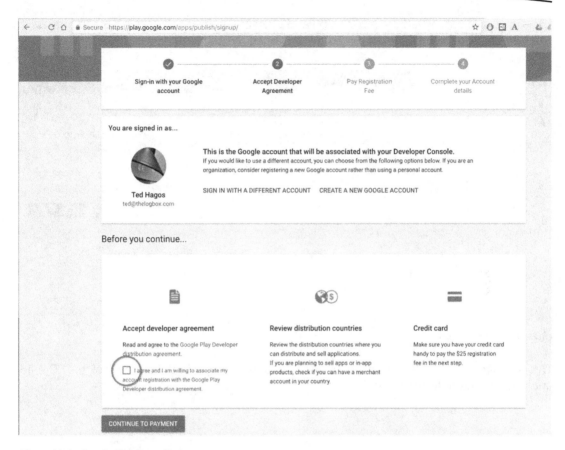

Figure 11-8. Google Play Console sign-up

Once you have completed the registration and payment, you will now have access to the Google Play Console.

Figure 11-9.   Play Console

This is where you can start the process of submitting your app to the store. Click the "Create application" button to get started.

Introduction to Java

The Java platform consists of a couple of things: a programming language, the virtual machine, and a set of built-in libraries and technology frameworks. I would imagine that most people would think of Java only as the programming language: that is quite understandable since the language is probably the most prominent part of the platform and hence has the most mind share. Just remember that Java is an umbrella term we use to refer to the platform.

The Java Language

The Java language is not so old, as far as programming languages go. James Gosling worked on it in the early part of the 90s and released it in 1995. It is barely 22 years old at the time of this writing. In contrast, the C language is almost 47 years old (C was released in 1969).

If you have background in other languages such as JavaScript, C++, or C#, Java may look familiar because all of them share some semblance to the C language. By the way, Java is in no way related to JavaScript. JavaScript is not a derivative of Java nor was it inspired by Java. Java is related to JavaScript the same way as car is related to carpet. They just have common letters in their names.

Java is a high-level language. It provides a fair amount of abstraction above the physical machine that it runs on. But you can dive down and perform some decent low-level operations on the bit level if you want to. It is also a general-purpose language. It wasn't designed just to program web applications or anything specific. It is not a domain-specific language the way Sinatra (Ruby) or Express (NodeJS) is. You can build pretty much anything you can imagine.

© Ted Hagos 2018
T. Hagos, *Learn Android Studio 3*, https://doi.org/10.1007/978-1-4842-3156-2

Virtual Machine

Java is a compiled language. Like other languages such as C or C++, you will write your programming instructions in a source file using a somewhat English-like language. This source file will be compiled into an object file. An object file contains a set of instructions that a machine can understand and execute. In Java, an object file or executable file is called **byte code**. The byte code is what a Java virtual machine, or JVM, can execute.

Byte codes, however, cannot be executed directly by the operating system (OS). They do not contain the same instructions, nor are they structured like the regular EXE files or other forms of portable executable. The OS does not know what to do with byte code. They should be executed within a virtual machine. The Java runtime engine (JRE) is such a machine.

Java is portable at the byte code level. You can write and compile your program in one OS, say Windows, and run it on another OS without requiring any modification. Sun Microsystems, the former custodian of the Java technology, came up with the WORA (Write Once Run Anywhere) slogan during the early days of Java.

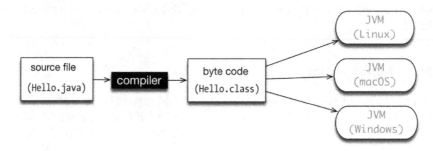

Figure A-1. Work cycle

The basic idea is to write the program source in a file that has a *.java* extension. A compilation process which results in a byte code (*.class* file) happens. The byte code is executed within a JRE. A JRE is also known as a JVM. Each operating system has its own version of the virtual machine, but what runs on one virtual machine will run on all.

Editions

You can use Java to build applications for a variety of architectures. Java comes in several editions. The Java SE (Java Standard Edition), which is the topic of this book, can be used to build desktop applications. Java Enterprise Edition (Java EE) can be used to build web applications, web services, high-availability back-end processes, and so on. Java Mobile Edition (Java ME) can be used to build apps for mobile or embedded devices. However, for mobile devices like Android phones/tablets, you might want to consider the Android SDK. By the way, the native language for the Android platform is Java.

Setup

The JDK installer is available for Windows, Linux, and macOS. The installer package can be downloaded from the Oracle download page for Java. Currently, the stable version of the JDK is v8.

`www.oracle.com/technetwork/java/javase/downloads/jdk8-downloads-2133151.html`

You must agree to the license agreement before you can download the installer.

To install the JDK on macOS, double-click the downloaded dmg file and follow the prompts. The installer takes care of updating the system path, so you don't need to perform any action after the installation.

To install the JDK on Windows, double-click the downloaded zipped file and follow the prompts. Unlike in macOS, you must perform extra configuration after the setup. You need to (1) include java/bin in your OS system path and (2) include a CLASSPATH definition in the System Path.

Tip   If you want to be able to invoke the JDK tools from anywhere in your system, add the full path of "JDK\bin" to the system PATH variable. If you accepted the default settings during the JDK setup, it would have been installed on "C:\Program Files\Java\jdk.18.0\bin". Here is how to set the path variable in Windows 10.

---

1. Click Start ➤ Control Panel ➤ System

2. Click Advanced ➤ Environment Variables

3. Add the location of the bin folder to the system "PATH" variable.

4. It is typical for the PATH variable to look like the following

5. C:\WINDOWS\system32;C:\WINDOWS;C:\Program Files\Java\ jdk1.8.0\bin;

If you are a Linux user, you may have seen the tar ball and rpm options on the download; you may use them and install it like you would install any other software on your Linux platform. Alternatively, you may install the JDK from the repositories. This instruction applies to Debian and its derivatives: Ubuntu, Mint, and so on.

```
sudo add-apt-repository ppa:webupd8team/java
sudo apt-get update
sudo apt-get install oracle-java8-installer
sudo update-alternatives --config java
```

Hello World

We'll start with the basic task of writing a simple program. This may seem like a silly program that lacks any real-world value, but it does have some educational value. The program is instructive on how to compile and run Java programs. There will be a couple of things that may not be immediately obvious nor will they make sense when we write the code, but we won't be bogged down by those details (at least not yet). We will sidestep some details and behaviors of the program, but we will circle back to them in later sections.

Here's what you will need for this exercise:

■   A programmer's editor. It doesn't have to be very advanced or fancy. Notepad, GEdit, or TextEdit would do but there are plenty of other choices for a decent programmer's editor: Sublime, Atom, and Visual Studio Code are decent choices. If you are already using a programmer's editor and it's not on this list, use that. Go with the one you are most familiar with

■   A terminal application. For Linux and macOS users, go for the terminal of your choice. For Windows users, this will be cmd.exe. You can launch this by clicking "Start"; then type `cmd.exe` and press Enter

Choose a folder where you can save program source files. The best location is one where you have read/write and execute permissions; this location is most likely your home folder.

Windows	`\Users\yourUserName`
macOS	`/Users/yourUserName`
Linux	`/home/yourUserName`

1. Launch a terminal window and go to your home folder

2. Create a folder named "practice". You can do this with the commands md practice and mkdir practice, for Windows and Linux/macOS, respectively

3. Switch to the "practice" directory you that you just created—cd practice

4. Create a file named "Hello.java"; this can be done with the command touch Hello.java. There is no simple way for Windows to create a named empty file, so you may just have to create the file using your program editor and save the file in the "practice" folder

5. Edit "Hello.java" and write our first program

This program, while short and simple, is hard to explain to beginners because it contains language elements that can be dense if you deal with them with sufficient detail. So, we need to take this at face value for now and trust that this is how things are done in Java. Nevertheless, we will skim through some of program elements.

Listing A-1.   /practice/Hello.java

```java
class Hello { ❶
  // Let's print something to STDOUT ❷
  public static void main(String[] args) { ❸
    System.out.println("Hello World\n"); ❹
  }
}
```

❶   `class` is special word. This means you want to create a class. "Hello" is the name of that class. It is a name chosen by the programmer (us)

❷   This line begins with //, which is a comment. Anything after the slashes until the end of the line is ignored by the compiler. So, this is a good way to leave breadcrumbs of information inside your program

❸   `main` is function, but Java doesn't call them as such. Instead, functions are called methods; let's get used to that. A method is a named collection of executable statements. You will create lots of methods in the future but just remember that the `main` method as shown here is special. It is the entry point to the program. All programs must have entry points. If a program does not have an entry point, the runtime engine will complain and you will get a runtime error

❹   `println` is a method that takes a String argument (it also takes other kinds of arguments, but in this case, it took a String) and prints it on the screen. Inside the `println` method are the worlds "Hello World" enclosed in double quotes. In Java, words like these are called Strings and make up a kind of data that we will use quite a lot. Also, this line is a good example of what a statement looks like. Note that this statement was terminated with a semicolon. Statements in Java are like sentences; they need to be punctuated. The Java compiler knows that you are finished with the statement when it sees the semicolon. We could have written more println statements in this example, but we only wrote one. It needs only one for now

The only interesting piece of code in Listing A-1 is the one that outputs something onscreen. The rest of the code is just scaffolding, but the scaffolding is necessary. We cannot do away with it. The next steps are to compile and run the program; you can do that with the following commands.

```
javac Hello.java
java Hello
```

The first command reads the Hello.java source file, compiles it to byte code, and produces the executable file named "Hello.class". If you look inside the "practice" folder, you will find this class file. The second command launches the JVM and runs the "Hello" program inside it. Notice that we didn't include the .*class* extension when we ran our program.

This is a good time to mention that Java is case sensitive, so "`java hello`" is lexically and materially different than "`java Hello`". The latter would run and work as expected and the former will result in a runtime error.

If you typed the sample code as shown in Listing A-1, you should not encounter any kind of error and the program would have worked as expected. You should be able to see the string "Hello World" on your screen.

Program Structure

When you are learning a foreign language, you probably started with the parts of its speech, what kind of rules govern them, how you can put things together, how are they punctuated, and so forth. When learning a programming language, we will have similar concerns. We need to learn what the parts are, along with how they are organized and put together.

Statements   Statements are the equivalent of sentences in the English language. These are executable statements in Java. Statements are terminated by a semicolon. In our earlier example, you have seen System.out.println("Hello World");—such is an example of a statement. Not all statements are as simple as that; some statements may contain multiple expressions joined by multiple operators

Comments   Comments are ignored by the compiler. It's a good way to document program code and it can benefit other people who read your code. It can even benefit you. Comments allow us to dump our thought processes and intentions at the time of writing the code. There are three ways to comment codes

```
// THIS IS A COMMENT
```

A single line comment, sometimes called an inline comment. The compiler will ignore everything to the right of the two forward slashes until the end of the line

```
/*
   Statement here
   Another statement
*/
```

This is the C-style comment. It is called that because it came primarily from the C language. You can use this multiline style to comment multiple lines of statements

```
/**
   Statement here
   Another statement
*/
```

This is almost the same as the C-style multiline comment. This type of comment, though, can be used to generate Java API style documentation

White space   Java is tokenized language; it doesn't care about white or blank space, so you can write your code like this

```
class Hello { public static void main (String [] args) { System.out.
println("Hello\n");}}
```

Or like this

```
class Hello {
public static void main (String [] args) {
System.out.println("Hello\n");
}
}
```

The compiler doesn't care. So, write your codes for the benefit of humans who may be unlucky enough to maintain our programs. Forget the compiler; it doesn't care about spaces anyway. Use white spaces to beautify the code and make it extremely readable, something like this:

```
class Hello {
  public static void main (String [] args) {
    System.out.println("Hello\n");
  }
}
```

Blocks   Oftentimes, you may need to write a bunch of statements and you will need to group them together. Blocks allow us to do just that. The lexical symbol for blocks are a pair of French braces; they are also sometimes called curly or squiggly braces. Blocks are used by classes, interfaces, and methods. Occasionally, they are also used to define static and instance blocks; these last two are not very common but you may need them from time to time

Variables

A variable is something that we use to manipulate data, or more precisely a value. Values are things that you can store, manipulate, print, or push or pull from the network. For us to be able to work with values, we need to put them inside variables.

```
String name;
```

The preceding statement *declares* a variable named "name", supposedly to hold the value of a person's name. In Java, when we declare a variable we must tell the compiler what kind of value it is expected to hold. In this case, it's a String value.

```
name = "John Doe";
```

The preceding statement *defines* the "name" variable; we assigned it the literal String value "John Doe". The assignment of value was facilitated by the equal sign (assignment operator). The declaration and definition of variables could be done as a two-step process, as you have seen in the preceding, but it doesn't have to be. The declaration and definition can be written in a single statement.

```
String name = "John Doe";
int age = 35;
String email = "jdoe@gmail.com"
```

The concept of variable as they relate to values might be easier to grasp if you visualize the variables as some sort of a named location and the location is a box, the contents of which holds the value

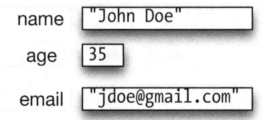

Figure A-2. Variable representation

Operators

Operators are easy to grasp because what they do will look immediately obvious. They behave like how you would expect them to. There are various kinds of operators in Java: some you can use for arithmetic, some are used for testing equalities (or inequalities), and some are even used for low-level data manipulation.

assignment	=
arithmetic	+ - / * %
unary	+ - ++ − !
equality and relational	== < > >= <= !=
conditional	&& || ? :
bitwise and bit shift	~ >> << >>> & | ^

Methods   Methods a.k.a. functions are a collection of executable statements. Java
programmers don't refer to these as functions, so you better get used to calling
them methods. Anyway, these collections of statements are packaged as one unit,
and whenever you need to execute those collection statements, you only need to
invoke the name of the method. Methods may or may not return values; they may or
may not also accept arguments.

Listing A-2.

```
public static void main (String []args) {
}
```

The method as shown in Listing A-2 accepts arguments, an array of Strings to be
specific:

Listing A-3.

```
int getSum(int a, int b) {
    int result = a + b;
    return result;
}
```

The method shown in Listing A-3 accepts two integer arguments and returns an
integer result

Classes   The class is a collection of variable and method declarations. When classes are
instantiated, objects are created as a result; this is the reason why classes are
sometimes called object factories

Listing A-4.

```
class Person {
    String fname;
    String lname;
}
Person p1 = new Person();
```

Listing A-4 defines a new data structure called Person by declaring a class with
the same name. It has two properties, "lname" and "fname", for last name and
first name, respectively. An object named "p1" is created from the definition of the
Person class

keywords   There are several reserved words in the Java language. You cannot use these words in your program because they have been, well, reserved. They mean something special when the compiler sees them in your program. Best not to use them as class, method, or variable name.

Table A-1. Java Reserved Words

byte	for	Protected	this	break
short	if	Package	super	continue
int	else	import	final	strictfp
long	switch	extends	throw	synchronized
float	class	implements	throws	new
double	interface	try	transient	native
char	abstract	catch	volatile	assert
boolean	void	finally	static	const
while	public	Instanceof	enum	goto
do	private	Return	case	default

Other Considerations

Let's consider some programming good practice and update some of the previous example (Listing A-5).

Listing A-5. Hello.java

```
class Hello {
  // Let's print something to STDOUT
  public static void main(String[] args) {
    System.out.println("Hello World\n");
  }
}
```

It is written in a file named "Hello.java" and it bears the same name as that of the name of the class. It is considered good practice that the name in the class definition is the same name as that of the file which contains it. You can however, choose not to follow this practice. Listing A-6 demonstrates this.

Listing A-6. Hello.java

```
class World {
  // Let's print something to STDOUT
  public static void main(String[] args) {
    System.out.println("Hello World\n");
  }
}
```

This code will still compile but it will not produce "Hello.class"; instead, it will yield the file "World.class". So, the way to execute it is not java Hello, but rather java World.

You may have also noticed that in all our code samples, there is only one class defined inside a Java source file. This too is considered good practice. Again, you may choose not to adhere to this practice. Listing A-7 shows how to do this.

Listing A-7. Hello.java

```java
class Hello {
    String text = "Hello";
}

class World {
    String text = "World";
}
```

When you compile this code with javac Hello.java, it will result in two class files named "Hello.class" and "World.class".

Having shown you the two ways in which you can break away from what is considered good practice, I urge you not to do it. The reason these deviations were shown here is because it is instructive to understand the rules behind source compilation.

Variables and Data Types

A programming language like Java relies on its ability to create, store, and edit values; these values need to be manipulated arithmetically or by some other means. Java allows us to work these values by storing them in variables; so, put simply, a variable is a named storage for values or data. A variable is created using a two-step process. First, you need to declare a variable, like so:

```java
int num;
```

In the preceding statement, "num" is the variable and "int" is what we call a type. A type determines the variable's size in memory and what kinds of operations you can do with them. In our preceding example, you can add, multiply, divide, or subtract from "num" because Java defined the arithmetic operators to work numeric types like "int".

The next step after declaring a variable is to define it. Defining a variable assigns a value to it.

```java
num = 10;
```

In the preceding statement, the integer literal "10" is on the right-hand side of the equal sign, which effectively assigns its value to the variable "num".

Alternatively, we can declare and define a variable on the same line, like so.

```java
int num = 10;
```

After a variable has been declared and defined, you can change its value at any later time.

```
int num = 10;
num = 20;
```

What you cannot do, however, is to assign a value to "num" that isn't an "int", like so.

```
int num = 10;
num = "Hello";
```

We cannot assign the String "Hello" to num, because we've already declared it as an "int" type. Java, being a strongly typed language, does not allow type coercions like this.

Primitive Types

Java has two data types: primitive and Reference. The primitive types are the ones that are built into the language; Java has eight of those.

Type	Size in Bits	Sample Literals
byte	8	−128 to 127
short	16	−32,768 to 32,767
int	32	2,147,483,648 to 2,147,483,647
long	64	−9,223,372,036,854,775,808 to 9,223,372,036,854,807
float	32	1.23e100f, −1.23e-100f, .3f, 3.14F
double	64	1.23456e300d, −1.23456e-300d, 1e1d
char	16	0–65535 or \u0000–\uFFFF
boolean	1	true, false

Java is a statically typed language; this is why we need to declare the types of variables before we can use them in our program.

Reference Types

A reference type value is anything that is not a primitive. Reference type values are created by instantiating classes, which means that reference type values are objects. Some examples of reference types are String and java.util.Date. When you create a class or an interface, you are creating a new reference type.

Creating a reference type value is not that much different from creating a primitive type value; it also involves the two-step process of declaring the variable and then defining it, for example.

```
Date date;
date = new Date();
```

In the preceding statement, the variable name is "date" and the type is "Date"; more specifically, it's "java.util.Date", which is one of the classes in the Java platform that comes with the installation of the JDK. The date object is created by using the "new" keyword plus the name of the class (Date) with parens. The name of the class plus parens is called a constructor method. This will be discussed in the section titled "Classes and Objects". When this statement finishes, the "date" variable will contain a reference to the location of a newly created Date object.

Constructors are not always empty; sometimes you can pass values inside the parens. See the following example.

```
String hello = new String("Hello");
```

The preceding statement creates a new String by passing a series of characters enclosed in double quotes to the String constructor. Strings values are very common in programming and are quite indispensable, but despite that, Java did not make it a part of the primitive types—String is a reference type. Another way to create String objects is shown in the following.

```
String world = "World";
```

In the preceding statement, we did not need to call the constructor of String to create a new object. We simply assigned a String literal the char variables "World".

Operators

Like many programming languages, Java programs are composed of variables, operators, and statements that are put together in a way that achieves very specific goals. Something you would commonly do in programming is to perform operations on values or data; sometimes you may need to do arithmetic operations, and other times, perhaps compare one value to another. Java has a rich set of operators that we can use to perform those functions.

Operators allow us to create expressions and statements which will be the building blocks of methods and classes later. This section details the various operators that you can use in Java.

Assignment   The equal sign (=) is used for simple assignment operations. The value on the RHS (right-hand side) will be assigned to the variable on the LHS (left-hand side)

Arithmetic   Arithmetic operators are straightforward. They do what you expect them to do

+   Addition. Works for number types (byte, short, int, long, double, and float)

```
int a = 1 + 2;  // adds two int literals
String a = "Hello";
String b = "World";
String c = a + b;
```

The additive operator also works on Strings. It results in concatenation

-    Subtraction

*   Multiplication

/   Division

%   Modulo operator is used to get the remainder

```
int a = 11 % 2; // results to 1
```

Unary   Unary operators work on a single operand. When used, it changes either the sign or the value of the operand

+   Signifies that the number is positive, which is the default, however, so numbers are positive even if you don't explicitly say they are by prepending them with a plus sign

-    The unary minus negates an expression

++   Increment operator. Increases the value of a variable by 1

```
int counter = 0;
counter++; // add 1 to the value of counter var
```

- -   Decrement operator. Decreases the value of the variable by 1

```
int counter = 100;
counter -; // subtract 1 from  counter
```

!   Logical complement operator. Inverts the value of a boolean variable

Equality and Relational	==	The double equals checks for equality of two operands, e.g.

```
int a = 1;
int b = 1;
if(a == b) {
// True
    }
```

Take care not to confuse single equals with double equals: the former is used to assign a value to a variable and the latter is used to test for equality. The equality operator works on all the primitive types (byte, short, int, long, double, float, char, and boolean). Confusingly, it also works on String values

```
String a = "Hello World";
String b = "Hello";
String c = "World";
If ((b + c) == a) {
// statement
    }
```

The code above will compile without problems, but it is not working the way you think it works. This is not the proper way to compare String values

	!=	The not equal operator. Does the opposite of ==
	>	Greater than
	<	Less than
	>=	Greater than or equal to
	<=	Less than or equal to
Conditional		Conditional operators are also known as logical or boolean operators. Its basic form is as follows

A operator B

Where operands A and B are boolean types. The logical operator joins and combines two boolean values into a single boolean value.

	&	Logical AND. Operation will return true if A and B are both true
	|	Logical OR. Operation will return true if either A or B is true
	&&	Conditional AND. This is the same as &, but if the operand on its left side is false, it will return false right away and it will not evaluate the other operand any longer. That's why this is called a short circuit operator
	||	Conditional OR. Same as logical OR, but if the operand on its left is true, it will immediately return true and won't be bothered to evaluate the second operand

Type Comparison	All the operators available in Java generally work only for the primitive types. You cannot compare reference types using equality operators, not without some serious work involving some method overrides. But there is one operator we can use that works for reference types: the *instanceof* operator. Its basic form is as follows

```
A instanceof B
```

Where A is an object reference variable and B is either a class or an interface, *instanceof* will be true if

A is an object that was created using the constructor of B

A was instantiated using the constructor of one of B's subclasses

A was instantiated using the constructor of a class which *implements* B (if B was an interface)

Bitwise and Bit Shifting	Bitwise and bit shifting operators are used if you need to work with data at the bit level. This is low-level programming. It is usually employed if you need to squeeze out every ounce of performance from your code. Working at the bit level makes the expression or operation very performant, but these kinds of code aren't very common among application developers because these codes tend to look pretty terse

Program Flow

Program statements are executed sequentially by default, one after the other, in a linear fashion. There are some statements in Java that can cause programs to deviate from a linear flow. Some statements can cause the flow to fork or to branch, and others can cause it to go around in circles, like in a loop. These statements are the subject of this section.

Decisions

These control structures allow the programmer to execute some statements when certain conditions are true and optionally run some statements when the same condition is untrue. There are two statements we can use for program decision making.

if then else

This construct is straightforward to implement: if a condition is met, do one thing, if not, then do another. The simplest form of the if construct is as follows:

```
if (<expression>) {
    STATEMENT
    STATEMENT
}
```

Where

- *expression* is mandatory. You cannot have an if statement with an empty pair of parens

- *expression* must resolve to a boolean value. This means you can put anything inside the parens as long as it resolves to a boolean value: for example, a method that resolves to either true or false, an equality expression, a variable that holds either a true or false value, and even the true or false literal

The following are some examples on how to construct expressions that test for equality. Remember that the single equal sign (=) is the assignment operator, it is what you will use when you want to assign a value to a variable. Confusing the equal sign with the double equal sign is a rookie mistake, and quite a common one.

```
a == b     // a is exactly equal to b
a != b     // a is not equal to b
a > b      // a is greater than b
a < b      // a is less than b
a >= b     // a is greater than or equal to b
a <= b     // a is less than or equal to b
```

If you need to account for multiple pathways, the if-then construct can handle that too by using the optional else if clause.

Listing A-8. else if Clause

```
import java.util.*;

    class Elif {
      public static void main(String[] args) {

        /*
        What the next 4 lines do:
        1. Create a calendar object
        2. Create a date object, which holds
           the current date
        3. Get the current day of the week which
           is basically an int 1..7
        */
        Calendar c = Calendar.getInstance();
        Date d = new Date();
        c.setTime(d);
        int dayOfWeek = c.get(Calendar.DAY_OF_WEEK);
```

```
    // Next, print out the friendly name for the
    // current day of week

    if (dayOfWeek == 1) {
      System.out.println("Sunday");
    }
    else if (dayOfWeek == 2) {
      System.out.println("Monday");
    }
    else if (dayOfWeek == 3) {
      System.out.println("Tuesday");
    }
    else if (dayOfWeek == 4) {
      System.out.println("Wednesday");
    }
    else if (dayOfWeek == 5) {
      System.out.println("Thursday");
    }
    else if (dayOfWeek == 6) {
      System.out.println("Friday");
    }
    else if (dayOfWeek == 7) {
      System.out.println("Saturday");
    }

  }
}
```

switch Statement

The switch statement has a slightly different structure from the if-then statement, which makes it in some cases more readable than an if-then construct that needs to handle multiple pathways. The basic form of the switch statement is as follows:

```
switch(expr) {
    case value:
        STATEMENT;
        break;
    case value:
        STATEMENT;
        break;
    default:
        STATEMENT;
}
```

Where *expr* is either of type *byte, short, char, and int*. When JDK 1.7 was introduced, the *String* type was added to the capabilities of the switch statement . Listing A-9 shows an example of how to use the switch statement.

Listing A-9. Switch Statement

```java
import java.util.Calendar;
import java.util.Date;

class Switch {

  public static void main(String[] args) {

    Calendar c = Calendar.getInstance();
    Date d = new Date();
    c.setTime(d);

    int dayOfWeek = c.get(Calendar.DAY_OF_WEEK);

    String day = "";

    switch(dayOfWeek) {
      case 1:
        day = "Sunday";
        break;
      case 2:
        day = "Monday";
        break;
      case 3:
        day = "Tuesday";
        break;
      case 4:
        day = "Wednesday";
        break;
      case 5:
        day = "Thursday";
        break;
      case 6:
        day = "Friday";
        break;
      case 7:
        day = "Saturday";
        break;
      default:
        day = "Dunno";
    }

    System.out.printf("Today is %s", day);
  }
}
```

Loops

When you need to execute some statements repeatedly, you can use any one of the three looping constructs: the *while*, *do-while*, and *for* statements.

while statement   The while statement allows us to execute a group of statements while some conditions are true. The basic form of the while loop is as follows:

```
while (cond)  {
    STATEMENTS
}
```

Where cond can be a variable, literal, or expression that resolves to a boolean value. While cond is *true*, all the statements inside the block will be executed. You need to take care and be mindful that there is something in your code which will make cond untrue (or *false*) at some point in time, lest you will have a loop that does not terminate.

Listing A-10. Simple Use of While Loop

```
class While {
  public static void main(String[] args) {
    int count = 0; ❶
    while(count < 11) { ❷
      System.out.println(count);
      count++; // ❸
    } ❹
  }
}
```

❶   A countervariable is initialized to zero

❷   The guard condition of the while loop is evaluated for the first time; at this point, the value of the count variable is zero, the condition evaluates to true, and we enter the loop's body

❸   The count variable is incremented using one of the shorthand operators; count is now equal to 1

❹   We reach the closing curly brace, which is the end of the while loop. Program control goes back to the beginning of the loop, and the condition is evaluated for the second time. The count variable is still less than 11, so we enter the loop again. This will go on until the value of count will be equal to 11, at which point, we will no longer enter the body of the loop and program control will transfer to line number 10 (the closing curly brace of the main method)

do-while statement

The *do-while* statement is almost the same in format and in function as the while statement, with the important distinction that in the do-while construct, the condition is checked after the body of the loop. This has an important effect on your execution; the statements in the loop body are guaranteed to be executed at least once, no matter if the condition is true or false.

Listing A-11. do-while Sample

```java
class DoWhile {
  public static void main(String[] args) {
    int i = 0;
    do {
      System.out.println(i++);
    } while (i < 0);
  }
}
```

The preceding code will still print out one output even if it fails the condition test.

for statement

The basic form of the *for loop* is as follows

```java
for (<initial value>;<condition>;<increment/decrement>) {
  STATEMENT
}
```

Where

"initial value" is a statement that sets or defines the initial value of a counter

"condition" is an expression that will be evaluated every time the loop completes or circles back. As long as this condition is evaluating to true, all the statements inside the loop block will be executed. Again, you need to be mindful that this condition will result to false at some point in time

"increment/decrement" is a statement that increases or decreases the value of a counter

Listing A-12. For Loop Sample

```java
class For {
  public static void main(String[] args) { /
    for(int count = 0; count < 11; count++) { ❶ ❷ ❸
      System.out.println(count); ❹
    }
  }
}
```

❶   A counter variable named count is initialized to zero

❷   A conditional expression (count < 11) is set to determine how many times we will go inside the loop

❸   The count variable's value is increased by 1 using one of the shorthand operators

❹   Value of count is printed on the screen

Simple Application of Control Structures

Let's see an example of control structures in action.

The FizzBuzz Problem

This is a popular exercise for beginning programmers. You may encounter many variations of this problem, but the basic idea is to use a branching control structure which routes logic when a number is either odd or even. The basic version of this problem is as follows:

1.   Count from 1 to 100

2.   If the current value of counter is exactly divisible by 3, print "Fizz" to the screen

3.   If the current value of the counter is exactly divisible by 5, print "Buzz" to the screen

4.   If the current value of the counter is exactly divisible by both 3 and 5, print "FizzBuzz" to the screen

Listing A-13. FizzBuzz.java

```java
class FizzBuzz {

  public static void main (String [] args){

    for (int i = 1; i <= 100 ; i++ ) { ❶

      if ( i % 15 == 0) {
        System.out.printf("FizzBuzz %d ", i); ❷
      }
      else if (i % 5 == 0) { ❸
        System.out.printf("Buzz %d ", i);
      }
      else if(i % 3 == 0) { ❹
        System.out.printf("Fizz %d ", i);
      }
    }

  }
}
```

❶ Count from 1 to 100; that's easy enough to do with a for loop

❷ Check if the current value of *i* is divisible by both 3 and 5, if it is, print "FizzBuzz"

❸ If the number is not divisible by 3×5, is it divisible just by 3 then? If it is, print "Fizz"

❹ If the number is not divisible by 3×5 and not divisible by 3, is divisible by 5? If it is, print "Buzz".
This is the last condition that we will check, because only these three conditions are stated on
the problem

How to Print a 5×5 Multiplication Table

This is an exercise on nested loops. The goal is output something like this:

1 × 1 = 1	1 × 2 = 2	1 × 3 = 3	1 × 4 = 4	1 × 5 = 5
2 × 1 = 2	2 × 2 = 4	2 × 3 = 6	2 × 4 = 8	2 × 5 = 10
3 × 1 = 3	3 × 2 = 6	3 × 3 = 9	3 × 4 = 12	3 × 5 = 15
4 × 1 = 4	4 × 2 = 8	4 × 3 = 12	4 × 4 = 16	4 × 5 = 20
5 × 1 = 5	5 × 2 = 10	5 × 3 = 15	5 × 4 = 20	5 × 5 = 25

Listing A-14. Multiplication.java

```
class Multiplication {

  public static void main(String[] args) {

    for (int i = 1; i <= 5; i++) {
      for (int j = 1; j <= 5; j++) {
        //System.out.printf("%d\t", i * j);
        System.out.printf("%d x %d = %d\n", i, j, i*j);
      }
      System.out.println("----------");
    }
  }
}
```

The code doesn't need a lot of commentary. There are two loops; one is embedded on the
other to generate the matrix of values in a 5×5 multiplication table.

Methods

A method is a named collection of statements. Think of it like a heading for a bunch of executable statements such that when you call the heading, you get to execute all the statements that are inside it. It's some sort of a shorthand. A method definition looks something like the following:

```
[access modifier] [special modifiers]
  <return type> <method name> ([parameters ...]) {

}
```

The access modifier (optional), when defined, could be either public, private, or protected. When it is not defined explicitly, the method has package access. We'll discuss access modifiers in the "Object Oriented Programming" section.

The special modifier(s), when defined, could be something like static, transient, volatile, synchronized, and so forth. We will discuss the static keyword in the "Object Oriented Programming" section. The other special keywords mentioned will be important to you when you're dealing with concurrency, but that is beyond the scope of this book.

A method must always declare a return type. This type can be primitive (byte, short, int, long, double, float, char, boolean) or a reference type (e.g., String, Date, Math, or a custom type). If the method is not expected to return anything, you can use void as the return type.

A method must have a name. This name identifies the method uniquely within the class where it is defined.

A method may or may not accept parameters. When it does accept parameters, it will always be passed by value, meaning that the method creates a copy of the passed parameter within the method. So, any change you make to the value of the parameter while within the scope of method doesn't affect the original variable outside the method. Of course, this is true only if the parameter is a primitive type. If the parameter is of a reference type, that's a different story.

> **Note**   Whenever you create a class or an interface, that becomes a custom type. So, a custom type is nothing more than a UDT (user-defined type).

It may seem from the preceding list that we need to keep a lot of things in mind when constructing and working with method—and there will be quite a few more—but this next rule about methods should be probably on the top of our list. You need to always remember that methods are part of either an object or a class. Whenever a method is called, it is never invoked in a vacuum; it is always invoked from a context. In OOP, methods constitute the behaviors of objects. So, they always linked to objects (or classes). We'll discuss this dichotomy of classes and objects in the next section, but for now let's deal with the context issue.

Listing A-15. Method from the Same Context

```
class Test {

  public static void main(String []args) {

    System.out.print("Main");
    Sample obj = new Sample(); ❶
    obj.one(); ❷
  }
}

class Sample {

  void one() {
    System.out.print("One");
    two(); ❸
  }
  void two() {
    System.out.print("Two");
    three(); ❹
  }
  void three() {
    System.out.print("Three");
  }
}
```

❶   The Sample class was instantiated; the object reference was stored in a variable named obj

❷   Method one was invoked on the Sample object (obj ref variable). There are two statements defined in method one: the first statement prints out "One"

❸   The second statement in the method invokes another method named two. It may seem the invocation for method two is done without a context because nothing is prepended to it. There is no variable and a dot symbol before the invocation. But this is not true because method two is being invoked by an instance of the Sample class (the same class where method two is defined). When the main method of the Test class called method one, it is from the context of an explicit object reference (the Sample object which is held by the obj variable). When method two is invoked, it is still from the context of the same Sample object that invoked method one. We simply don't need to write this context anymore because method two and method one are defined on the same class, and method one is invoking method two from example the same object context

❹   Method two called three. Method three is also defined within the same class as two and one, so invoking method three from anywhere in class Sample does not require an explicit object context

Listing A-16. Method Invocation from a Different Context

```
class Test {
  public static void main(String[] args) {
    Foo objFoo = new Foo();
    objFoo.doSomething(); ❶
  }
}

class Foo {
  void doSomething() {
    System.out.print("Foo");
    Bar objBar = new Bar();
    objBar.doSomething();  ❷
  }
}

class Bar {
  void doSomething() {
    System.out.print("Bar ");
  }
}
// prints out Foo Bar
```

❶   Nothing surprising; doSomething is a method defined in another class (Foo). We need to create
     an instance of Foo before we can invoke doSomething in it

❷   We want to invoke doSomething again, but this doSomething is a method defined in a class
     other than Foo (it's in Bar). We need to create an instance of Bar before we can invoke any of its
     methods

Listing A-17. Pass by Value

```
class Test {

  void fooBar(int a) { ❶
    a = 3; ❷
    System.out.printf("fooBar a = %d\n",a); ❸
  }

  public static void main(String[] args) {
    Test obj = new Test();

    int a = 2;
    System.out.printf("a = %d\n",a); // prints a = 2
    obj.fooBar(a);
    System.out.printf("a = %d\n",a); ❹
  }
}
```

❶ The value of the a variable when it was passed from the main function was 2. When fooBar accepts the integer parameter, fooBar creates a copy of the a variable inside the method body, and the variable a became an automatic variable (they are called automatic variables because they are defined by the function automatically, without explicit help from you)

❷ fooBar alters the value of the a variable, but what it changed is its copy of the variable and not the a variable as defined inside the main function

❸ fooBar prints the value of the a variable, and it tries to resolve where it is defined. It will look first inside the method where println is called; naturally it will find the copy of the "a" variable, so it will stop looking any further (if println didn't find the a variable within the method, it will look further outside the method and into the class body). What follows this statement is already the end of the fooBar method. Everything that was declared and defined within the method will vanish as soon as the method reaches its end of definition—programmers would say that the method has already gone out of scope

❹ Now that fooBar has gone out of scope, the control passes back to the main method. The next statement to execute is printing the value of the a variable again. This statement will still print "a = 2", because this variable a was practically untouched. Whatever fooBar did to its copy of the a variable did not affect the original a variable as it was defined in the main method

Object Oriented Programming

Different programming languages organize data and functionalities quite differently from each other. The way a language handles computations bears a significant influence on how the programmer designs the code: it affects the way he abstracts the problems and how he crafts a solution. Some languages use function, modules, or subroutines as a primary means to organize data. It enables the programmer to decompose a problem into more manageable chunks. Java is an object oriented language; its primary means of abstraction is by using objects.

It wouldn't be wrong to think of an object as a data structure, but that notion of an object would be incomplete because it is more than just a collection of simple types that's clumped up into one.

An object encapsulates data, behavior or operations and usage semantics. If we were to work on an Account object, we shouldn't bother how that object was constructed internally, and we care less about how it does withdrawal or deposit. The only thing we care about is that we can call the methods deposit and withdraw against an account object.

```
Account objAccount = new Account();
objAccount.deposit();
objAccount.withdraw();
```

The user of an object should only focus what he wants done and how it is done. The details of behavioral implementation and the internal data structure of the object are not the concern of the object's users or clients. This characteristic of an object is one of the tenets of OOP. There are many other characteristics of Java which make it an OOP language, and they will be pointed out in later sections of this appendix.

Objects are created by instantiating classes. You can think of a class as some sort of a template for creating objects, because a class's primary responsibility is to facilitate the creation of objects. A class is generally constructed like this:

```
class <Name of Class>  ❶ ❷
{ ❸

} ❹
```

❶ The word `class` is special: it's one of Java's reserved words, and when you use it in a construct such as the preceding one, it denotes the creation of a new type—a class

❷ What follows after the class keyword is the name of a class. Most classes in Java require a name or an identifier which will make it unique and identifiable in the region of your program

❸ The opening French or curly brace marks the start of the block for the class definition

❹ The closing French brace closes the block

> **Important**   Like all blocks and parens in Java, an opening curly brace must always be paired with a closing curly brace, lest you will have a hard time with the compiler.

Listing A-18. A Real Code Example

```
class Hello {
  public static void main(String []args) {
    System.out.println("Hello World");
  }
}
```

Listing A-18 should look familiar because we used this code in earlier sections. It's a very basic class definition with a main function.

The source file should be written in a file that has a ".java" as an extension. We could store this in a file named "Hello.java" but we don't have to. Unless the class is declared public, the name of the class and that of the source file where it is written don't have to be the same. It is only by convention that this is so. Nonetheless, it is a good practice to observe that the name of the class definition and the file name are the same. Makes it easier to manage files because the file name is descriptive of the class it contains

When we compile the code in Listing A-18, it will result in a file named "Hello.class". The resulting byte code takes after the name of class definition (class Hello) and not the file name where the class is stored.

It's generally not a good idea to put more than one class definition in a single source file, but that is not illegal to do (see Listing A-19).

Listing A-19. Definition of Three Classes

```java
class Apple {
}
class Banana {
}
class Orange {
}
// When this is compiled, it will produce
// 3 files, "Apple.class", "Banana.class" and "Orange.class"
```

The foregoing should take care of the basics of class compilation and some basic practices to observe when creating source files for class definitions. Listing A-20 shows the basic structure of a fictitious Account object. The code is stripped off any guard conditions or validations to facilitate the explanation of basic concepts. So, please don't use this as a basis for your real-world projects.

Listing A-20. Definition of an Account Class

```java
class Account {                       ❶ ❷

  Account() {                         ❸
    initialize();
  }

  private String accountNumber;  ❹
  double balance;

  void deposit(double amt) {     ❺
    balance = balance + amt;
  }

  void withdraw(double amt) {
    balance = balance = amt;
  }

  private void initialize() {...}     ❻
}
```

❶   class keyword denotes that we want to create a new type

❷   We've given this class the name "Account"

❸   This called a constructor. It looks like a method but it really is not. This part of an object is what's responsible for creations of object. When an object is created, one of the first few things that gets called is the constructor. This is a good place to write initialization codes

❹   This class defines an accountNumber property. We marked it as private, which means this variable can only be accessed from within the class which defined it. This variable is only visible from within the Account object. By the way, some programmers call a class's property as "state." We can use the two terms interchangeably

❺   This class also defines some methods. Member methods are bound to the class in which they are defined. This method can only be called from within the context of an Account object. Member methods gives the objects their behavior

❻   Another member method of the Account object, but this one isn't meant to be called from the outside; that's why it was marked private

The creation of an object can be facilitated as shown in the following code snippet:

```
Account objAccount;        ❶
objAccount = new Account(); ❷
```

❶   Create a variable and declare its type using the name of our Account class

❷   Define the variable as shown in the preceding. The word new, like the word class, is special. It's one of Java's reserved words. The new keyword will call the constructor of the Account class

More Details on Classes

The foregoing describes the typical creation and use of classes. For the greatest part of your programming tasks, this is most likely how your code will be structured. However, there will be times when you will need to use the more advanced facilities of Java for constructing classes. The following code snippet describes a more detailed form for constructing classes.

```
[access modifier] [special modifier] class <Name of Class>
    <extends <Name of Another Class>>
    [implements <Name of Interface(s)] {

}
```

- **access modifier**—a class can specify the region in your program where it will be bounded or visible. A top-level class (a class that is not nested in another class) can use the keyword public to increase the scope of its visibility. The access modifier is optional; when it is not defined, the default visibility for a class is package-private, which means the class is only visible from other classes that are on the same package

- **special modifiers**—a class may be declared as abstract, final, static, or strictfp. We'll discuss some of these things in the next sections. Unlike the access modifier, when a class does not declare any special modifier; it means it is just a regular concrete class. A concrete class is something that you can use readily, pretty much how we created the Account object (e.g., `Account objAccount = new Account()`)

- **extends**—a class extends the definition of an existing class; it doesn't matter if it is a user-defined class or part of the Java library. The keyword extends is also reserved word. Extending an existing class means we want to inherit that class. Whatever (nonprivate) variables and methods it has, we will also have. In OOP, this characteristic is called inheritance

- **implements**—the implements keyword, like extends, is used for inheritance. When we inherit from an interface, we inherit the type (all its behaviors) but not much else, because the methods of an interface don't have any implementation. All its methods are abstract

Constructors

A constructor is an executable code that is called during object creation; each class has at least one. A basic constructor looks like this.

```
class Account {
  Account() {   ❶

  }
}

class Person {
  Account acct = new Account(); ❷
}
```

❶ The no-arg (no argument) constructor; it's called no-arg because the constructor doesn't take any argument or parameter. A constructor is named after the class, and it has parens like a method, but unlike it, it doesn't have a return type and it contains no "return" statement in its body either

❷ The "new" keyword calls the no-arg constructor of the Account class

Constructors are so important, that even if you don't explicitly write your own constructor, the compiler will provide one for you. See the following code.

```
class Account {
}

class Person {

  Account acct = new Account(); ❶

}
```

❶ You can still call the no-arg constructor even if you did not explicitly write one. The compiler will provide the no-arg constructor as a default

Overloading

A constructor may appear more than once in a class definition; this concept is called overloading. It's the ability of constructors (and methods) to appear more than once in source file. When constructors (and methods) are overloaded, they still need to be unique, and that uniqueness is determined by the constructor's signature. The uniqueness of a signature is determined by the number and type of parameters that a constructor accepts.

```
class Point {
  int x;
  int y;

  Point(int mx, int my) {
    x = mx;
    y = my;
  }

  Point() {
    x = 10;
    y = 10;
  }
}

Point p1 = new Point(20,20);   ❶
Point p2 = new Point();        ❷
Point p3 = new Point("foo");   ❸
```

❶ When we pass two integers to Point, this will match the constructor definition, which takes in two integer arguments

❷ This will match the no-arg constructor

❸ This will be a compilation error because it doesn't match any constructor definition. We don't have any constructor that takes in a String parameter

> **Note**   The no-arg default constructor is only available if we don't have any constructor definition at all in our class. Once we implement our own constructor(s), the compiler will no longer provide the default constructor.

Packages

Packages are a named collection of related or grouped types. It's essentially a namespace that you can use in order group types that are related by function or any other type of grouping that you want to achieve. A package may contain a combination of classes, interfaces, and modules (you can embed a package within a package).

To create a class that will be within a package, we will use the package directive.

```
package com.apress;

class Foo {

}
```

> **Important**   The "package" directive should be written as the first executable statement in a source file. The only things that can appear before the package statement are comments.

In the preceding example, the package name is "com.apress"; it is the reverse DNS equivalent of "apress.com". We don't need to use reverse DNS notation but it will be wise to follow this practice, especially if you want to distribute your Android applications to the public at some point in time. The package name is usually your company name + project name in reverse DNS notation. When the preceding code gets compiled, the created class will be in the folder com/apress/Foo.class. You can no longer use the Foo class using the simple name (Foo) because it is now part of a package. To use the Foo class, we should use its fully qualified name "com.apress.Foo", as shown in the following.

```
com.apress.Foo foo = new com.apress.Foo();
```

Our coding experience would be cumbersome if we always have to use the fully qualified class name instead of the simple name of classes; thankfully, Java has an "import" mechanism. To keep using Foo's simple name, we can use the "import" keyword.

```
import com.apress.Foo;

Foo foo = new Foo();
```

Multiple Types in a Package

Packages usually have more than one type in them; as we said earlier, a package is a named collection of types. Let's say that our package "com.apress" has two more types in it.

```
package com.apress;

class Foo { . . . }
class Boo { . . . }
class Goo { . . . }
```

For us to use the simple names of the types inside this package, we could write an import statement for each type, like so:

```
import com.apress.Foo;
import com.apress.Boo;
import com.apress.Goo;

Foo foo = new Foo();
Boo boo = new Boo();
Goo goo = new Goo();
```

Or, as a shortcut, we can import all the types in the package using a single statement, as shown in the following:

```
import com.apress.*;

Foo foo = new Foo();
Boo boo = new Boo();
Goo goo = new Goo();
```

When We Don't Need "import"

We don't need to use the "import" statement when

1. We are referencing types that are on the same package, and when;

2. We are referencing types within the "java.lang" package

Let's look a sample code.

```
package com.apress;

class Foo { . . . }

class Boo {
  Foo foo = new Foo(); ❶
}

class Goo {
  Goo() {
    String out = getClass().getSimpleName(); ❷
    System.out.println(out); ❸
  }
}
```

❶   We don't need to use the fully qualified name of Foo because we are referencing it from the Boo
    class, which is in the same package as Foo. If you need to use types that are within the same
    package, you can use the simple name

❷   If we had to write the fully qualified name of the String class, we would have written this
    statement as java.lang.String out = getClass().getSimpleName(); luckily, Java automatically
    imports all the types within the "java.lang" package

❸   The System class is also within the "java.lang" package; that's why we can use its simple name

Inheritance

As an object oriented language, Java allows us to reuse the capabilities and characteristics
of an existing class: this concept is called inheritance. It involves two classes: the base class
and the derived class, sometimes also known as the parent and the child class, respectively.
Inheritance allows the child class to "inherit" the behavior and properties of the parent and
consequently change or modify them if it needs to provide some specialized behavior. The
child class inherits from the parent class using the "extends" keyword. Let's see what this
looks like in code.

```
class Employee {
  String employeeid;
  void doWork() {
    System.out.printf("%s is working\n", getClass().getSimpleName());
  }
}

class Programmer extends Employee {  ❶

}
```

```java
class Company {
  public static void main(String []args) {
    Employee emp = new Employee();
    Programmer prog = new Programmer();

    emp.doWork();  ❷
    prog.doWork(); ❸
  }
}
```

❶   The class Programmer inherits from Employee using the "extends" keyword. This means that the Programmer class automatically inherits the properties (employeeid) and behaviors (doWork) of Employee

❷   We invoke "doWork" on the Employee object; it will output "Employee is working"

❸   We can invoke "doWork" on the Programmer object as well even if we did not define it in the Programmer class. The "doWork" method was inherited from Employee. This statement outputs "Programmer is working"

Object as the Root Class

Whenever you create a new class, you have to extend an existing class, because every class in Java must always have a parent; orphans aren't allowed. This rule is so important that even if you don't explicitly extend a class, the compiler will automatically assume that want to extend java.lang.Object. This object is what you might call the root class in all of Java, because every class in the Java library and all the classes that you will create will be a descendant of java.lang.Object, directly or indirectly.

```java
class Hello extends Object {

}
```

We don't have to write extends Object, because the compiler will do that for us

We don't need to write the fully qualified name of the class (java.lang.Object), because the package java.lang is implicitly imported for us

Single Rooted Class Inheritance

Inheritance is a good mechanism for reusing existing functionality that already resides on existing classes. However, Java imposes some limitations on this mechanism. A class is only allowed to extend at most, just one class. You cannot extend multiple classes. So, the following code would be illegal:

```java
class MultiFunction extends Printer, Fax {

}
```

Java however, allows us to inherit from more than one interface. So, in order to achieve multiple inheritances, you need to use interfaces. The following is a pseudocode that depicts how this might be done:

```java
interface Printer { ... }

interface Fax { ... }

class MultiFunction implements Printer, Fax {

}
```

Polymorphism

Child classes can provide specialization of behavior by either adding or completely changing the implementation of their inherited behaviors (methods). This concept is called polymorphism.

```java
class Employee {
  String employeeid;
  void doWork() {
    System.out.printf("%s is working\n", getClass().getSimpleName());
  }
}

class Programmer extends Employee {
  void doWork() {
    System.out.printf("%s is coding\n", getClass().getSimpleName()); ❶
  }
}

class Company {
  public static void main(String []args) {
    Employee emp = new Employee();
    Programmer prog = new Programmer();

    emp.doWork();  ❷
    prog.doWork();  ❸

  }
}
```

❶ The "doWork" method is reimplemented on the Programmer class; this effectively overrides the inherited "doWork" from Employee

❷ This still outputs "Employee is working"

❸ This outputs something else now; it prints "Programmer is coding" because "doWork" was overridden in the Programmer class

Interfaces

A Java interface is similar to class because it defines a type, but unlike a class, it doesn't implement or define any behavior, it only declares it.

```
interface IPhone {    ❶

  void answerCall(); ❷
  void dial();

}
```

❶ An interface is created by using the "interface" keyword. This declares a new type called IPhone with two behaviors: "answerCall" and "dial"

❷ The methods of an interface do not have any implementation; notice that the body of the method is missing (the pair of curly braces). Instead, method declarations in an interface are terminated by a semicolon. Methods that don't have implementation are called abstract methods—all methods inside an interface are abstract

An interface cannot be instantiated like a class, so you cannot write codes like the one following:

```
IPhone phone = new IPhone(); // this is illegal
```

To use an interface, you should "implement" it in a class. Let's see how this works:

```
interface IPhone {
  void answerCall();
  void dial();
}

class SomePhone implements IPhone { ❶
  public void answerCall() {         ❷
    System.out.println("answering call");
  }
  public void dial(){

  }
}
```

```
class Test {
  public static void main(String[] args) {
    IPhone phone = new SomePhone(); ❸
    phone.answerCall();
  }
}
```

❶   A class uses an interface by "implementing" it

❷   The method "answerCall" is overridden in SomePhone, which effectively makes it a concrete method

❸   The "phone" variable is declared an IPhone (left-hand side) but ultimately defined as an instance of SomePhone (right-hand side). This code works because SomePhone is a kind of IPhone. When SomePhone implemented IPhone, it inherited its type

When a class implements an interface, that class is essentially bound to the interface in some kind of a contract wherein the class "agrees" to provide concrete behavior to all the methods declared on the interface. This is the reason why we needed to override all the methods of IPhone.

> **Note**   Methods in an interface are by default always public, so when they are overridden, they need to be declared public, because you cannot reduce the visibility of inherited methods.

Multiple Inheritance

Unlike class extension, we can implement more than one interface in our classes. This is how Java does multiple inheritance. The following sample code illustrates this.

```
interface IPhone {
  void answerCall();
  void dial();
}

interface IPrinter {
  void print();
}

class Fax implements IPhone, IPrinter {
  public void answerCall() {}
  public void dial() {}
  public void print() {}
}
```

```
class Test {
  public static void main(String[] args) {
    Fax fax = new Fax();
    fax.answerCall();
    fax.dial();
    fax.print();
  }
}
```

The class "Fax" agrees to implement all the behavior or IPhone and IPrinter. When implementing more than one interface, you need to separate them by comma.

Exceptions

Despite our best efforts get the program right and behaving as predictably as possible, it can still fail because of various reasons. When a program fails because of abnormal conditions in its environment, the Java runtime throws an exception. When an exception is thrown, the normal flow of the program is disrupted, and if the exception is not properly handled, it may cause the program to terminate in an ungraceful manner. There two ways to handle exceptions: either we handle it using a try-catch structure or we rethrow it and let it be somebody else's problem. In this section, we will look at how to handle exceptions using the try-catch block.

The general form of the try-catch is as follows.

```
try {
  // statement that can throw exceptions
}
catch(ExceptionType1 obje) {
  // error handling statement;
}
catch(ExceptionType2 obje) {
  // error handling statement;
}
catch(ExceptionTypen obje) {
  // error handling statement;
}
```

The try-catch, like the if-else, routes program flow. It branches program control when some conditions become true. When an exception is raised inside the body of the try block, the program flow automatically jumps out of that block. The catch blocks will be inspected one by one until a type of exception thrown is properly matched to any of the catch blocks. When a match is found, the error handling statements on the matching catch block are executed. Let's see how that looks on a real code.

```
String filename = "something.txt";
try {
  java.io.FileReader reader = new java.io.FileReader(filename);
}
catch(FileNotFoundException e) {
  // ask the user to input another filename
}
```

In the preceding example, we only have one catch block; that's because the statement inside the try block can only throw a "FileNotFoundException" and nothing else. If we had other statements in the try block that can throw other kinds of exception, then we should write the corresponding catch blocks for those. You might ask "how do we know if an exception is going to be thrown by a method call?". The answer to that question is "by reading the documentation". If you read the Java language API reference for the FileReader class, you will learn the details of how it is used and what kinds of exceptions some of its methods may throw, among other things. Another way you may find out the kinds of exceptions that can be thrown by the FileReader (or any other method/constructor call) is to simply write it like a regular statement, that is, without any error handling structure, like so.

```
java.io.FileReader reader = new java.io.FileReader(filename);
```

As soon as you try to compile the source program where this line is written, you will find out that the FileReader constructor may throw a "FileNotFoundException" because the Java compiler will complain loudly.

The try-catch structure is usable for many situations, but if you want to be thorough in handling the error, you may to use the more complete try-catch-finally structure. The general form of try-catch-finally is

```
try {
  // statement that can throw exceptions
}
catch(ExceptionType obje) {
  // error handling statement;
}
finally {
  // this code will execute
  // with or without encountering
  // an error
}
```

In a try-catch structure, if an exception happens, the program control will jump out of the try block, leaving the remaining statements inside the try block unexecuted. If one of those unexecuted statements is critical to the program, for example, closing a file or database connection, that may introduce another problem. This is the kind of situation where you need to use the "finally" clause. The codes written inside a finally clause are guaranteed to execute whether an exception happens. Let's see the file reading code sample again, but this time, with a finally clause.

```
String filename = "something.txt";
try {
  java.io.FileReader reader = new java.io.FileReader(filename);
}
catch(FileNotFoundException e) {
  // ask the user to input another filename
}
finally {
  // close any connections you may have
  // opened e.g. "reader"
}
```

Index

Get the eBook for only $5!

Why limit yourself?

With most of our titles available in both PDF and ePUB format, you can access your content wherever and however you wish—on your PC, phone, tablet, or reader.

Since you've purchased this print book, we are happy to offer you the eBook for just $5.

To learn more, go to http://www.apress.com/companion or contact support@apress.com.

Apress®

CPSIA information can be obtained
at www.ICGtesting.com
Printed in the USA
BVHW011256010719
552389BV00005B/74/P